My Mother's Voice

By Sally Callahan

Elder Books
Forest Knolls, California

My Mother's Voice

Library of Congress Cataloguing in Publication Data
Main Entry Under Title:

My Mother's Voice
Callahan, Sally

1. Alzheimer's disease 2. Aging 3. Family relationships
4. Caregiving

ISBN 0-943873-49-5

LCCN 98-073890

Cover by Susan Shankin

Production by Margot Comstock/McArt Communications

Cover photo by Ben McCoy

Printed in the United States of America

This book is dedicated to

♥ *My mother*, that remarkable woman who, even as she was fading, gathered what wits she had left to show me the way; supervising, encouraging, and nurturing me to the point where I could stand on my own two feet, speak her words, fight for her rights to quality and loving care, and finally, for her right to die.

Table of Contents

List of Tables

Acknowledgments

While I realized that I would need help completing *My Mother's Voice*, I had no idea of the level and types of assistance that would be required. There were dozens of people along the way who offered a helping hand through reading, encouragement, support or the willingness to share an objectivity and perspective I could not possibly have reached on my own.

I am eternally grateful to the many angels who miraculously appeared to pick me up, dust me off, dry my tears and help me back to the place where I could remember and hear my mother, the real one, the well one, the lost one, as though she was standing beside me, guiding me through the telling of our journey. *I am grateful to all who have opened their hearts,* shared their often clearer thinking minds and spoken their thoughtful, supportive words throughout the project.

There were literally dozens who provided loving, respectful care for my mother over the years. To you competent, compassionate aides, activities directors, doctors, lawyers, nurses, support group leaders, and others we encountered along our journey who offered such rich material for this book, I am also grateful.

I am especially grateful to the many brave Alzheimer family members for providing invaluable feedback on this manuscript. Thanks also to the family members who have come through the South Dennis Support Group over the years. Your courage, compassion and commitment to your loved ones are an ongoing inspiration.

Thanks to the many medical, spiritual and Alzheimer's professionals who have offered their wisdom, knowledge and unflagging support; the dedicated professionals at the Alzheimer's Association

of Eastern Massachusetts whose caring and professionalism are a
model to all of us, and those at the Bedford, VA, GRECC whose wonderful work in late-stage issues touched my life as a caregiver and
since, and to all at the Alzheimer's Association of Cape Cod & the
Islands for their ongoing gifts of time, hard work and commitment.
So many of you have aided my transition from daughter-caregiver to
supporter of patients and caregivers.

Without Eileen and the crew at the Harwichport Post Office, the
drafts of this manuscript would never have made their way around
the country. Thank you for your unflagging patience, courtesy and
service.

Cheerleaders, friends and readers of early drafts generously
offered support and encouragement. My thanks to all.

Some must be singled out. To each I offer my undying gratitude.

- ♥ Thomas J. Veasey the lighthouse in many a raging storm for
  his love, support and wisdom.

- ♥ Judy Taylor for her friendship and many miles through the
  years.

- ♥ First reader and wise friend, Isabel Pounder.

- ♥ Debra Redalia for her editorial input.

- ♥ Dot Sweeney for feedback that provided hope when I most
  needed it.

- ♥ Ellie Ryan and Jan Kavanaugh for keeping me honest.

- ♥ Sally Connolly and Nancy Smith, co-captains of the cheer
  leading squad.

- ♥ All who offered hugs, hankies, meals and clean-sheeted beds
  —you know who you are.

- ♥ The courage and steadfast support of my uncle and my now
  former husband for their patient guidance through the land
  mines of Alzheimer's.

- ♥ Colin C. Moran for his incredible support through the years.

- ♥ President Robert R. Rose for his encouragement and support
  which helped put the "community" back in community college for me.

- ♥ The seventy plus people who made the "Lifting the Veil"
  Project at the college a reality. Particularly Margie and Jim

for your courage and those brave souls who took the first *Stroll Down Memory Lane* and Joanne Jones, Jennifer Rudolph and Linda Rose for their hard work and creativity. Their contributions have touched hearts and offered hope to so many!

- Julie Noonan-Lawson for her courage, friendship, encouragement, honesty and love.

- Georgia Heard and her '97 and '98 poetry class warm welcomes—that Vineyard Vaccine is potent!

- Marie Cantlon and Andrea Peraner-Sweet for their patient guidance and wise counsel.

- Gail Sarahs and Gloria Bell for listening, advising and reminding me to breathe.

- The MAC crew who came to the rescue at the end of a very long process. Thank you Sharon, Helen, Phil, Mike, Bonnie, Bruce and Frederic.

- Dorothy Handel and Natalie Palmer Stafford respectively for the sunset photo and cover.

- Anne Seeley and Tim's mom for your very special stories.

I would also like to acknowledge my brothers and sisters and others in the family. Thanks for your many sacrifices in support of our mother, the encouragement, support and love that provided the impetus to continue in the most discouraging of times. Although we were jaded, angry, hurt, and grieving at many points in our journey, we are still a family. That is due, at least in part, to the courage each of us has found to listen, learn and grow. It is also, I am sure, the result of the love we learned at our mother's knee. For these things I am grateful, as I could not have been without the pain of having lived them.

Finally, I must acknowledge and thank my parents, who provided a solid start in a loving home, the advantages of a classical education, the courage to strive for excellence, the confidence to grow, and a college education that challenged me to become (and remain) a life-long learner. ♥

Preface

We are all pioneers when it comes to this relatively new disease called Alzheimer's, which has become epidemic in America and around the world. As family and professional caregivers we are, in many ways, ill equipped. Alzheimer's is long and exhausting, and has the potential to take more than the patient as its victim.

Over 4 million American families live with Alzheimer's. They cross socioeconomic, racial, religious and all other boundaries. Alzheimer's families are wealthy and poor. Caucasians, persons of color, republicans, democrats and libertarians, conservatives and liberals, men and women, gay and straight are affected by Alzheimer's.

Alzheimer's caregivers are our neighbors, cousins, parents, grown children, aunts and uncles, brothers and sisters, co-workers, strangers, doctors, lawyers, custodians, gardeners, former presidents, teachers and their spouses and children. They do what they do because they want to, or because they must. Living their commitment, they give love to a person who once was like most of them—well, whole, and able to care for themselves. Courageous, loving and weary, Alzheimer's caregivers are special people who deserve our assistance and support.

Others who care for Alzheimer's patients and support their families are professionals of many sizes and shapes: home health care workers and certified nurses aides, directors of activities, nurses, doctors, lawyers, clergy, social workers, and researchers. The best of them are worth their weight in gold.

Although much has changed since the early eighties, when I began my journey as a caregiver, some things remain much as they

1

were.   And like other family caregivers who have survived Alzheimer's, I have written about my journey.   This is a book about conflict, faith, loss, grief and letting go.   But, above all, it is about the triumph of the human spirit and the power of love.

When my mother's doctors gave us the diagnosis of Alzheimer's, we received no instruction manual.   They didn't tell us how to care for ourselves as well as our mother, or how devastating and exhausting this process can be.   They told us what to do, but not how to survive doing it.

Even as the end approached, I was by my mother's side, working with those who provided personal care on a daily basis, agonizing over decisions, crying tears of frustration and grief.   Until November 3rd, 1994, the day we buried my mother's body, at every funeral I attended I thought surely the next would be hers.   Meanwhile, I trudged on for nearly a decade-and-a-half, still standing, but barely.   I stumbled from one decision to the next, moving in fits and starts, each becoming somehow more difficult.   I cried and fought.   I threw my hands up in despair, but I came to learn the meaning and practice of unconditional love.

While I would not change my decision to accept the role of caregiver, nor most of the decisions I made, I definitely wish I had known then many of the things that I know now.   Perhaps the most important of these is to seek more support much earlier in the process and to understand that love was my strongest ally.   There have been professionals, family members, colleagues and friends who were constructive and supportive.   There have also been some from each of these groups whose input was destructive and counter-productive.   That has been true from the beginning and is true today.   I learned many things about my mother, my husband and my siblings; about myself, my strengths, and my weaknesses; and about the medical maze—a complex, often contradictory system I was challenged to learn quickly.   I had to face my personal value system on a regular basis and compare it to my mother's eventually silenced voice and ever-more-distant values and wishes.

I wish I had found resources to normalize the experience of Alzheimer's.   In the early and middle years of our journey, aside from support groups, there were few who understood the experience.   Although the entire family was journeying the same road, and we were all struggling to make sense of the experience and fit it into our lives, others were not able to normalize it for me, particularly those who saw it so differently.   If they tried to convince me that I was doing it "wrong", I only dug my heels in deeper. We were rarely able to help each other or provide comfort. We were too close, too involved, struggling too hard to ease each others' or our own horror and grief.

It has been difficult to share our story. The fact that caregivers must go on for so many years, often without a break, makes it very hard to put such personal experiences and feelings on paper for others to read and critique. But unless people start talking about what is happening, start sharing experiences and strategies, and let others know that there is a way to survive the strenuous journey of Alzheimer's, how else will something positive reach those facing the problems? It would be wrong for more people to be left in the dust or become lost in the overwhelming swamp of emotion, bureaucracies, and too little support when those who have survived it could help.

The anecdotes related in these pages are taken from my own and others' experiences with Alzheimer's. I have changed names, gender, and other specifics so the flavor of the experience will be kept without particular individuals and families being identified. This isn't a guide book. It rarely offers advice. It is not a "how-to" but rather a "how-I-did-it" book.

For almost 15 years, I struggled to make correct decisions for my mother. I do not know what may be right for anyone else. Nor do I believe that I, or anyone else, should make judgments about the rights, wishes, and needs of others. I believe all people on such a journey have similar needs: however people's personalities, resources, life experiences, values, and skills make them unique.

I know now more than I care to know about ethical and moral issues, although I have no formal training, per se. I do not profess to have answers for others. In my case, I know that there have been many who have helped. Some have been unseen; others I consider angels in the clothing of professionals, friends, colleagues, family and, at times, strangers. I know now what I did not know so many years ago: I had a very deep need for spiritual sustenance in order to survive this journey intact. I also wish there had been more support for my mother in the early stages of Alzheimer's, and for me and for those who supported me.

I was, and still am, most concerned by people (professionals and family members alike) who profess to know without a doubt what is right and who claim to have all the answers. I am still wary of those who cannot or will not listen or take the time to work through the issues in light of the patient and her wishes. These are the attitudes that rob the Alzheimer's patient of her self-determinism.

So, if these words help just one patient, one family, one professional, or one friend who wants to support someone going through Alzheimer's, then risking my vulnerability was worth it. As Robert Kennedy said, "If not us, who? If not now, when?"

Why My Mother?

At one point, *Frontline* the documentary program aired on national public television, had a representative sit in on a support group in which I participated. I was talking about the problems I had been having with Medicaid and *Frontline* asked if I would speak to them. After an interview, they asked if they could tape my mother and me. I agreed, as long as none of my siblings objected. The reporters came to the nursing home on my mother's 76th birthday where my husband and I were giving her a frappe, a card and a gift. The 12-foot long microphones, which were within a foot of my mother's face, and the people behind the large cameras, were apparently invisible to her. She never once acknowledged them.

The *Frontline* producer asked for a still photograph of my mother and me sitting on the bed to be used in *TV Guide*. When I said my mother wasn't able to sit up, the nurse propped her on the bed next to me and sat on the floor in front of us. She kept asking my mother, who had been completely uncommunicative, who I was. In apparent annoyance, my mother yelled, "That's my Sally." The only thing that interested her that day was the frappe! Gifts and cards had apparently become a thing of the past. After the nursing home visit, my husband and I were interviewed for four hours at home. Several days later, we were still exhausted. The process of reliving the ins and outs of our journey was overwhelming to both of us.

After the interviews, I said to the support group leader, "I agree this needs to be done, but why should it be my mother, a beautiful, elegant, proud woman who has degenerated into a toothless aged hag, dressed in sweats, who doesn't know what's going on, especially on national TV?" The group leader said, "If not your mother Sal, then whose?" I have asked, "Why my mother" more than once.

Part of my resistance was that I did not want to air the family's dirty laundry, or expose the dysfunction we denied, or thought had been well-hidden. I subsequently came to believe that if publicity about our plight helped just one person, then it served a worthwhile purpose.

I must admit however, that over the years, I heard the words "If not your mother, Sal, then whose?" ringing loud and clear, again and again. And almost always the words have been enough to make me dig a little bit deeper for the courage to speak of my mother, myself, and those we love.

While Alzheimer's is always terminal (and not pretty in the process,) Alzheimer's caregiving is survivable. All is not lost—there can and will be good moments. Trust yourself, BREATHE, and remember that when all else fails, LOVE WORKS.

My Prayer

It is my hope that families and patients will take hope, find meaning, and receive courage from this book. I also hope that it will be helpful in moving professional caregivers forward in ways that allow all involved to reach their fullest potential. I pray that with distance and perspective, all family caregivers will come to view this experience as more of a blessing than a burden.

To professional caregivers who read these words, I ask you to open your hearts and minds, to stretch your professional envelope, to dig deeper and deeper for compassion, kindness, patience, courage, openness, and respect for those you serve. I ask you to remember that you are not the patient, you are not her family, you are not God. I ask you to raise the issues in appropriate forums and start talking, writing and searching for ways to guide your clients to correct decisions. And please remember to say to yourself occasionally, "There, but for the grace of God, go I."

And finally, I pray for you, dear reader, the openness of heart and mind to embrace the ebb and flow of the tides of your journey.

How to Use This Book

These pages cover the entire spectrum of Alzheimer's. While they do not cover all things that all people experience in each stage, neither do they white-wash or water down my experiences with Alzheimer's. For this reason, I strongly recommend that you respect your learning style and where you are in this process. Although some may want to read this tome from cover to cover, perhaps in a single sitting, most will not. In fact, you may want to take it in bits and pieces, the size of each bit and piece to be dictated by your emotional and physical state.

If you find yourself getting too tired, upset or overwhelmed by what you are reading, please put the book down, or skip to another section. But then find someone to talk to about what you found difficult. You can always go back later when you are more ready, or after you have talked over what bothered you with a supportive friend, family member, or professional.

Throughout these pages I use feminine pronouns because I was a daughter caring for her mother. I mean no disrespect to anyone and invite those who wish to substitute male pronouns wherever it is more comfortable for them. ❤

Chapter 1:
My Mother's Voice

And so the years go flying by
With all that had to be,
While memories of my mother's voice
Come back to comfort me.
—Carrie Jacobs-Bond

Though told by her first grade teacher that she was a "listening bird," my mother's voice was almost lilting. Sweet in timbre, cordial, courteous and lady-like in word and tone, it was comforting, welcoming, nurturing—my mother's voice was almost always smiling. While never hard to hear, especially when expressing displeasure with one of her five children, her voice was tempered—never shrill or rude. Though shy, and sometimes reticent, my mother could speak with authority, unruffled assurance, and certainty.

Despite being raised in a poor, Boston Irish Catholic family, she spoke with gentle breeding, impeccably correct grammar and enunciation that was clear as a bell. My mother could caress, cajole, challenge, command, encourage, control, soothe, scold, admonish or praise with the slightest adjustment to her voice which was silenced long before her death. I never thought that I would be the one who would have to speak for my mother when she was no longer able.

Rita "Puppy" Callahan was a warm, loving woman who loved hats (her mother had worked for a milliner) and was devoted to her family. Although born and raised in the city, she made a wonderful life

7

for her husband and children in the suburbs. She was happiest, however, at their home on Cape Cod. She managed to lead an active social life while keeping up with the activities of five kids. Sometime in the early 1980s, when she was in her late sixties and living the busy, independent life of a widow, her children became aware of changes in Puppy. The changes were subtle at first, and they were slow to acknowledge them. When confronted, Puppy became fiercely protective of her independence.

Although they did not immediately recognize it, Puppy and her children had been hurled into the murky, confusing waters of Alzheimer's disease.

There are many misconceptions about Alzheimer's and how it relates to dementia, both in the public and even still within the medical profession. Dementia is a grouping of symptoms that include cognitive decline, loss of memory and judgment, and changes in personality and behavior.

Dementia of the Alzheimer's Type, also known as DAT in the medical literature, is a particular brand, or flavor, if you will, of dementia, which is caused by specific changes in the brain. It cannot be cured, or prevented. Dementia of the Alzheimer's Type is terminal. But the progression is variable and often relatively slow. The patient's need for care can last for as little as a year or for two or more decades.

Alzheimer's patients—those who must make this journey alone in so many ways, those whose world is rearranging itself into foreign places, losing all connection to that which they have known before—come from the ranks of our friends, families and co-workers. They are once well people whose disease moves them slowly to a life of dependence on the compassion, care, and love of others.

At some point in the disease process, victims of Alzheimer's lose the ability to make decisions for themselves. This is not a discrete event that happens at a particular moment in time. Rather it is a process that renders them able in one moment but unable in another. When this happens, the patient needs a voice through which to be heard, particularly when she can no longer speak for herself.

Many years before my mother stopped speaking, she passed her voice to me. The process of growing into and accepting her voice, and sorting it out from my own voice and the voices of my brothers and sisters and others, is what is described in this book. It is my experience of speaking for my mother when she could no longer speak for herself—it is the story of accepting, assuming and using my mother's voice.

Denial and Acceptance

One of the most difficult aspects of Alzheimer's is the waning judgment it inflicts on its victims. Along with this comes an inability to recognize one's own difficulties. While it may be eminently clear to others, it is sometimes impossible for the patient to realize that she is losing judgment. As part of this process, it is common for patients and their families to go through a period of denial.

Patients know something is wrong long before they will allow others to become aware. Sometimes, though, it is a matter of simply not remembering, or being incapable of understanding, that the symptoms are an indication of a serious problem. Patient denial is often exhibited as excuses for actions, thoughts, and feelings. As one daughter says, "these excuses are her battle to keep from sinking into this disease."

Another mechanism that patients use is confabulation. Confabulation is making up a story to fit the circumstances or to provide an answer. Confabulation adds to the early confusion family members encounter. There were times when I underestimated my mother by thinking she was telling me a story. It wasn't until after her death that I found out that the visitor she so desperately tried to tell me about was an old friend who had actually come to see her.

Families often deny strange behaviors, refuse to acknowledge poor judgment, and shrug away dangerous situations. Failure to attach significance to the fact that Mother shows up at a family funeral with a plastic bag on her head, or that Father speaks to the television, or that Aunt Jane laces her tea with dish washing soap is a protection against the harsh reality that something is wrong. Otherwise rational, intelligent people can allow fear and emotions to render families unable, or unwilling, to deal with the evidence that others may see so clearly—at least for a time.

Occasionally, medical caregivers are in cahoots with the patient's and family's denial. Family doctors may tell concerned children that the patient may have "a touch of Alzheimer's," and they may recommend that they do nothing because they are unlikely to get permission or cooperation from the patient. While well-meaning, these approaches often rob patients of the precious time they have left to become meaningfully involved in decisions about their own futures.

These decisions then fall to their spouses, children, or others. I was always a step or two behind in terms of recognizing, acknowledging and accepting my mother's deficits.

Due to the fear and paralysis that Alzheimer's often invokes in families, denial is a tough nut to crack. While protection of the vulnerable can be necessary, it can also be carried too far, resulting in adversarial relationships between people and agencies that would better serve the patient through cooperation, trust, and open communication.

Complicating this is the fact that Alzheimer's patients may suffer hallucinations (hear or see things that are not there,) delusions (distortions in thinking) and become mistrustful, paranoid, and combative. This behavior is variable and ranges from nonexistent to complete or partial loss of touch with reality, followed by confusingly lucid times.

Family members are often confused, worried and angry at the strange behavior exhibited by their loved one. Their fear can result in less-than-clear thinking, and defenses can be fast to appear. Professionals, who may be more used to making decisions for others, can be insensitive to the process of denial, terror, and anger within the families, who are likely doing their best to cope. Family members are vulnerable, too.

I still vividly recall a conversation in June of 1984 with the first neurologist. He said, "I know it must seem at times as though your mother is being manipulative, clear one minute and confused the next. Please believe me, not only does she not have control over this, she also doesn't realize it is happening." It was as though he flipped a switch in my mind that made me able to see the situation for what it was, evaluate my mother's moods and clarity, and find the patience and courage to deal with her in respectful, productive ways. His words opened the door to my compassion and to abilities I never knew I possessed.

Habilitation Therapy

We live in a society that values cognitive abilities, productivity and speed above all else. For those who are losing these abilities, their value falls quickly and others view their strange behaviors, faltering speech, and confused thought processes as though they are now lepers—people to be shunned, tossed aside.

Human beings are not intellect alone. In fact, in some ways—the onset of Alzheimer's offers unusual opportunities to patients and caregivers to reacquaint themselves with other aspects of the human experience. As reason and verbal communication are eventually lost, other ways to communicate are needed. Since Alzheimer's patients can not be returned to the land of cognition and speedy task completion, since they can not retain facts such as the day and date and time—they experience life very differently than they used to and than others do. And while these losses are certainly sad, they offer opportunities for patients and caregivers to experience other human qualities like feeling more deeply, living at a slower pace and using different modes of communication. The losses leave patients and caregivers with the opportunity, if only they will accept it, for a heightened awareness of the magic of the universe so many late twentieth century Americans have lost. An experience that values, above all else, nature, love, peace, emotions, spirituality, and quiet. For those caregivers who are willing to find ways into their patient's world, many gifts and blessings are there for the taking.

To see the joy on my mother's face, to feel her calm, peaceful breathing as we held hands while I read a poem I had written was a gift unavailable to my well mother and me. The opportunity to be in relationship with an undefended mother, and to offer the protection, advocacy and love she had showered upon her children were indeed gifts. To find ways to keep her safe while maintaining her independence and those abilities that remained was challenging. To exercise and rely on my humanitarian and emotional rather than cognitive skills, to honor my mother's wishes for herself, stated clearly when she was well, was an honor. To find ways to make my mother feel loved, valued and useful was both a challenge and a gift.

Habilitation worked for me long before Dr. Paul Raia and Joanne Koenig-Coste coined the term for this instinctive, successful approach to Alzheimer's caregiving. It is an approach in which the caregiver is willing to enter the patient's world and relate to her on her own terms, according to the rules of her world, even as they are changing.

> The aim of habilitation therapy is not to restore people with a dementia such as Alzheimer's disease to what they once were (i.e., rehabilitation), but to maximize their functional independence....[1]

From the early days of this journey, I had a certain fascination with the changes in my mother. There were times when I was able to

stand back from the emotion of it. It was then that I marveled at
how she coped. I also began to find ways to change as my mother
changed.

I accepted what I was told by medical people—that the losses my
mother suffered could not be reversed. But did that also mean we
couldn't find other ways of relating, other ways of just being? I also
believed, as I had been told, that she couldn't learn new things, but
somehow she and those around her were adapting. She provided a
map of sorts by asking me, in her own way, to let her be, not to
"quiz" her. In my attempts to stay connected with one of the most
important people in my life, I began to change how I interacted with
her, how I viewed her, how I viewed our relationship. I began to
accompany her into her strange new world.

Victims of Alzheimer's live with different views of the world.
They see and understand differently than they once did and than we
do. But this does not make them wrong and us right. It does not
make them worse and us better. It makes them different. They are
making the best of what they have left.

Although professionals used to believe in trying to orient Alzheimer's patients to the real world, my mother vehemently resisted
these efforts. And I saw that they did not work. So we tacitly agreed
to journey through Alzheimer's my mother's way, focusing on her as
an individual, respecting her dignity and right to determine how to
live out the rest of her life, how to die. We instinctively knew that
the bottom line was *her rights and wishes* even though she now had
a disease which would, in time, kill her.

Eventually I learned that we were both happier if I didn't try to
change her perceptions and thoughts, both of which were real to her,
no matter how bizarre they may have been to me. Habilitation is
what we, as a family did to preserve and redefine quality relationship
and living. If memory serves, the root of Habilitation is from the
Latin word, *habilitare*, meaning, to make fit or able." The definition
of Habilitation, according to Paul Raia and Joanne Koenig-Coste, two
eminent Alzheimer professionals in Massachusetts, is:

> In this view, individuals respond to their disease
> according to how supportive their environments are.
> Here, the emphasis is on active treatment of the symp-
> toms of the dementia through a careful focus on the uti-
> lization of those capacities which remain, particularly
> the person's psychological capacity. Developing a bet-

ter understanding of the psychology of dementia—how a person thinks, feels, communicates, compensates, responds to change, to emotion, to love—may bring some of the biggest breakthroughs in treatment.[2]

The emphasis on this journey was on process rather than product. The quality of the journey would define the quality of my mother's, and, to some extent, my life. Her body and mind were sick and slowly being destroyed, but her essence, her spirit would emerge more clearly and brilliantly as the journey unfolded, but only if I was willing to journey with her, through and into her world, and be open to her spirit.

Choosing a Surrogate Voice

I am the fourth of five children. I found myself at the beginning of this journey at the tender age of 30, when I received a Durable Family Power of Attorney in the mail with a note, "Weather great, 80 degrees, sun shining —Love". When I called to ask what was wrong, my mother said, "Nothing honey, put it away, the others don't know you have it and won't know until you pull it out in a hospital. You're in charge. Late for bridge, have to run."

At the time, I did not understand what the Durable Family Power of Attorney meant or why I had received it. My mother made it clear immediately and consistently that the document must remain hidden until it was needed. What was to come was a long and difficult journey.

But I was lucky. My mother was clear about her wishes from the time I was six, when she expressed her beliefs and values on life and death following her father's death after a long battle with cancer. Quality of life, compassionate, kind care of the sick and dying were spoken of often, always in calm, clear, unemotional terms.

My mother was neither ambivalent nor afraid of end-of-life issues. She was vocal, firm and matter of fact about them. Doctors and attorneys were consistently clear that my obligation was to honor my mother's wishes, not my own, my family's, medical professional's or anyone else's.

Although the consistent advice to honor my mother's wishes gave me grist for the mill from which to make correct decisions for her, it did not give me the emotional protection, the clarity of mind, or the knowledge and facility to make decision after decision with certainty and peace. *I struggled*. I was blessed with two doctors, a priest, attorneys, several nurses, hospice, counselors, support groups, and a few colleagues, family members and friends who showed a willingness to listen and struggle with me. "Alzheimer-friendly" professionals were open and honest about the options and consequences. All listened again and again as I muddled my way through the hazards of facing and understanding the issues, evaluating alternatives and making decisions. These were not easy things.

Toward the end, hospice repeated to me what I had heard with increasing horror numerous times over the years—that due to modern technology, my mother could be kept alive almost indefinitely. It is clear to me that ethical and moral issues are not as highly defined as the medical technologies available. I am sad to say that I had to fight for her right to die, to stop the prolonging of this process. I sought resources to educate those who cared for my mother about her rights and how those rights translated in their care of her.

Qualities to look for in a surrogate voice

People diagnosed with Alzheimer's become increasingly vulnerable to the vagaries of others' values and morals. Some children, spouses, and others can, and do, take advantage of failing elders. This causes professional caregivers and providers to become vigilant in places and situations that neither patients nor their loved ones expect or welcome. Families often state that "the system" was threatening or unhelpful, or tried to wrest control from those with whom it rightfully belonged. It is patient vulnerability that necessitates naming a surrogate.

In naming a surrogate, a person chooses and legally names another person or persons to make decisions when they are no longer able. There are many vehicles which can accomplish this, which are state and locality dependent. Durable Family Powers of Attorney, Health Care Proxies and Living Wills are a few.

Although there may be more than one surrogate voice, and those surrogates may have responsibility for different aspects of the Alzheimer's patient's life, throughout this book I will describe the surrogate voice as a single person.

If a surrogate has not been named before the onset of Alzheimer's, it is not necessarily too late. Patients can and do have moments of clarity, times when they are aware of their difficulties, sometimes excruciatingly so.

My mother's decision to give me a Durable Family Power of Attorney was not out of character for her. She understood, and was not upset by, the need for such measures. She knew they needed to be legalized and she acted. As far as I know, my mother acted prior to her descent into Alzheimer's. If this was not the case, then it was at the very beginning of the disease process.

Determining who is friend and who is foe can be difficult for patient, family, and professionals. But it is imperative that the qualities for a surrogate voice be identified, understood, and sought *while the future Alzheimer's patient is still able*, for it is her surrogate who will make life and death decisions that affect the quality, length, comfort and ultimate value of her final days, months, and years.

Regardless of a person's ability to vocalize feelings and her awareness of potential surrogates, people usually have a sense of who to trust and who not to trust. However, as Diana Friel McGowin wrote in *Living in the Labyrinth,*

> Although I had three grown children, the very thought of becoming a burden to any one or all of them appalled me. Additionally, of course, I had the attitude of most mothers, that should I need to fall upon any of my children's care, God help me. Although adults, they still appeared as children to me. Children, not caregivers.[3]

While a surrogate voice may have many qualities, those listed below are crucial.

A surrogate must have the intellectual capacity, language and willingness to face and to name the issues, and evaluate options. She must be willing and able to work constructively with others, share decisions, and seek input. She must have the moral fiber to question her motives without crippling her ability to decide. A personal code of ethics and morality either in line with the patient's, or at least able to differentiate from the patient's, is critical. While prior experience may provide a frame of reference, it is not critical, and may even cloud things for the surrogate.

An innate ability to understand the patient's wishes and desires is essential. The surrogate must also have the capacity to evaluate confusing alternatives and to communicate under emotional stress. Some people decide to go outside of the family to find a proxy who will be "true" to their wishes rather than swayed by sentiments within the family. In this sense, objectivity and "tough-mindedness" can be helpful.

It is important for the surrogate to be capable of avoiding dangerous comparisons to other situations that *seem* similar but are not
comparable. It is hard to meld heart and head to make appropriate
decisions. I had difficulty with dangerous comparisons when facing
the decision to stop the use of antibiotics for my mother in 1993. In
a previous situation in 1987 my husband's life had been saved by
massive doses of intravenous antibiotics over a period of several
months. Although I knew intellectually that the situations were different, they did not *feel* different. Essentially, I was afraid I had chosen life for my husband, but was choosing death for my mother. It
took many conversations with a variety of people over an extended
period of time to clear this up. Although I knew that only one organ
was involved in my husband, that he could live a long, productive life
of quality, and that was not the case with my mother, it was a particularly tricky and difficult decision for me.

Essentially, the surrogate must be *self-aware* and *reflective*. The
surrogate must have resolved painful issues and history with the
patient. Unresolved emotional issues between patient and surrogate
can cloud appropriate decision making. This can be detrimental to
following patient wishes.

Another characteristic of the surrogate voice is her *ability to stay
for the long haul*. Although I was a slow starter, and more emotional
in the earlier stages than my siblings, I persevered. In fact, as I
maneuvered my way from one decision to the next, I found strength
I never knew I had. In fact, I "built myself up" to the point where I
could face the increasingly difficult challenges and decisions being
my mother's surrogate required.

The chart at the end of this chapter (Table 1. Assessing Potential
Surrogates) is designed to help the patient evaluate potential surrogates. Write the names of people being considered as surrogates over
the last five columns, then rate them on each category to add some
objectivity and uncover concerns with individuals being considered. This can help the person naming the surrogate identify issues
that need to be discussed with her potential surrogate and perhaps
others. Some might even decide to name two people as surrogates
who between them will "cover all the bases."

The bottom line comes down to trust, integrity, and respect: trust
that the surrogate voice will be true to the patient's wishes; integrity
as an intrinsic character attribute of the surrogate voice; and respect
by those who provide care of the honorable intentions of the surrogate. The ability to work cooperatively and speak convincingly are

clearly important. A courageous, clear thinking, moral person who can be objective and maintain clear boundaries is needed.

The surrogate's *ability to withstand pressure from family members who disagree with the patient's or the surrogate's decisions* is critical. Alzheimer's disease changes roles within a family, roles that may have been played out for years (mother-daughter, leader-follower, traditionalist-rebel, peacemaker-fighter). The changes to the patient leave a void, which the rest of the elements of the system struggle to fill. Differing styles, conflicts of the past, denial, fear and grief all play into the scenario of a family system rearranging itself because of Alzheimer's.

Another area of difficulty for many is the facing and communicating of decisions that are counter to the advice or opinion of professionals; be they medical, ecclesiastical or psychological. If the surrogate has unresolved authority issues, argues for the sake of arguing, is a "know it all" (is either mis- or uninformed) or simply one who wants to be important, she is likely to cloud the issues, lowering effectiveness as a surrogate. While admittedly difficult, it is the responsibility of the surrogate to advocate for the patient's wishes and desires. The surrogate must always make decisions that are respectful of those wishes. It is the patient—not the surrogate—who matters most, comes first, is in and belongs in the limelight.

Sometimes decisions are controversial. Emotions within the family, emotions of professional caregivers and emotions in society at large about care issues can create a cacophony in which it is hard to hear oneself think let alone make decisions for another human being. But this is exactly what the surrogate must do, oftentimes against great odds. It is a lonely, exhausting responsibility, yet one that is of paramount importance to the patient.

The task of surrogate decision making can be eased greatly by the patient herself. Frank discussions between the patient and surrogate about what being a surrogate means, and when and how it is to be used can be of enormous help. However, it is not unusual for the patient to be unable or unwilling, or for the surrogate not to be open to such discussions. This results in the need to be guided by past conversations and other indicators of the patient's wishes. In the case of those who never mentioned such issues, it can be more difficult for the surrogate to determine what is appropriate. Complicating this responsibility are the changes in the patient.

Because the surrogate voice may run into opposition from others, and conflict within herself, whatever can be done to protect her legally, emotionally and for the long term should be done. My mother was vigilant about preparing her surrogate voice. She used the time she had left to guide and ease me into this difficult role. She stood at my elbow when I spoke for her in the early days in the nursing home. She commented on my progress, encouraging and nurturing her fledgling decision-maker. She made it clear in ways only her children could interpret and understand that she was of the same mind she had always been, despite the fact that her mind was fading. However, despite her help along the way, the process was incredibly difficult for me, and, I believe for all of us.

The ideal choice for a surrogate would be a family member who will share information and actively involve and seek the feelings and opinions of other concerned family members and those who love the patient. One woman told me she tape recorded doctor's consultations during the diagnostic process to send to her brothers who lived out of state.

My husband and an uncle were consistent voices with a personal knowledge of and love for my mother. They had the courage and tenacity to stay by my side, offering what those on the outside could not. They brought my real, well mother back to life by reminding me of her words and wishes when she couldn't do so herself. Ultimately, this enabled me to repeat my mother's words and wishes to the professionals who cared for her.

The policy of most long-term care facilities to require a single family member contact is understandable. But the primary contact person must have the right to include additional family members in discussions of import. In our case this happened on certain occasions, providing opportunities for the rest of the family to hear it "directly from the horse's mouth" as well as showing the nursing home a united front and reminding them that our mother was loved by five children.

A word about showing emotion

Caregivers are sometimes judged as weak when they express their emotions. The willingness to show these emotions can, in fact, be the sign of a healthy, fully functioning human being. A carefree, happy go lucky person who is always optimistic can be the sign of someone who is not in touch with reality, one not willing or able to face life's difficult, painful side.

Although I think of myself as a person with a sense of humor, and I recognize that it got me through many tough situations, humor alone is not a healthy, respectful coping mechanism. There is nothing worse than taking the risk of sharing a particularly difficult thought or feeling and having it met with a humorous parody or being told to "lighten up." Certainly I could not have survived what I did without humor, but there were too many times when people tried to use humor inappropriately. It was not helpful. It was not respectful. When humor was the only strategy, it denied my grief and horror at the disease that was killing my mother. Over or exclusive use of humor as a coping or supporting strategy should be avoided.

Alzheimer's is difficult and painful. It is not a disease for sissies or for ostriches. Strength, conviction, and courage come in many guises. All are in the job description of the surrogate voice. Showing emotion in reasonable, respectful ways is appropriate and healthy. Non-judgmental respect for each person's way of dealing with Alzheimer's is crucial.

When to pass control to the surrogate

A final word about surrogates is warranted. Although it can be a heady experience for a child or spouse to have control over their parent's or mate's life, it is of the utmost importance that the power not be used until absolutely necessary. And never for the sake of power itself.

In fact, it is better for patient and surrogate, and perhaps for medical providers, if the reins are shared before they pass completely and irrevocably to the surrogate. Easing into the role, hearing and participating in discussions that lead to decisions can help all involved to develop into better decision makers. False starts, unclear wishes and fears can be corrected in a slower, more calculated process that includes patient and surrogate in a team effort. It also acclimates both patient and surrogate to discussing issues in each other's presence, supporting one another along a difficult path. Although the journey through Alzheimer's is unavoidable, it can be infinitely more comfortable for patient and surrogate if they have experience and history where they are equal or partners.

Failing to make things clear, refusal to declare a legal surrogate and unwillingness or inability to share those decisions with all concerned have long term effects on the family as well as the patient and sometimes even professionals. Professionals will hopefully provide the impetus for and support the patient in facing and making these hard decisions while they are still able.

Choosing from among conflicting family members

Sometimes, old feelings of guilt and unresolved sibling rivalries make the patient a Ping-Pong ball in the match over which her children finally have control. Existing attitudes, old battlegrounds and significant emotional pain and denial can combine to produce a disastrous situation. The patient, once afflicted, needs security, structure and support.

Under the best of circumstances, productive discussion and assessment is difficult. Family history can not help but play a part in what happens. For some, Alzheimer's is seen as an opportunity to ease guilt, repay old debts, or finally correct things that have been broken for years. The surrogate can't afford to take things too personally.

In our situation, I continued to include my siblings way beyond the point where professionals deemed it productive. I was dually motivated in this. Although my mother had five children, each of her five children had but one mother. I would not have wanted to be left out, un-consulted or un-informed in such important decisions. Despite the difficulties I faced by including my siblings in decision making, for the most part, I would do it the same way again.

Families

Alzheimer's disease can be a slow, confusing process. In dealing with their Alzheimer's-afflicted loved one, the caregiver will become greatly impacted and emotionally involved. It is inescapable. Objectivity becomes almost impossible.

My brother recently told me of the Halloween night he received a call from our frightened mother. Since she was unable to tell him what was wrong, he drove to her house and spent the night. His willingness to take her as she was, and meet her need for security was exactly what our mother needed. Thank God she called him. Thank God he responded in love.

As I look back on my mother's needs and listen to the frustration of today's caregivers, I am struck by the conflicting needs and mixed messages in the lives of Alzheimer's families. As technology has transformed a society that wants more faster into a society that *expects* instant gratification, the Alzheimer's patient is cast in an ever more difficult light.

How is a family, whose adults may well be working full-time and may also have the responsibilities of children, to accept and manage well the responsibility of an Alzheimer's patient? People work in their cars, at home, and even on vacations bringing laptop computers, phones, beepers, and fax machines to the beach. How can people who function at that pace, driven by the need to compete and survive in a world that is more and more competitive, stop to listen to or to help an Alzheimer's patient?

Alzheimer's patients slow down in every aspect of their lives, as their caregivers feel pressured to move faster and accomplish more in an absurdly paced world. How can people embroiled in the opposing forces of living in late twentieth century America, survive as an Alzheimer's family? If they do not try to become a caregiving family, or can not continue as a caregiving family, who will care for that Alzheimer's patient? Who will pick up the pieces of that family?

Throughout my mother's illness, the decisions made were mostly correct for my mother but sometimes less correct for her family and her children's families. While all of my mother's children *did* live in that fast-paced world, we somehow continued to care for her. But most of it fell to me, a child making decisions for a parent, in the context of a complicated, sometimes difficult family dynamic among my mother's five children. Oftentimes, a confusing array of opinions—both covert and overt—from professional and family caregivers combined to make decision-making a treacherous road, fraught with potholes of doubt, traffic jams of ambivalence, and occasionally grid-locks of opposing and conflicting opinions. All of this was in the midst of my internal cacophony of loss, grief, anger, and despair.

Having the responsibility for the life of another thrust upon you is a demanding, exhausting, gut-wrenching task. It is a journey few would seek, and one that some refuse.

It would be a lie to say that my mother's journey through Alzheimer's did not strain the relationships of her children. It did. It was painful, it was sometimes destructive, but we survived it. We are still a family. The world in which I grew up was not perfect, but it was stable and secure. The family of which I was a part was not perfect, but it was, and is, a family of love.

I know how difficult I found my siblings to be at points in time. But I also know that I was at least as difficult for them to deal with, if not more so. We were dealt a tough hand. We were firmly entrenched in a family long before Alzheimer's showed its ugly face.

We had suffered losses prior to the onset of our mother's disease. We had love, but we had lots of pain too. Some of the ways we dealt with one another in difficult situations were less than healthy.

Early in the journey I particularly wished my father were alive so the burden of decision making would be his rather than mine. But I also knew it would have been unbearable to watch his pain at the changes in my mother. By the end, I realized that spouses have a difficult time with Alzheimer's decisions too. I recognize that though the issues are the same, approaching caregiving from a different relationship to the patient must change some of the caregiver's personal issues. I do not presume to speak to those with different relationships as though I know, for I don't. Yet I hope sharing my experiences may be of some help to them, too.

Religious and extended family support structures, (with the exception of one uncle and one aunt) were not available to our family, at least initially. While not scattered across the country like so many American families, we were scattered across 150 miles in the same state and, for a period of time, across 1500 miles. Few of us were in close proximity to our mother, or to each other. With the exception of one sister, none of us was practicing the religion of our childhood. Our father was deceased, and most of our aunts and uncles were either dead or out of contact.

The use of phones typically meant that two of the six of us spoke at a time, until our mother no longer used the phone; then it became two of five. Communications were often misrepresented, but that was mostly due, I believe, to the fact that each of us was constantly struggling to assimilate and process the changes that had become part of our lives. Our emotional, intellectual, and temperamental reactions were varied. We were on a roller coaster that rarely slowed long enough for us to catch our individual or collective breath.

We were simultaneously trying to cope with the strange loss of our mother and the stresses of being parents, spouses and workers in a hectic, high-pressure world. In many ways, we were not up to the task; yet in others, we performed admirably. But our family system eventually broke down. Our ability to calmly and rationally identify, discuss and evaluate issues, alternatives, and appropriate solutions for our mother was lacking. Our family was not unusual. We were, in many respects, the typical American family whose lives were being irrevocably altered by the intrusion of a long-term, fatal dementia. Like most American families, if statistics are to be believed, we were dysfunctional.

> ...The blaming family is only too commonly found in
> the Alzheimer world. Instead of uniting to form a battle
> strategy to deal with the disease, working out family
> approaches and coming to consensus, the family breaks
> apart. This division tends to continue for years after
> the crisis, separating siblings and other relatives. It
> happens both because there has previously been a pat-
> tern of divisiveness but also, because of the family's
> inability to face loss, fear and the pressures of role
> change. Family members blame each other instead of
> confronting their own feelings about the disease.[4]

My mother's children were unable to work effectively as a group.
Except on a few occasions, we were unwilling to accept professional
assistance to facilitate, support, ease and enhance a group decision-
making process. We rarely agreed on the *specifics* of carrying out
her wishes, which on the surface, we all agreed upon. Emotions ran
high.

All of my mother's children are intelligent, vocal, strong willed
people. Despite the fact that we ranged in age from late twenties to
early forties at the beginning of our mother's illness, we often, like
many families, were trying to work through unresolved childhood
issues with one another and with our mother. Issues of control, love,
alliances, and being correct frequently clouded the issues we faced
for our mother. Changing our view of Alzheimer's from chronic to
terminal was a painful but necessary process. We went through the
process at different rates, in different ways, with different resulting
behaviors.

Inclusion of others can support or hinder the primary family
caregiver. Personality conflicts, disagreements over issues of care,
and lack of patience can cause serious difficulties for the family
member in the role of primary caregiver or surrogate. It is critical, if
at all possible for families to meet to identify old issues, in an
attempt to minimize their effect on the decision-making process. A
family who is able to do this well, is much more likely to support one
another and their afflicted loved one than a family who cannot do it
at all, or does it less well. In our case, unfortunately, as my mother
became worse, her family became less able to work together and I
felt increasingly isolated and alone.

The rocky ride of Alzheimer's forced me out of the security and
love within which I had been raised. It pushed my mother and her
children into a whirlpool of conflicting emotions with fast-moving

tides to an unseen, unknown shore. The descriptions of the destination were not encouraging. The decisions that our mother made
and, finally, that I made *for* her were hard and lonely. They were
heartbreaking. But we didn't run from them. We stayed side-by-
side, often bobbing and weaving, as difficult as that was. And I
learned from my mother throughout the process.

I grew up through this process. I matured as I developed my
innate abilities to be just and fair through mothering my mother.
But I felt alone and abandoned, sometimes solely responsible, and
more often than not overwhelmed.

A Path to Love

I learned without a doubt, that I loved my mother uncondition-
ally through all the stages of this horrible disease. I have lived Scott
Peck's definition of love.

> ... real love does not have its roots in a feeling of love.
> To the contrary, real love often occurs in a context in
> which the feeling of love is lacking, when we act lov-
> ingly despite the fact that we don't feel loving.[5]

With the grace of God, I felt love much more often than Dr. Peck
indicates is often so. As my love for my mother was tested and grew
I came to better understand Dr. Peck's words. Loving my mother as
I did was hard work, not fun. It aged and moved me along the road
toward maturity. Alzheimer's provides a caregiver with many challenges, but it can also be a path to love. The person with Alzheimer's
gives us perfect opportunities to grow and change.

From this vantage point, I am reminded of the agony and the
ecstasy. During the journey it seemed that I only felt agony, yet with
the perspective of distance and time, I realize that I experienced
ecstasy not only during the journey, but *because* of the journey.
Growing up, I remember my mother saying, in response to one of us
complaining about one ache or another, "It's just growing pains."
While the Alzheimer's journey caused much pain, without it I would
not have grown, or grown in the same ways.

Many normal experiences were lifted to the heights of ecstasy,
because they were in such stark contrast to the agonizing losses and
experiences of Alzheimer's. Turning on my outside shower in April
and leaving it on through November so I could shower beneath the
stars each night was a great source of comfort and joy to me. Seeing
a whale and her calf breaching 50 feet off the bow of the boat was an

incredibly amazing and moving experience. My appreciation for the normal and not so normal events of life was heightened. The move to a new home, reveling in a large construction project, finding a wonderful new author were very different experiences than they might have been because they were a break from the drudgery of my mother's illness. Pleasant, everyday experiences were highlighted; the sight of a cardinal, seeing a rainbow as I crested the hill on the highway. Crossing the bridge to the Cape, which had always been a relaxing and joyous experience for me became the breath of fresh air that cleared the storm clouds of grief and burden that weighed so heavily in other parts of my life.

Each of us, in our own ways found that daily pleasures could reach *great moment* status; events that would be important became celebratory. My sister recently told me that taking time out from teenage kids and a pile of papers to correct, to play three holes of golf at six o'clock was a refuge that forced her concentration away from the problems in her life. The graduation of her son became a source of intense joy. The agony of my mother not allowing her to leave the nursing home was offset by my mother's giggle at some joke only she was privy to.

♥

The primary thing I wish I had learned earlier was to trust myself—my heart, my mind, my gut—but perhaps most of all to trust my mother's decision for me to speak for her. Had I learned this up-front, I would also have learned to assess the trustworthiness of professionals by looking in their eyes and by being direct, and listening with my whole being to what they said and how they said it. Although my rusty faith in God, family and myself was shaken to its very roots, it held and over time strengthened.

I also wish I had learned very early on the importance of taking care of myself. I was a lay person, forced to learn lots of foreign material, fast. I was constantly juggling my own feelings of grief and loss while reversing roles, supporting my mother and dealing with professionals who were in various states of ignorance vs. knowledge, insensitivity vs. genuine caring. I learned that the issues are complex and the answers elusive. In most cases, the best solution for my mother was the result of candid, cooperative communication among staff, doctors, sometimes family, and myself.

There are many things I wish people had told me earlier in this process. There are also many things I wish I could have talked

about, or talked about more openly. The journey presented challenge after challenge:

- ❤ Finding the courage to face and accept what was happening
- ❤ Grieving
- ❤ Educating myself, professional caregivers, family, friends,
  neighbors and even strangers
- ❤ Learning ways to love and respect my mother as she was
  changing
- ❤ Finding ways to stay connected to and communicate with
  her as she moved further into her Alzheimer's world.

Changes

I was forced to release my well mother. But, in her place was a
mother who was, in many ways, easier to get along with. No longer
the parental mother, but the loving one—delightful and fragile, but
that was OK. It made us feel protective and able to take care of her.

I found it particularly difficult to accept the changes in my
mother. My senses told me she was the same person I had always
known and loved. She looked the same, sounded the same, walked
and dressed the same, yet she was somehow different. Of course
that "sameness" didn't last, but it lasted long enough to thoroughly
confuse me for a good long while. She was not the only one changed
by this disease.

At some point more than halfway through this journey, I remember being angry and horrified when a support group leader said,
"you'll be different when this is over—you can't help but be different." Despite my protests and rage, she was right. As difficult as this
has been, it has also been an extraordinary opportunity for the
growth of my spirit, mind, heart and soul. I am irrevocably changed.
I am different than I was and I can't go back. It is like the Cape Cod
shore; it will never be tomorrow as it was today!

The stronger appreciation of small things—the treasuring of
moments of calm not previously even noticed are changes with
which I was blessed. So you see, dear reader, although I fought the
Alzheimer's experience, it was, in many ways a blessing in disguise.
Through it, I changed in positive ways as I learned to be less hurried,
to appreciate the smaller joys of life, to love above all else.

Perspective had much to do with how I experienced my mother and her Alzheimer's disease. For a long time and sometimes still, I refer to and think of my *well* mother, my *real* mother, the one known as "Puppy" as someone different and distinct from my *other* mother, the *sick* one, the one known as "Rita." Upon reflection of these names, which describe apparently distinct and different people, I begin to wonder if perhaps my perspective has been skewed.

If I look at photos and think of how others, and I, change over time, why is it I differentiate so with my mother, as though she were actually two different people? Perhaps it reflects a changing reality, changing roles. Perhaps the changes in my mother's name is an honoring, an acknowledgment that my *well* mother was changing so much that a *different* mother, but my mother nonetheless, was taking her place.

I often wondered which person was the real person. I wanted to shout, "Will my *real* mother please stand up?! How can I make appropriate decisions when it's been so long since I've heard her voice I can't even remember it? What if she changed her mind? What if it no longer applies? What if I make a mistake? What if I can't do it? What if..."

My mother's essence never left although at times, I was less open to experiencing it due to my grief and exhaustion. And I had forgotten my well mother, we all had to some extent. It was not until her wake that people who had not made this journey with us, began to point out to my mother's children how she had been. We had been too close to the reality of the struggle, and the agony to remember for ourselves. We had forgotten the reality of who she was and who we used to be—the ecstasy.

Heartspeak

Because we are so oriented to communicating with words in our culture, it is often assumed that when an Alzheimer's patient loses the ability to make sensible speech, she can no longer communicate. But while the standard door of communication may close for Alzheimer's patients by lack of speech or lack of the ability to make their speech understood, the window of the heart opens as they become very sensitive to the feelings of others. Anyone who has been involved willingly with Alzheimer patients knows the end of speech is not the end of communication, though it may appear so to the uninitiated or insensitive.

As an educator, my first inclination was to function in my brain; I was much less in tune with and cognizant of the intelligence of my heart and my spirit. I had not yet learned, or perhaps had long since forgotten, the importance of looking people in the eye for the truth of their intentions, and the power of body language and hugs to communicate.

Without my being aware of it, my mother and I began early on to hone the skills of what I later dubbed *heartspeak*. Perhaps we simply moved backward in time to ways we had known and used before I could speak. Heartspeak was only one of many intelligences that came to support us through the process.

In the beginning, I knew intuitively that I would see my mother through this, *but I did not know that she would also see me through it*. I did not know then about "eye hugs" and hand-holding as ways to stay connected. To this day, I do not have words to describe the connection that somehow remained intact, but I know of its importance. I know that it provided the invisible map by which we together navigated the twists and turns of her dementia.

Although I didn't understand it at the time, I was embarking on the most difficult, costly, rewarding, and enlightening experience of my life. Still in the thick of it, after 13 years, I looked back, both grateful and horrified that it had presented itself. I am confident that I have made decisions according to my mother's wishes, and out of love.

While I look with a strange sort of pride at what I have done for my mother, I also look with horror at the toll it has taken on her family. But I played the hand I was dealt, although I never seemed to find the "Rules according to Hoyle" and I'm still looking for the manual that Alzheimer's caregivers should be given upon acceptance of the role.

There is no doubt that a diagnosis of Alzheimer's is bad news. The disease is progressive, degenerative, terminal, and if carried to its end, capable of stripping away the very things that make one unique. But the news needn't be all bad. For at some point, the victim loses the ability to sustain knowledge of the Alzheimer's thief, and some become quite peaceful and content. And though the horror stories people tell are based in fact, the truth is that no one can predict the course of the disease. No one knows how it will affect one person or another. Caregivers can *choose* a more healthy, less painful response to this experience with adequate and appropriate support.

The changes that result from Alzheimer's, though heartbreaking, can be blessings in disguise. Some people actually improve when the stress of being "as they always were" is removed. While the lengthiness of Alzheimer's is terribly stressful, it offers time for patients and families to heal old wounds, complete unfinished business, and grow into their humanity and personal spirituality.

Though no one knows for sure, and some would disagree, I know that the essence of my mother was always present, even through all those losses. And we were lucky, we learned to stay connected and to grow in ways that would have been denied us if it weren't for her Alzheimer's.

My mother went through many stages—we all did. Without our mother's Alzheimer's and my sister's resultant fear of it, she may never have gone back to school or taught. This growth has had a ripple effect on her family. Without our mother' s Alzheimer's I might never have begun writing poetry, or have written an article or this book. In my Alzheimer's work since my mother's death, I have rediscovered a passion I had lost since my days as a young teacher. So you see, my mother and her children *grew* into our future. And while never comfortable, it was rarely as bad as I had feared.

When we emptied my mother's home, I was awarded her plaque that said, "Today is the Tomorrow You Worried About Yesterday." It was an apt award. I now know the hundreds, perhaps thousands, of times I worried for naught. For my mother did not go through all of the same stages that others I knew of went through. And when we arrived at other stages over which I had worried endlessly, I was ready, and so was she. ❤

Table 1: Assessing Potential Surrogates

	Name	Name	Name	Name	Name
Is he or she willing and able to:					
Evaluate options					

Work constructively with:
   family members
   patient
   professional caregivers					

Seek input from:
   family members
   patient
   professional caregivers					

Share information with:
   family members
   patient
   professional caregivers					

Communicate decisions to:
   family members
   patient
   professional caregivers					

Be honest with:
   family members
   patient
   professional caregivers					

Listen and hear
   family members
   patient
   professional caregivers					

Marshall Resources					
Persevere					
Follow through					
Seek and Accept Support					
Can he or she:					
Honestly review his or her motives.					
Avoid crippling his or her ability to decide with guilt?					
Does he or she possess the requisite:					
Intellectual Capacity?					
Communication Skills?					
Code of ethics?					

1. Paul Raia, Ph.D., Joanne Koenig-Coste, MEd., "Habilitation Therapy: Realigning the Planets", *Alzheimer's Association of Eastern Massachusetts Newsletter*, Spring 1996, Volume 14, Number 2, p.3.

2. Paul Raia, Ph.D., Joanne Koenig-Coste, MEd., "Habilitation Therapy: Realigning the Planets", *Alzheimer's Association of Eastern Massachusetts Newsletter*, Spring 1996, Volume 14, Number 2, p.3.

3. Diana Friel McGowin, *Living in the Labyrinth, A Personal Journey through the Maze of Alzheimer's*, Delta Publishing, New York, NY, 1994, p. 104-105.

4. Frena Gray Davidson, *The Alzheimer's Sourcebook for Caregivers A Practical Guide for Getting Through the Day*, Lowell House, Los Angeles, CA, 1993, p. 42.

5. M.Scott Peck M.D., *The Road Less Traveled A New Psychology of Love, Traditional Values and Spiritual Growth*, Simon and Schuster, New York, NY, 1978, p. 88.

Chapter 2:
The Nature of Decisions

*The Alzheimer's patient asks nothing
more than a hand to hold, a heart to
care, and a mind to think for them when
they cannot; someone to protect them as
they travel through the dangerous twists
and turns of the labyrinth.*
—Diana Friel McGowin

The decisions required by Alzheimer's are many and varied. They fall within social, personal, medical and spiritual realms. All decisions must be driven by the patient's wishes and values. They must strive to maintain a quality of life consistent with the patient's beliefs.

Although issues of safety must sometimes be evaluated and addressed immediately, the first hurdle is denial. Patients and their loved ones experience denial. At some point, denial must be ferreted out and abandoned, so that conscious decision making can begin— the sooner the better.

While many feel that it is not necessary to go to the expense and put the patient through a full diagnostic work-up, it is critical to have a correct diagnosis from a multidisciplinary team who specializes in diagnosing dementias. Two important reasons: the symptoms may be the result of some disease other than Alzheimer's that is reversible. If it is Alzheimer's, you want to know as soon as possible so you can begin to plan for the future, with input from the patient.

Naming a surrogate voice, giving a proxy so that another can make decisions when you are no longer able is also essential. Throughout the disease, patients and caregivers are faced with quality of life issues. Legal and financial decisions must also be made. As the person with Alzheimer's progresses into the disease, she will need more and more assistance. Those who live many years, will require changes in their living arrangements.

In order for caregivers to survive, they must make a commitment to care for themselves. The Alzheimer's journey challenges all involved to let go at many points in time. As the disease progresses, end stage issues arise such as initiating, continuing or withholding medical treatment. The definitions of such terms as comfort measures, extraordinary means and heroic measures become very important. Finally, death and dying issues and the future of the caregiver must be considered.

Decision-Making as a Process

Decisions are the result of a process of evaluating alternative courses of action, reaction or non-action. If made well, decisions are an act of love, an affirmation of the person who is afflicted, a final statement to God and the world that this patient was a person before being robbed of personality, judgment, speech, mobility and eventually life itself and she will remain a person to her dying day. That she is worthy of time, thought, and love is the underlying belief and message the decision maker-caregiver must communicate.

Decisions sometimes appear to have little effect but usually do have long term and lasting effects, which can be frightening. They can be made in the urgency of crises or be well-thought-out. Decisions about and for the individual with Alzheimer's are rarely easy— usually, they are heartbreaking and exact a toll on those who make them.

Very few individuals, if any, are emotionally, intellectually and educationally equipped to move without assistance through the maze of decisions required for an Alzheimer's patient. Decisions involving Alzheimer's disease are by nature difficult. The correct decision for any given individual or group depends on many things, including the perspective of the one evaluating the decision. The society in which we have been raised and live has not prepared us to clearly fathom, let alone make, such difficult decisions, and society often fails to offer support once decisions are made.

In our society, feelings and emotions are often unwelcome. People frequently see themselves as "experts" in any number of subjects; thus expect definitive, fast decisions. Sometimes, decisions change and, often, initial decisions are emotional rather than carefully thought out. These are not conditions conducive to making the often muddy, emotionally charged decisions required by, of, and for the Alzheimer's patient.

The decisions I made for my mother fell into the medical, religious, spiritual, social, financial and personal realms. They were made in isolation, and in groups. Sometimes decisions were directed by authorities such as judges, lawyers, doctors and other professionals. The process was never easy.

Create a Multidisciplinary Team

It was only with time and through a baptism of fire that I found the need to develop a multidisciplinary team to support the decision making process; central to my role as my mother's surrogate.

In retrospect, I wish that from the outset, I had had access to systems and strategies to support discussion of the issues. Such access would have provided a milieu in which we could explore options and come to loving, moral decisions. I needed help sorting through the various, and sometimes conflicting, philosophies of care that would impact, and at times define, my mother's future. I wish hospice had been available from the start to assist me in translating my mother's wishes and to facilitate team building. In my mother's case, it took years, but eventually, a multidisciplinary team evolved. Unfortunately, I was the one primarily responsible for developing it.

A multidisciplinary team seeks input outside of the medical profession and the family. Our team included clergy, a social worker and a chaplain in a hospice setting. Those outside of the medical systems offered some understanding and skill that supported and presented different perspectives. This helped me to understand, and further define and accept the multiplicity of roles required of me. It greatly enhanced the odds that my mother's wishes would be examined and followed in a "moral community."

Multidisciplinary teams are not always, and in our case were never, all together physically. Individual team members may never share the same viewpoint. This is not necessarily bad, and in fact may strengthen the decision maker, as long as each is clear about her role and responsibilities. Finally, the makeup of multidisciplinary teams is affected by many factors—an urban team in a teaching hospital might have a much different makeup than a suburban team.

By their very nature, decisions are emotional. It is painful to see a once vibrant woman deteriorate to the point of total dependence. Family caregivers are emotionally involved because of their relationship to the patient. They have a history with the patient and other family members. They are struggling to assimilate drastic changes in the personality, abilities, and physical appearance of the patient. Many factors come into play that I leave in the bailiwick of mental health professionals. But I noticed, over time, a strategy for dealing with the emotionality of the decisions I made for my mother.

The process of decision making

Although not consciously aware of it until late in the game, I did go through a series of definable steps in making each decision.

I was not aware of the relatively clear description of the process outlined below while I was making decisions. I was too involved, too upset, too overwhelmed and too exhausted. Although the decisions themselves became more difficult, my skill in the process that evolved increased. The steps were sometimes in a different chronological order, but each step was part of each decision. I had to respect my need to:

- ❤ Adjust to the change or changes that raised the need for the decision
- ❤ Mourn the losses accompanying the change
- ❤ Experience emotional reactions that took the form of tears, or depression or anger and sometimes, thank God, laughter
- ❤ Gather data
- ❤ Discuss the alternatives and evaluate their consequences
- ❤ Mentally prepare myself (and perhaps others) for the consequences
- ❤ Search on a spiritual level
- ❤ List the pros and cons to alternatives and
- ❤ Sometimes defend the decision.

These steps could happen in a moment, or an hour or they could take months. In some cases, they took years. The time it took to make the decision was not necessarily related to my comfort with the decision. I rarely felt comfortable. But it was important for all of the steps to occur. When a decision was attempted skipping one or more of the steps, it was not possible to accept it as a decision, relate it to those who had to be told and defend it to those who objected.

Some of what I went through was instinctive. I knew, at some deep level, that my decisions would be right, that I would be able to see them through, and that I would survive this burden. And through the process, I discovered I had a deep faith, which I had been denying for many years; a faith which carried me when I could no longer carry myself.

For me, the bottom line was always Rita Callahan's rights and clearly stated wishes. I was forced to face these issues "where I live." I was challenged by courageous, loving, supportive, highly moral, mature individuals to love my mother enough to make decisions as she would, to protect her independence, quality of life, dignity and eventually her right to die. I was challenged and learned to let her go.

There were so many things I doubted but there were also some things I knew. Without a doubt, I knew my mother would not want to be alive like she was for the last several years of her life. I knew, if able, she would have gone to Jack Kevorkian, the Michigan physician who assists people to end their life. I knew she did not want to "go to the home." She would have been mortified at how she looked, and what she had lost, what she had become. I knew my mother would be furious at the burden her Alzheimer's disease had placed on her family.

Supports for decision making

Keeping my mother's wishes, rights and best interests as the goal was paramount to establishing and maintaining a cooperative, constructive team milieu in which to discuss the issues and guide me as the primary family caregiver. I found it helpful when others:

- ❤ Gave me respect as the decision-maker
- ❤ Were willing to listen and support without labels and judgment

❤ Conveyed a clear, sincere message that they too cared about my mother, would see this through with me, and support me in making the right decision

❤ Shared their own, similar experiences

❤ Provided references when necessary for outside support

❤ Were open to the fact that medical professionals may not have all the answers.

During my mother's years in the nursing home we had two doctors who were incredibly compassionate as I tried, through tears, to tell them of my mother's clearly stated wishes. They showed unflagging respect for those wishes and my struggle to make decisions that honored them.

Gretta, a long time nurse, assured me that it was fine for me to take a respite break. She assured me that my mother would be fine and reminded me how important it was to care for myself. Her willingness to share her caregiving experience early on eased my feelings of responsibility and loneliness. She had lived and survived the caregiving role. This was my first experience with a medical professional who faced the same struggles and emotions as I did. This nurse's candor established the base upon which a very important supportive relationship was to be built. I learned much from Gretta over the years.

The Professional's Role

The fact that many professional caregivers feel the attachment, the right, and the responsibility to "safeguard" the patient can lead to conflict and stress in decision-making.

I watched professional after professional give glib, pat answers to questions they had obviously not faced directly or personally. I dealt with some professionals who were condescending and judgmental and other professionals who hid behind labels that were inaccurate and counter productive. I struggled for the courage to ask for their understanding that we were talking about my mother, a very strong, once clear-thinking woman who had expressed her ideas in no uncertain terms. When it didn't work, I found other avenues for her voice to be heard, her wishes to be known and her rights to be respected and protected.

It is a common pitfall for health professionals to judge a decision by their own value system rather than the value system of the patient, family caregiver, or surrogate voice. It is incumbent upon everyone, as much as possible, to give the patient (or her surrogate or caregiver) the options, consequences and other pertinent knowledge about the situation, and then to accept his or her decision.

I remember a particularly difficult conversation with a nurse I knew fairly well. She insisted that it was to be her decision whether or not my mother would be sent to a hospital, despite the fact that the family had made the decision that she was not to be sent. This person clearly believed that it was a judgment call that she would make, regardless of my mother's wishes as stated by me.

Another very difficult situation arose when a nurse approached my brother several weeks after we had notified the doctor that no antibiotics would be used, under any circumstances. My mother had been fighting a fever and hematuria (blood in the urine) for over a week when my brother was approached. The nurse told my brother that the decision we had made was wrong because my mother was a Catholic, and she was a Catholic. When my brother told the nurse she was a nurse first, and a Catholic second, she disagreed. He very calmly said she would no longer be working with our mother, then notified the supervisor on duty.

As upsetting as those incidents were, I was often more concerned about those who quietly disagreed and covertly undermined our decisions rather than those who challenged them directly. It became clear, over time, that some of the facility staff did not share my mother's value system regarding health care issues.

Facility staff, like family, can become attached to the patient. This reduces their ability to be objective. Although very difficult to prove, I believe that some staff were unwilling to honor my mother's wishes. Since covert disapproval is not open, it is difficult to confront. In situations where I felt strongly that my mother's rights could be compromised by such attitudes and beliefs, I talked about the issues with the director of nursing or with another person of some authority. It was my hope, and is my belief that they dealt with some of the staff by not assigning them to my mother and in some cases, by removing them from the end-stage floor altogether.

About a year after my mother's death, I had a very interesting conversation with a veteran community college nursing professor who had designed and instituted into the curriculum a course on death and dying. Her statement to me was, "Unless and until nurses face death and dying in their own lives and come to terms with it, they will be unable to deal with the issues surrounding death and dying in their professional lives." Her simple words cast my years of concern into a clearer light, revealing a world of scary motives and actions that can jeopardize patients' rights to self-determination.

What Guides Decision-Making?

Looking back, I can honestly say that I made the best decisions I was able to make at each step of the way. That is not to say the decisions felt right. In fact, I wish I had made some decisions earlier than I did. But in retrospect, I see that I was true to a process honed over the period of my decision making. I used certain criteria on a regular basis and my motive was always how my mother would act and choose, if speaking and deciding for herself. It is only with the benefit of hindsight that I fully appreciate the complexities of the systems that converged to become my environment for decision-making. I now know what hard work decision-making is for the Alzheimer's patient.

Because the disease robs the patient of the ability to identify and evaluate issues and make decisions, it is imperative that the patient be involved as early as possible in discussing her wishes. We must never lose sight of the fact that it is her life and death that are the subject of decision-making.

Like many Alzheimer's patients, my mother fought with all her might to maintain control over her life. Family members and professionals were astounded at her ability to do this, given the degree of her impaired abilities. She defied those who spoke of taking control. Her tenacity and protective nature allowed her to do what the "experts" found so amazing. In fact, I believe my mother was aware of and involved in decisions, albeit more passively than had been her style, throughout her disease, long after she was able to communicate in customary ways.

I heard the same thing again and again over my years of decision-making. Doctors, lawyers, counselors, clergy, and others to whom I looked for advice told me decisions should be made based on my mother's expressed wishes. They pointed out that my own and my siblings' feelings, thoughts, and opinions were not of consequence. My responsibility was to honor my mother's desires—period. Hearing these words from so many different people gave a strong initial message that was continually reinforced. It is the only consistent advice I encountered.

Even though it is infinitely easier to describe this advice than it was to make the actual decisions, I did heed it throughout. In fact, the advice pointed out how muddled things get when one assumes another's voice. The process of sorting through and assigning owner-ship to thoughts, feelings and opinions was ongoing.

> Quick neat fixes which our society seems so addicted to, should not be used to make care decisions for the patient with Alzheimer's. Those family and friends who are willing are often ill equipped themselves to provide the spiritual, medical, ethical, moral and psychological guidance needed. The development, over time, of a team of people who are willing and able to provide dif-ferent perspectives is critical.[1]

Time must be taken to sit with the information, the differing opin-ions, and the patient's wishes. Caution must always be taken to avoid agendas that are not in the patient's best interest. Power strug-gles and professional over-involvement should be avoided. It is imperative that the exchange between professional and family care-givers, and between caregivers in each group, not be polarized so that they end up in a tug-of-war over the patient. Unfortunately, this can and does happen.

Rapid, unthinking, unfeeling decisions by anyone should be ques-tioned by all professional and family members of the patient's care-giving team. "Monday morning quarterbacks", those who seem to have all the answers at their immediate disposal, the quick fixers and savers must be cautiously heeded, if at all.

My decisions were based on my mother's wishes that were expressed for decades before she got sick. My mother had been clear and consistent about her wishes regarding the end of her life. My first recollection was in 1956 after the death of her father. I was six years old. Over the years, she spoke of such things, always with clear, calm certainty.

My mother's definitions of the terms quality of life and quality in dying were woven over decades through scores of conversations as she commented to her family about this situation or that, what one person and their family or another was challenged to face. She was clear about what she would want and what she would not want.

As many people do, my mother made general statements about her wishes such as; "let me go", "no heroics", "comfort only", "keep me comfortable but let me die!" But she also told us over time, in a variety of contexts, what those statements and phrases meant to her. From her early statements about the nuns unplugging her father at the end of his long battle with cancer to not wanting to eat baby food like her toothless uncle, to her dread of being unable to move, drool and to depend on others for care, to her greeting to me on the night my own father died.

On that night, she greeted us at the door with a smile, "Your father died quickly, with no pain, in his own bed. Thank God every day for that gift." At the time I was stunned by her words given the fact that her mate of over forty years had just died next to her. But fifteen years later I fully understood my mother's words.

The last to die within the family that my mother spoke of in these terms was her sister. Although my mother was into Alzheimer's, it was early on and she was as clear and calm as she'd ever been. She supported the involvement of hospice and accompanied me to see my aunt the night before she died. My mother was typically peaceful and I was amazed at her reactions and comfort with death.

My mother's final statement to me about the end of her own life was little more than a month before she entered the nursing home. She said, "Oh Honey, my biggest fear—the one thing I couldn't handle is to lose my mind." I was grateful that she was unaware that she was already headed down that sad road, and that she could still tell me about her wishes.

Things are much more difficult if the patient has never expressed her wishes and then starts after she has become ill. Alzheimer's by it's very nature affects the patient's ability to make decisions. Caution must be exercised when the patient's wishes might be knee-jerk reactions based on exaggerated effect instead of the ability to problem solve, reason and see the "bigger picture." However, early stage patients still have these capabilities, though not consistently.

Who Communicates Decisions?

Initially, my mother herself communicated decisions. When she was no longer able to do so on her own behalf, I, in my role as surrogate voice, communicated decisions officially and legally. However, it was not uncommon for my siblings, my mother's professional caregivers, and others in support roles to communicate decisions and be sure they were carried out. Having many people share the role of caregiver complicates the communication of decisions. Once my mother was institutionalized, decisions were sometimes ignored, unknown, or countermanded. Often, it was the fact that decisions were not followed that clarified them.

Things change if or when the patient is institutionalized. In our case, the decision-making process was often uncomfortable within the family and between the family and facility. It led, eventually, to ever-clearer markings on my mother's chart that I was to be consulted and only my instructions were to be followed. It had been agreed upon within the family that, though I was the "official" decision-maker, all members of the family were advocates. In our advocacy role, each of us would speak on behalf of our mother, if we felt it necessary.

Due to the size of our family and the dynamics within it, all incidents were not shared with all involved. However, serious incidents and issues were communicated within the family so that a united front could be presented to professional caregivers and to increase the likelihood of decisions being carried out. This was especially true for decisions that were not fully understood or accepted by all professional caregivers.

Even after she became non-verbal and seriously demented, I kept my mother apprised of decisions. Since I believed that it was my mother's life and, ultimately, her death, I insisted on being honest with her and always introduced new caregivers. On rare occasions another caregiver or I would forget our manners and speak of my mother and the issues as though she were not there. Even in the end stages, this agitated my mother greatly. At times, when I was too tired to work through the unnatural language of discussing things as though my Mom were participating, I would tell her up front that we would be talking about her in the third person, but meant no disrespect. I was always aware of my mother's reactions. Although her reactions were sometimes absent, more often, I found them revealing. I always took them into account before final decisions were made.

I observed such a revealing reaction from my mother just weeks before her death. I had asked the new Director of Nurses to come in so I could introduce her. My mother did not look good. Her face was flushed and her eyes were at half-mast. The Director of Nurses yelled her greeting to my mother, as though she were deaf, then expressed concern over her appearance, saying she looked feverish and sounded congested.

I told her my mother was a hospice patient, and she replied, "Well, we'll use antibiotics to keep her comfortable." I said no, only palliative measures would be employed to maintain comfort. After several minutes, the woman yelled her good-byes and left.

Immediately, my mother opened her eyes wide, looked directly at me and laughed, as though to say, "You've got it under control. Better you than me, kid."

By that time, I was comfortable with my interpretations of my mother's reactions and knew, without a doubt, that she was aware of and in agreement with the involvement of hospice.

Speaking with professional caregivers in front of my mother provided an opportunity for her to remain involved, no matter how unlikely that may have seemed. Offering her a chance to concur or object also gave me comfort. In a way, it was almost a sanctioning of my interpretation of her wishes and the decisions I made for her.

Who Is Affected by Decisions?

Decision-making for and by patients with Alzheimer's affects many people. Oftentimes, many of these people are in a system called a "family." Systems theory is very clear that when one element of a system changes, the system changes; when one element of a system is stressed, the system is stressed.

There are many people affected by each case of Alzheimer's disease. Of course, the patient, and her family and friends are the most affected. Her children, if grown, are parts of other families with hopes, dreams, stresses and responsibilities. Children and grandchildren are also affected, and their experience around the disease will affect their values, development and future. This experience will affect their future choices and decisions about their own lives and the lives of those around them.

The needs of the patient, while paramount, must be weighed against the needs of other individuals and families. The sacrifice of a family or another's life to caregiving and the challenges of the disease must be carefully weighed.

It is within the purview of the primary caregiver to gather, analyze, balance and fit the patient's wishes, current situation, medical and professional advice and the consequences of various alternatives with the feelings of those involved. This juggling is tricky and exhausting, but it can be done, and it can be done well.

The importance of taking the time to sit with ideas, feedback, options, and needs cannot be stressed enough. Although difficult, solutions and alternative methods of caregiving can be found that are not destructive. This requires time and energy. The cost is high, but so is the reward.

I struggled constantly to re-evaluate what was important. It required a recognition and acceptance of how the disease was affecting my mother. I was less aware, however, of how it was affecting me. I struggled for years to learn to live the serenity prayer: changing what I could, accepting what I couldn't change, and seeking wisdom to know the difference.

I learned that there were things I could control, such as, how I interacted with my mother, and things I couldn't, for example, how the disease would progress and how others acted towards me and my mother.

Ethics

Dr. Kevorkian was not in the news when my mother and I began this journey, but he hit the scene with a splash while I felt myself drowning in life-and-death decisions. His notoriety raised social awareness as well. In some ways, this made things easier, because it provided a framework in which to discuss issues related to my mother's care. In other ways, it was more difficult because emotions were particularly high when people were challenged by open discussion of quality-of-life issues, withholding treatment and death and dying. I did not realize when I first heard of Dr. Kevorkian that his first patient was a 54-year-old woman with Alzheimer's.

I had not spent a lot of time thinking about ethics until I was faced with a stream of decisions about my mother and her Alzheimer's, all of which seemed to have ethical implications. These decisions ranged from seeking a diagnosis, to driving an automobile, to changes in living arrangements, to treating infections. All had long term effects on my mother and others as well.

Although I eventually came to my own paradigm for dealing with ethical considerations, I am not sure that others with whom I discussed decisions had. Nurses and nursing aides in facilities, doctors, emergency medical personnel and family members must all face the ethics of their decisions along the way.

In my mind, ethical and moral issues run the gambit all the way from the specific issues of care to ways of thinking, analyzing, communicating, and deciding. As I thought about what I faced because of Alzheimer's, I realize that many more decisions and processes fall into the category of ethics and morals than I initially thought. Prior to my mother's illness, I believed that ethics and morals were the amorphous stuff of theologians and philosophers. It took many years for me to find, and also to create for myself, forums and strategies so that appropriate, ethical, moral decisions could be made that honored my mother's wishes.

I assume my ethical and moral values are a combination of my family and religious upbringing, but during my tenure as caregiver, my father had been dead for many years, and my mother was fading fast, and all too soon, she was unable to participate or communicate. Furthermore, I had become a stranger to the church in which I had been raised. I considered myself a "recovering Catholic." But I viewed things like thoughtful decisions, honesty, and telling my mother the truth as ethical, and necessary. I believed in trust, but not in blind faith.

❤

Nurses, doctors, aides and emergency medical personnel have beliefs, value systems and opinions. Their roles differ in terms of the patient, but there was no doubt in my mind that they should all be bound by the same overriding premise by which I was bound—my mother's clearly stated wishes. Of course, for post-Alzheimer's caregivers (those who met my mother after she had Alzheimer's) this required that I fill them in so we were all on the same page—my mother's page.

However, this was not an opinion shared by everyone we encountered. My own expectations and standards for the medical, legal and other professionals will be described in greater detail in subsequent chapters, but it is important to note two things at this point. 1) Some people intentionally undermine decisions made for the Alzheimer's patient. Not only is this wrong, it also adds an additional stress to the caregiver, and it can be confusing and destructive for all involved. While it is always wise to pick one's battles, this is one that cannot be ignored. 2) The other important piece of the puzzle is that professionals have a right and need to have their beliefs and values respected. This requires a mechanism for professionals to freely share their concerns and for them to be supported in not caring for a particular patient if it conflicts greatly with their values.

Managing Disagreements

Methods must be found to manage disagreements, whether they are between family members, professionals and the family, family members and the surrogate, family members and the patient, or the patient and her surrogate.

In a situation like mine, where there were many people, it was not likely that we would agree on all matters. Unless one of us had a major problem with a decision, one that was in great conflict with our understanding of our mother's wishes, we tried to manage differences of opinion within the family.

Occasionally, one of us would not agree with our mother's decision, meaning that we would not choose that specific course or withholding of treatment, for ourselves, for our children, or spouses. But if we knew it to be her wish, we were ethically bound to honor it, and make decisions accordingly. It is almost impossible for a large family to be perfectly in sync all the time. But that does not make consensus impossible. Unless the person who is not in agreement in the group has a major ethical problem with a particular decision or believes it is against the patient's wishes, it is not in the best interest of the patient to block the decision. Continual self reflection and review of motivation is required of family caregivers to be sure that the issues that raise disagreement are really about the ethical implications of a decision rather than some old or current issue among family members being battled out through Alzheimer's.

The family who seeks resources to help them progress beyond impasses, resolve conflicts, and make decisions by consensus will fare better than the family that does not. If caregivers are to truly face the issues raised in the caring of an Alzheimer patient, they will have times of confusion, discomfort and pain. Over time, I evolved a code of ethics for myself and others who cared for my mother that would, stated in the simplest terms, provide comfort at all levels, physical, emotional, spiritual, social and psychological. This required introspection, definitions of dignity, quality of life and belief in the right to self-determination. And while I acknowledged differing values and views and the right of others to hold them, I knew care must be true to my mother's wishes.

Diagnosis

Although it may seem obvious, obtaining a diagnosis is very important and sometimes overlooked. A definitive diagnosis of Alzheimer's is not possible without examining brain tissue. This is not done until after death. For this reason, a diagnosis of Alzheimer's is a diagnosis of exclusion. That is, all other possible causes of the symptoms of dementia are excluded leaving a probable diagnosis of Alzheimer's. Some people, some medical professionals included, suggest that going through the somewhat lengthy, expensive process of diagnosis is unnecessary and presents a hardship to patients and caregivers. I find this irresponsible except under the most unusual of circumstances.

There are two primary reasons to seek a full diagnostic work-up from a group of Alzheimer's professionals who specialize in the diagnosis of dementia.

The first is that of the hundred or so conditions that can mimic Alzheimer's Disease, a goodly number of the "mimickers" of dementia can be corrected, reversing the dementia. Vitamin deficiencies, depression, malnutrition, anemia, infection, thyroid, sleep disorders and drug reactions are a few of the causes of dementia that can be reversed or cured. Reversal of the dementia caused by some of these depends upon early detection.

The second reason to seek a thorough work-up is so the afflicted person can be as involved as possible in the decisions that must be made about her future. Although Alzheimer's eventually robs persons of the capability and judgment to make decisions for themselves, this does not happen at a discreet point in time. People can be in the early stages of dementia for quite some time and still have lucid periods when they are able to make judgments. The importance of a complete diagnostic work-up cannot be stressed enough.

An interdisciplinary medical group that specializes in the diagnosis of dementia of the Alzheimer type is warranted. Unless you are out in the hinterlands, a larger facility is likely to be the better choice, but the National Institute on Aging has some programs designed to reach remote populations. Large city hospitals that have been doing this type of diagnosis from the beginning would still be my first choice, but things are changing. The local Alzheimer's Association is a place to begin your search for a specialized diagnostic team.

Diagnosis is simply too important to shortchange yourself and your loved one with a diagnostic group who does not have the experience, expertise and commitment of those who are truly dedicated to Alzheimer's. Experience, training and a multidisciplinary team approach is warranted. But the sad fact is that people who do not have the experience or the commitment have hopped on the Alzheimer's bandwagon. Precious time has been lost to patients and their families, causing hardship and heartbreak that could have been avoided had a better choice for diagnosis been made earlier.

Perhaps the saddest story I have heard about the lack of an appropriate diagnosis is that of a young family. The couple lived close to the man's mother who was in her fifties. At one point, the woman's sister enrolled her in a local research program where she was given a "diagnosis" of Alzheimer's. The couple became more and more involved as the patient's condition worsened. By the time they called me, they said no diagnosis or legal and financial planning had been done aside from the "free diagnosis" by the researchers.

At my urging the couple took the young man's mother to the city dementia unit and began working with an attorney who specializes in dementia long-term planning. Through this process, they found out that a local family doctor had made notations in her chart of "probable Alzheimer's" six years earlier. By the time they got to the point of making decisions about changes in living arrangements and medical treatments, the woman was unable to participate. This left the couple to make devastating choices, their only guidance from professionals who knew neither the patient nor her family. Within little less than two years, the woman was institutionalized and the young couple divorced. Early diagnosis could have provided time to plan and take advantage of some appropriate intermediate steps before institutionalizing this patient. Early diagnosis might also have preserved a marriage.

When seeking a diagnosis, avoid groups whose primary focus and function is research rather than diagnosis. Some advertise a "free diagnosis". While research is certainly important, research facilities whose primary emphasis is on research are more likely to do a screening rather than a full diagnostic work-up. The family doctor that claims he can do the work-up alone should be avoided. While the family doctor may begin the process by ordering some tests and making referrals, the diagnosis from a group who specializes in dementia diagnoses has many advantages.

The Anatomy of an Alzheimer's Diagnosis

There are several things that are necessary in order for a dementia diagnosis to be considered comprehensive. Unless each of these steps occurs, the chance remains that something that can be cor-

rected will remain undiscovered, hence uncorrected and the diagnostic process will be incomplete.

1. Complete Neurological Examination

2. Complete Psychiatric and Psychological Assessment

3. Complete Social Workup

4. Complete Physical Examination

5. Blood Tests

6. Brain Scans (CT, MRI, and maybe PET and SPECT)*

7. Extensive family and patient history

8. Other indicated tests and work-ups

9. Communication with the patient and family regarding diagnosis and the future

10. Appropriate referrals

Except in extenuating circumstances, a diagnostic work-up from
a team who specializes in Alzheimer's (and related dementias)
should be done. Time is of the essence. Some will say money is a
problem. I have heard all sorts of reasons why a diagnosis can't or
shouldn't be done but one that does not hold any weight is the issue
of cost because most insurance will pay at least 80% and the balance
can usually be negotiated down or completely removed. Resistance
is to be expected but those experienced in this type of diagnosis are
adept at handling reluctant patients and family members. Finally,
appointments can be difficult to get, so making an appointment as
soon as possible may leave time for you and others to acclimate
yourselves to the situation. I recently read of a hospital dementia
diagnostic team that is also offering continuing treatment for both
patients and families. This strikes me as a wonderful idea and I hope
that others across the country are considering it.

Diagnostic criteria and tools will change as research sheds more
light on the causes of and ways to detect Alzheimer's. Research
efforts have increased dramatically over the past few years and that
trend is likely to continue. This makes it all the more important to
go to those who have their hand on the pulse of new discoveries.

While a diagnosis of Alzheimer's was once thought to be a death
sentence by patients and families, Alzheimer's offers unparalleled
opportunities to those who are willing to grow from the experience.

*New and better diagnostic tests are being developed all the time. This is
another reason to work with Alzheimer's diagnostic specialists.

A diagnosis of Alzheimer's need not be the end of happiness, laughter and love. Assuming appropriate and adequate support, and a bit of courage and grace it can be the beginning of a new path, new growth and other blessings. ❤

1. Sally Callahan, "The dilemma of feeding end-stage Alzheimer patients", *The American Journal of Alzheimer's Disease*, Volume 10, Number 3, Weston, MA, May/June 1995, p.12.

Chapter 3:
Quality of Life

Quality of life, as defined by the patient, is the key to decision making. If decision-makers are not aware of the patient's definition of "quality of life," how can they make appropriate decisions? Unfortunately, too many decision-makers act in ignorance of the patient's understanding and definition of quality of life. Though aware of the patient's definition of quality of life, unfortunately some act according to their own definitions or the definitions of others, which may well be in conflict with the patient's definitions.

People often bandy the phrase "quality of life" about with great alacrity, moving merrily along in discussions without ever pinning down precise meaning, without forcing themselves and others to be specific about its essence. Within our family, we used the term without defining it. At some point, each of us came to believe that the quality of our mother's life had slipped away. But, I suspect the point in time was different for each of us. It is not clear to me whether this was because we did not share a common definition, or whether some one or the other of us thought about it more or less than another. Perhaps we were unable to think clearly about it since we felt almost helpless to alter the situation.

What is quality of life? Is it the ability to communicate, to share with loved ones? The ability to know oneself, to know loved ones, to know others? Is it the ability to contribute? If so, what constitutes contribution? Is it the ability to feel emotion, to be empathic, compassionate, share joy and sorrow? Is it the ability to experience love and hate, fear and security? Is it the ability to make decisions for oneself? Is it independence, dignity, safety? Is it control over one's body, mind, spirit? Is it respect and dignity? Is quality of life the absence of suffering (physical, emotional, spiritual, psychological) or is it more?

However you define it for yourself, it is the patient's definition of quality of life that matters. Despite my confusion and hesitation in making judgments, I clearly hold a person's right to self-determination sacred.

♥

I most recently faced my belief in a person's right to self-determination shortly after my mother's death. It was during a conversation with my brother who had recently completed chemotherapy and radiation. We were talking about his cancer, which he said was gone. He was cured, this cancer, he said, would not kill him. He also told me, as he had before, that he would not go through treatment again. He was not afraid of dying and did not want to live as a burden. He was very clear about what that meant and how he felt. Although I was not sure how I felt about his choices, I acknowledged immediately his right to make decisions for himself and said I would support any decisions he made. I also said I hoped he would make informed decisions.

My brother's words during our initial conversation, and over the many difficult months that followed, were frighteningly like our mother's. His clarity and conviction were also like our mother's. The difference was that he was whole, his mind was intact and he could communicate clearly. Our mother had not been whole, and she had lost the ability to communicate. She lived for many years beyond those losses.

This reminder of our mother's strong will and clear wishes caused some second thoughts about the decisions I had made for her. But I could not change the decisions I had made. And I recognized, yet again, that I had made decisions for my mother from a position of love, to the best of my ability at the time. And my decisions were made while she was still physically present. But she had changed so very much that it was almost impossible for me to remember her words and mannerisms. It was impossible for me to remember her well voice while I looked down at the 'baby in the bed' that she had become.

I know that the precise point in time when I was forced to face the quality of life issue at the core of my being was the evening I heard of a woman in her nineties who fought to stay "out of the home." When she was too defenseless to protest going to the nursing home, she took matters into her own hands by not sleeping there even one night. The woman died the day she arrived. Was this self-determination or fate?

Dignity

The definition of dignity is elusive. At the beginning of this journey, I thought dignity meant not being "exposed" in front of others, particularly strangers, and not trading physical beauty and independence for dependence upon others. But my definition of dignity changed as my mother changed.

One evening, within the first month my mother was in the nursing home, I was sitting in her room, stomach churning, unable to intercede as I watched a difficult scene unfold. My inability to act was a combination of the newness of the situation and my grief and horror at what I was witnessing. My mother needed to use the toilet and required assistance. I went to the nurses desk, which was right outside her door, to ask for help. The nurse said my mother's aide was occupied with another patient, she'd be in when she could. When I said my mother couldn't wait, the nurse sent an aide who was passing by into the room.

The aide was very young and impatient. Just as I was about to explode watching her yell at my mother who was unable to get up from the john, my mother's aide came in and took over. She too was very young, but her approach was entirely different. She walked in and bent down to my mother, and with a warm, genuine smile said, "Come on Rita, how about a great big hug?" My mother reached up and put her arms around the aide's neck, as she skillfully lifted my mother and pulled up her clothes, in a single, swift movement. Her intervention distracted my mother from her move toward hysterics, and led me to a sigh of relief.

Another evening, I went in to find a nurse rolling my mother onto her side to clean her after a bowel movement. My mother's face brightened as I greeted her and reached to help the nurse. A glimpse of the polite, social person she had been was offered as she used her eyes to indicate that the nurse and I should introduce ourselves. My mother was unable to speak and clearly not aware of what was being

done to her. I immediately assured her that we knew each other and
started chatting with the nurse.

Although one part of me is still horrified at the scene, another is
grateful for my mother's lack of awareness on one level and efforts to
share at another. I am also grateful for the skillful love the nurse and
I had developed over time, being able to include my mother in our
communication in a way that acknowledged and valued her being
and presence. This was a gift of dignity.

Perhaps the basis of dignity is truth. But when do truth and disclosure become more harmful than respectful. When if ever, would I
abandon these foundations of dignity? When would I learn the value
of "fiblets"?

My relationship with my mother was built on truth and trust. But
how was I to continue that relationship of truth and trust when I
thought the news I had to deliver would destroy her? How was I, the
child, to tell her, the mother, that our roles would soon reverse, that I
would make decisions and she would abide by them and her life
would be determined by them?

How could I explain to my mother what I couldn't understand?
How could I give her hope when I was terrified? Would there come a
point where I would be unable to follow her wishes? Would I allow
her to end her life as she threatened? Would I assist her? Would I
prevent her from taking her life? If I truly believed it to be her wish,
would I take her life if and when she was not able to take it herself?

Decisions about truth and disclosure are not one-time issues.
And there are others who can assist in these decisions and disclo-
sures. The reins do not pass all at once.

I recall the last time my mother was at the major city hospital in
which she was diagnosed. The doctor, in front of my sister and me,
had told her that she had probable Alzheimer's.

She was angry and frightened but had the presence of mind to
ask, "What medicines do you have to offer? What difference can you
make to my future?"

The doctor said that unfortunately, she had no medicine that was
proven to be effective in the treatment, retardation or cure of Alzheimer's. But she mentioned a research study going on "across the
river" in which my mother was welcome to participate.

My mother thanked the doctor for her time, rose and left. I followed as she told me, in no uncertain terms, that she would not be a guinea pig, nor would she go back to people who could not help her. With that, she entered the elevator and left the building, with me rushing after her. True to her words, she did not return until the night of her death.

Although my sister wanted to pursue the research, and was willing to be the chauffeur, I thought it not even worth discussing since my mother was so adamantly opposed. She was losing control of her life and knew it. She had little enough left to determine and her ability to do so was waning quickly. We did not pursue research at that time out of respect for our mother's feelings and decision. We were not however, opposed to research and as things progressed, we came to have more strength in our convictions that someone had to help the medical researchers to find the clues that would unlock the etiology of Alzheimer's and find a cure. But we did this in ways that were known to us to be acceptable to our mother.

❤

Recently my friend Jan invited me to accompany her to see her Mom in a nursing home. I had been there before. The Alzheimer's Unit, which was in a separate wing of the building, was one of the best in the area. It was comforting to me in some strange way to see Jan and her mother; their conversation as Jan put away the clean laundry she'd brought, and her mother's interest as they looked at the fifty year old picture of herself and her sisters. I was fascinated by her Mom's astonishment that she herself was in the picture. I was saddened by her flash of grief as she heard, as if for the first time, of her sister's death.

As we were leaving, I saw a lovely little lady with beautiful hair, her gnarled hands fretting the bottom of her johnny to almost indecent levels, by the community room. She was repeating "I'm lost, I don't know what to do, don't know where to go" like a litany when I approached her.

"No one's here. No one cares," she continued. Her piercing blue eyes held mine as I gently took her hand.

As we arrived at a vacant table, I sat down and coaxed her to sit with me.

She still held my hand as her sad voice, laced with anger, asked, "Why did God forget me?"

I grabbed her other hand. My heart and soul poured through my eyes and smile and I replied, "Oh no, God's not forgotten you."

We were sitting face to face, hands clasped and time just stopped.

I don't remember what else I said but I remember her turning my hands over and saying, "Your hands—they're so loving."

Then, after a while she smiled and said, "You're a good lady, thank you for coming. I'm much better now. Thank you."

With her tacit permission, I rose. On my way to dinner I said to myself, "God didn't forget her you see, he just sent me." I think often of that lady and send her healing energy, light and prayers that her journey will be eased by feelings of comfort and security.

The litany lady reminded me of the night the priest, with whom I had been discussing end of life issues, had come to the nursing home to pray and administer the sacrament of the healing. As had happened during previous anointing, my mother looked terribly frightened and concerned when he explained he was going to anoint her with the oils. I couldn't help but think that she knew what that meant in the "old days"—death. When the priest actually placed his hands on her forehead, she laughed, like she had at other times.

When the priest had finished, he told her God would take care of her, God was waiting for her. Again she became agitated and seemed frightened.

Without thinking, I rushed by the priest, rudely pushing him out of the way.

 I took my mother's hands and said, "It's OK Mamma, don't be afraid. Everything will be fine. There's nothing to be afraid of."

This was a strange thing for me to do since I was still stuck in a swamp of spiritual doubt and questions. I certainly would not have said that I believed there was a heaven waiting, and that everything would be fine. My instinctual reaction surprised me, not that I would act so swiftly to reassure her, but that I apparently believed what I was saying.

My mother was immediately calmed by my words as the priest smiled from several steps away.

❤

During her early months in the nursing home, my mother insisted on keeping her jewelry and clothing, as well as her checkbook. This insistence caused great difficulties for the nursing home.

They were quite clear that they could not be responsible for these things and were adamant that they be removed. My mother was equally, or perhaps more, adamant that she would follow them out the door.

I supported my mother's choices in these matters. Her happiness, her sense of independence, and her dignity were inextricably tied to these symbols in her mind. I accepted the fact that we were exposing them to the risk of theft or disappearance or damage. It was a risk worth taking for dignity and independence were far more important than the tangible assets, the things that were in dispute. I simply made an arrangement with the nursing home to accept whatever checks my mother wrote and call me to straighten out "real payment."

I could not stop the disease. And I could not change the fact that we had slipped into the percentage of Alzheimer's families who must turn to institutional care. But I could fight for the things that represented independence and dignity to my mother. I did fight, and we won. The things disappeared, some of them never to be found. But I would do it again in a minute. My decision was based on gut. My gut was right. Allowing my mother to keep these last vestiges of her former self eased her transition to nursing home living and allowed her a few last stands before she lost the wherewithal to fight for her rights, her independence, her dignity—the foundations of her life. But by then, I was ready to take up the gauntlet on her behalf.

Almost nine years later, during the last hours of my mother's life, she was receiving morphine sublingually on the hour. I was struck by the consistently caring acts and words of those who ministered to her. Without exception, each person spoke her name as he or she gently moved her. Without exception, each person explained what they were doing and why. These people treated my mother with the utmost respect and they loved her.

Respect

Respect is fundamental to quality of life. Respect means treating people with kindness and courtesy, as though they are valued. Using diminishing language is disrespectful. Telling people to stop feeling how they feel is disrespectful. Being impatient with people is disrespectful. Refusing to listen to someone because they are demented is disrespectful.

Shortly after my mother's death, I witnessed an example of respect at a local grocery store. An older gentleman was having difficulty describing what he wanted. Bob, the young man behind the counter was patient, courteous and kind. His smile was genuine as he helped the man by asking simple questions. Despite Bob's patient, respectful response, the man was clearly agitated and frustrated, but between the two of them, the man ended up with something with which he was satisfied.

After the customer left, I said to the young man, "I watched your encounter with that man. I guess you realized he was having difficulty making himself understood. My mother had Alzheimer's which caused her to have similar difficulties. Although I don't know that he has Alzheimer's I wanted to thank you for your patience and kindness. You made the encounter successful for him."

Bob said, "I tried real hard, I hope I did OK?"

"Yes," I said. "Your patience and assistance, your calm, kind response was wonderful and I just want you to know it makes a difference for people who are like my mother was." By the time I'd finished talking I was close to tears, but I know Bob appreciated the compliment.

As I left I wondered if I was overstepping boundaries by speaking to the young man, but I decided my motivation was good and part of my responsibility as a caregiver, albeit former, was to educate others. There is much confusion about Alzheimer's and the need for education is great. I decided I would try to be more aware of how people treated one another and thank those who were obviously caring and made an extra effort. I hoped my words shed some light on what must have been a confusing situation from the deli worker's perspective.

I couldn't help but hope that my mother met with people like the young man at the deli rather than those who are impatient and unkind. Bob's willingness to take time and make an extra effort to assist his customer is an example of respect. Dealing with the public can be difficult. Disgruntled employees can become problematic for Alzheimer's patients. Those who treat people with respect, especially Alzheimer's patients who have difficulty expressing themselves, add to the quality of the Alzheimer's patients' lives.

When a person is listened to, her feelings are heard and acknowledged, and she is accepted and valued as she is, without judgment. She has been validated. Validation is another way to show respect.

When an Alzheimer's patient or caregiver expresses frustration, the response they receive can be helpful or harmful. With patients, it is sometimes difficult to respond appropriately for their words often do not match what they are trying to convey.

Learning to "listen" to the emotion more than the words is a skill. Learning this skill better positions the responder. I found that responding to my mother's emotion, rather than her words was more productive. I assume that is because she then felt "truly heard" and validated. I worried that as her language left her, I would be less able to respond appropriately. But this did not happen, for as her language left, my skill at "listening" in other ways developed. Being truly heard and validated adds to quality of life and worth as a human and social being. Alzheimer's caregivers practice active listening and become skilled at reading body language. Emotions are one of the last things to leave an Alzheimer's patient. They learn to listen with their hearts.

Manners

For some reason, I found it difficult and never quite mastered the oft-proffered advice to Alzheimer's caregivers not to ask questions of the patient. Early on, I walked into my sister's house and asked my mother if she'd had lunch. Her angry response, "Don't quiz me about whether I ate, do I look like I'm starving?" caught me off guard but she was still enough of the mother, and I still enough of the child to respond with an apology.

Clearly it was unfair to "quiz" her, but somehow, I needed my mother's reassurance that she was OK, that all would be fine. Of course she was much wiser than I and not only avoided an answer to my hidden question, which she didn't have, but she also distracted me. In time, I accepted that things were not fine, that she was not OK. But I watched my Ps and Qs. Who would it be more natural than to a mother to insist on manners? And it was rude of me to ask her questions she couldn't answer.

My mother's insistence on manners never ended. One morning, well into her descent, I walked into the nursing home day room where her nurse was feeding her. Uncharacteristically, we started talking about my mother in the third person, as though she were not there. This made my mother quite angry, and despite her inability to speak and move, her fists came up vigorously shaking at me. I immediately offered a contrite apology as did the nurse.

With all my strength, I couldn't get my mother's hands down until she accepted our lame excuses. For years I had insisted that people not speak as though she were not in the room. I also introduced new people right up to the end. While some thought this foolish, I viewed it as a sign of respect, a way to maintain her dignity. Little did I know that my mother was as aware as she was. Thank God I did things correctly for the most part because, despite her disease, her displeasure was as severe and painful to me as it had been when she was well. Her Alzheimer's neither removed my buttons nor her ability to press them.

Disrespect

Although some people liken the descent into Alzheimer's to becoming a child again, I find this analogy insulting and dangerous. Patients of Alzheimer's disease are adults. They can never become children again although many behaviors become more childlike as they progress into the disease.

Although they lose memory, judgment and appropriateness of response, Alzheimer's patients remain adults who have experienced the progression from infancy to adulthood. To think of them, or to speak of them, or to treat them like children, is demeaning and unfair. It strips them of dignity. It lowers them to the status of less than full human beings. It implies that they are lesser or less worthy.

End stage, non-verbal Alzheimer's patients are still adults despite their regression to the dependencies of infancy. Perhaps the use by some family members, myself included, of language that is more childlike is confusing and sends the wrong message to others. But for me, it was a way to honor the changes in role and relationship and maintain my involvement. For me, the use of the term 'baby in the bed' was a term of affection, an endearment that provided a quick word picture of our role reversal although I would never use it with my mother. It was a term that recognized the changes and helped me to keep a loving relationship with my mother.

A Matter of Perspective

Not too long ago, I had a frightening glimpse into a distorted, changing and confusing world on the second of a two day Alzheimer training class I was conducting. Knowing that my eyeglass prescription had worsened each day I was without the contact lens I had lost five days earlier, I arrived early to be sure I could walk around without bumping into things. I could see, but nothing was quite in focus. The edges of objects and their relationship to each other and to me were askew. Something was wrong with my world and getting worse as each day passed.

When the hostess arrived and greeted me I said, "They've lowered the ceiling in here. I hope my claustrophobia doesn't get the better of me."

When she replied, "Nothing has changed," I wanted to shout, "What's the matter with you. This ceiling is so low I can barely pass under it without hitting my head!"

Of course in my mind I knew the ceiling was not lower but my eyes were telling me something different. This war that was waging inside my head left me frightened and unsure, agitated and impatient, working hard to keep my panic at bay. I had to pull myself together to function because I was the presenter, and as the morning wore on and I became engaged in the presentation and with the audience, my panic eased. But I told them of my experience and the glimpse it offered into what it must be like for the Alzheimer's patient. I found myself moving to the perimeter of the presentation area, touching the boundaries, trying to teach my body the new rules of my changing, scary world.

In light of this experience it is not surprising to me that persons with Alzheimer's get testy and angry. They must feel as though they are in a foreign country but they can't learn the language and customs. So as caregivers, we should heed the old adage—"When in Rome, do as the Romans do". When working with those with Alzheimer's, enter their world and adapt to it. Learn their language and customs. Respect how they are different and adapt rather than insisting that they adapt, which of course they can not.

The Alzheimer's patient has a constant need to determine the details and parameters of his new, frighteningly unstable world. Lost cues and forgotten connections can result in repetitive behaviors, agitation, restlessness, and constant dogging of their caregivers by asking the same question or following them around. Angry or repetitive behaviors are perhaps the most difficult of all. Caregivers often complain of their patient following them wherever they go. This is called shadowing.

If the caregiver is able to view this behavior from the patient's perspective, they might find a deeper well of compassion and patience than they thought possible. I know I did. Alzheimer's shifts a person to a different world where the rules have changed, the language is unfathomable and the people seem more foreign than familiar. They can't learn new ways or adapt so their caregivers must do these things for both of them.

Incessant repetition of actions, stories, or questions all present challenges to the caregiver. Redirecting and refocusing the patient from the annoying behavior often works. It breaks the pattern and can move them to a more positive activity. Failure-free activities (such as those described in the book *Failure Free Activities* by Carmel Sheridan) break the cycle of patient boredom while providing some relief to caregivers. Instituting and maintaining a routine that makes sense to the patient works.

The best medicine for these difficult behaviors is truly understanding that the patient has no control over them and that the caregiver cannot change the patient's behavior. It is only her own behavior over which the caregiver has control. However, establishing and sticking with a routine is helpful. In fact, routine is one of the most effective strategies caregivers have, because it is one of the patient's greatest needs.

Finally, keeping a log of problems can help identify the causes of problem behaviors and point the way to effective solutions. Consider using the Behavior Log at the end of this chapter to pinpoint problem behaviors. Reviewing the log with another person might offer support as well as solutions.

Comfort

Comfort and healing touch are things I wish I had known more about when I began my journey. Although I had a general idea about comfort, I could have done better for myself and my mother if I had been clearer on what it really meant. I had occasion to experience touch as a healing tool late in this journey.

When I look back, I realize that I used healing touch instinctively. But again, I wish I had known more, and had been more deliberate in its use since I suspect it has far greater potential than I realized, and is little used. Use of scented lotions and colognes can be comforting to both patients and family caregivers.

As my mother moved further into the disease we became more affectionate, initially to soothe anxiety, then later to communicate, and later still to maintain connection. In addition to being nice for her, it was nice for me too. It slowed me down physically and emotionally. It soothed my anxiety, and it met my need to communicate and remain connected.

Full Functionality

Allowing patients to function at as high a level as possible for as long as possible is an aspect of quality of life that is often overlooked. On that road to complete role reversal, the caregiver often takes over tasks that the Alzheimer's patient is still capable of completing on her own or with a little assistance and/or cueing. It is often easier for the caregiver to just "do it herself."

The struggles of a hectic world make patience and "longer than necessary" task completion a bone of contention. But the fact is that self-esteem, happiness and peace of mind are directly related to independence and doing for oneself what one can. Although it is difficult to strike the right balance between full functionality for the patient and manageable frustration for the caregiver, it is well worth striving for. I had a peek into the psychology of this after my unexpected major surgery.

My husband of many years, from whom I was separated at the time of my surgery, had taken me home. Upon arrival, I was upset that my woodpile had fallen. He immediately said he would restack the wood and was understandably astounded at my tears of rage and frustration. What was my problem? I guess it was the fact that it was my woodpile, I had stacked that wood, and I should be the one to fix it. He quickly stopped arguing and offered to take care of it under my direction. As silly as that must have seemed to him at the time, he instinctively knew the importance of my maintaining some control. I too had instinctively learned this with my mother but was unable to describe it until shortly after the surgery.

❤

In order to avoid excess disability, preserve self-esteem and maximize quality of life, caregivers must anticipate the patient's needs by becoming expert observers. They must also be willing to accompany them into their strange new worlds.

One aspect of Habilitation is to make the environment suitable or fit for the patient to function in, thereby giving him a sense of being able. The environment has to be ready to change with the patient's inner abilities and perceptions. For example, although David had Alzheimer's disease, he got a great deal of pleasure from fixing his own breakfast; cooked oatmeal which he would eat directly from the pan. When his wife realized the danger of this particular tradition, she convinced David to switch to dry toasted oatmeal, sliced banana, sugar and milk. He had a special knife that had been his father's for slicing the banana and a special cooking spoon that he liked to eat with.

At first he could:

- ❤ Take the bowl, knife, spoon, sugar bowl and milk from their respective storage places (his wife just had to make sure they were in their proper places.)
- ❤ Pour out a reasonable amount of cereal
- ❤ Cut the ends off the banana, slit the skin lengthwise and dispose of it in the garbage. (His wife's role became moving the garbage pail close enough so he wouldn't miss when he threw the skin.)
- ❤ Slice the banana in thin, uniform slices dispersed about the surface of the cereal
- ❤ Sprinkle sugar from the sugar bowl over every slice (It took a lot of sugar, but tests showed his blood and urine were not affected.)
- ❤ Pour milk from the bottle carefully over every surface. (He didn't seem to realize that the fluid would find its own level, despite having been an elementary science teacher.)
- ❤ Eat and enjoy every bite.

As time went on it became clear to his wife when she should intervene on single elements of his strategy. She took over in the following ways:

- ❤ Put the needed ingredients and instruments on the table, she later set the table
- ❤ Poured out a reasonable amount of cereal
- ❤ Gave him a pitcher with the right amount of milk. Later, she poured it on the cereal for him
- ❤ Took the banana skin to the garbage pail. Later, when he tried to slice the banana without taking off the skin, she peeled it for him. Still later, she took over the slicing.

He still kept the sense of managing his own breakfast and ate every bite. Of course the time did come when his wife had to gradually do some, then all, of the spooning. Still later David wanted a smaller portion. Still later they switched to cooked cereal which was easier to swallow. By then he was happy to be fed. But how awful it would have been to introduce these changes before each was needed.

The loving care David's wife took in finding safe alternatives, and anticipating and instituting changes maintained David's dignity, respected the capabilities he still had and added a quality of life that might have been lost with a less thoughtful, flexible caregiver. The changes were guided by the patients needs, not the caregiver's convenience.

Independence vs. Safety

The balance of independence and safety are faced by all Alzheimer's caregivers who wish to be true to their patient's definition of quality of life. These issues are often the source of conflict around and between caregivers and patients. With some luck and a lot of grace, correct decisions that are not harmful to others will be made.

Caregiver ambivalence compounds these issues. I used to think ambivalence meant feeling one way one moment and the opposite way the next. I came to realize that ambivalence is feeling opposing things simultaneously. Not a comfortable companion, ambivalence, but one with whom I became very familiar. Although we have never discussed it, I suspect that my brothers and sisters shared my ambivalence about this issue.

Since my mother was so clear about her wishes, there was a part of me that hoped she would act on them. Who was I to stop her? Who was I to trade her independence and dignity for dependence and indignity? Who were any of us to force her to accept safety over independence? She had not lived her life that way, why start now?

But there was the dilemma of knowing that Alzheimer's affects a person's judgment and that my mother was becoming the captive of a disease that would ultimately rob her of her abilities. And what was our responsibility to the safety of others? At what point would her judgment be impaired to the point that she would become a danger to herself and others? Who would decide when that was? What would be the consequences of accepting such decisions?

Many of these issues are compounded by the age-old dilemma, the rights of one versus the rights of many. These things are not simple. Rights and responsibilities vs. freedoms—specifically my mother's rights—were the issues with which I wrestled.

A simple but rather clear illustration of this dilemma is the question of giving flu shots to those who are in facilities. It took me several repetitions to finally grasp this, but I finally came to realize the common sense approach that underlines the losses with which the Alzheimer's patient and her family are faced. Because Alzheimer's patients are often physical with those around them, it makes no more sense to withhold a flu shot from them than it does from small children who act in similar ways. Kisses and the transmission of bodily fluids create a ripe atmosphere in which germs are passed and people become sick. So if the patient is mobile and in contact with others, while in day care or a nursing home, the good of the many comes before the rights of the one.

Those who are most likely to have knowledge of the patient's definition of quality of life, family caregivers, are all too often moving from crisis to crisis, without benefit of the time to think things through in light of their loved one's definition of quality of life. I found few professional caregivers with the ability, or perhaps the willingness, to discuss alternate treatments in terms of quality of life as defined by my mother. Of course occasionally, and more often with doctors in my experience, I found someone who not only believed in an individual's right to make decisions for herself, but was willing to explore them with me, someone who was mature enough to speak of and honor those decisions. But that is not, I fear, how most people in the medical professions are trained.

Medical professionals are programmed to save lives. Their mission is to help people. They go to great lengths and use extraordinary measures to cure, to fix, to in essence play God. Even though the technology now exists to support such an approach, and that same technology makes it easier to keep people breathing longer and their hearts pumping almost indefinitely, this approach can be antithetical to the right to self-determination and an individual's definition of quality of life. Traditional medical training and institutional "tension" may be antithetical to patient and family wishes.

❤

From the beginning, my mother's children were caught between her fierce declarations of independence and dignity and their own ever increasing concern for and need to provide safety. She was exceedingly adept at keeping the level of her impairment from us. But eventually, even we could no longer deny her problems. By respecting her wishes to remain independent, we kept her so, allowed her to be so, for a longer period of time. These issues are the ultimate societal and individual ethical dilemmas.

While in retrospect I agree with my sister-in-law, I also sometimes wonder if we were too protective of our mother's independence while being irresponsible about the rights of others to safety. We did not lose our mother to an automobile accident in which others might have been injured or killed. We were not left the legacy of suicide, for our mother did not act on her words regarding that. We did not lose her to an unknown fate as she wandered off one day. But other Alzheimer's families do face these tragedies.

Safety, while important, especially in light of the safety of others, is less clear to me. As I think my brothers and sisters did, I often viewed independence and self-determination as more important than safety. This view, I know, was my mother's view. And although we and she, and very possibly others were at risk, those risks were consistent with her values, wishes and decisions, both when she was well and after she became sick.

Although a part of me knew that my mother was not going to be the victor over Alzheimer's, another part of me was cheering her on. While I didn't welcome or encourage the behaviors that made her so difficult to confront, a part of me was secretly lauding her spirit, her independence, her strength and her courage. For this was my mother, the strong, clear woman I knew. If someone could beat this thing, surely it would be she.

But the issue of safety was there. In retrospect we know there were incidents we may have under-reacted to at the time. Unconsciously our inaction may have been intentional. But I can't help but wonder how many more incidents we never knew about.

❤

One evening, my mother caused great concern when she did not show up at my sister's house at the appointed hour. As time marched relentlessly on, concern increased. Eventually, my mother showed up, having walked almost ten miles.

It was a beautiful evening, and the pleasant one mile walk from our mother's condominium to her home of many years, through a neighborhood she had lived in for decades, was not unreasonable. But somehow, the path became unclear and she took the circuitous route, passing through two other towns. I remember a comment when concern was expressed that she was so quiet that night. "Give her a break, she walked almost ten miles, she was exhausted. Who wouldn't be?"

We know of times that my mother was lost in the car. Her late arrival at my nephew's birthday party was again cause for great concern. A phone call from an Alzheimer's-friendly woman in an office park cleared up this mystery. My mother had gotten "turned around somehow" and the woman was able to get enough information from her to call us to come to her rescue.

And what about the time my sister drove around the block after dropping my mother and me outside the Colonial Theater in Boston to pick up theater tickets?

While waiting for my sister, my mother headed down the street, ignoring my appeals to stay where we were. As she moved closer to the "combat zone," I became more concerned. When she removed her coat to cover a man lying in a doorway, I said we really had to return to the theater.

My statement was met with my mother's irate words, "I was born and raised in this city. I know it like the back of my hand. How dare you treat me like a rube."

With that she marched off, swinging her purse temptingly in front of undesirables lurking threateningly in a doorway. Thankfully, my sister arrived just in time to distract our mother from her march into serious danger.

❤

Perhaps we were too young, and our mother too strong, to truly go against her adamant wishes, but we constantly waged a battle between independence and safety. We took risks, some of which we were aware, others less so. And in the end, our mother won. She was independent for as long as, and in fact perhaps beyond, her ability to be so.

I wonder if that is why she was so cooperative when her independence was finally gone, for she chose a move to the nursing home over living in my sister's house with a companion. Perhaps at that point my mother had an inner sense of what was needed—in her own way giving in to her eroding abilities, taking the pressure off all of us.

I also wonder if our support of our mother's independence and courage to keep on fighting didn't solidify a base of trust upon which we stood for the remaining years of her life. When she did give in, she did so with grace, courage and strength. She had fought the good fight and gave up her independence like a true champion.

Driving an Automobile

Driving presents a particularly difficult dilemma for Alzheimer's patients and their families. Driving represents independence, freedom and maturity. Young people can't wait to "get their wheels." They dream about the new freedoms driving represents. They see driving as a sign that they are grown up. It affords them an independence they've never had before. Losing the right to drive is the opposite of this. Yet, along with independence, freedom and maturity, comes responsibility.

Over the years I have heard and participated in numerous discussions about Alzheimer's patients driving. One man in a support group described his father as the only one among his friends who was capable of driving. Yet the son was now wondering if his father was as capable as he and his friends insisted. There had been no incidents of which he was aware, but his father was changing and he couldn't help but worry.

From the support group, I went to a friend's house. While my friend was getting a snack for us, her husband and I were talking. His response to my retelling of the discussion at the support group affected me deeply.

He said, "It's very clear to me, Sal. I can't believe you were sitting around wondering about the appropriateness of his father's driving. Just think about how unfair, unjust, how wrong it would be, if, while you were discussing and debating the merits and difficulties of his driving, that man wiped out my family?"

I had grown up with this man's wife. I adored their children and had grown to love and respect him. I was struck by how clear his statement had made the issue over which I had agonized for my family and others. What was wrong with this picture? Why did it take me so long to comprehend the danger of impaired people continuing to drive? Had I lost my judgment along with my mother? Were we all so far into denial that we would risk the lives of innocent people?

Another friend had raised the issue of driving long before we acted on it. At that point in time I was too overwhelmed with the losses that were creeping up on us like a choking vine. I could not hear, let alone act on his warning of liabilities. How could he speak of liabilities when my mother's very self was threatened? Who cared about liabilities at that point? Certainly not I. Perhaps there were other warnings that we should have heeded earlier. Perhaps the day the State Police called our house was a warning.

The trooper asked my husband if he had a mother-in-law named "Puppy." Tempted to say no, he replied "yes." Well, it seemed that the policeman had stopped my mother for speeding, and asked her to back up. She started yelling that she had never been arrested before. The trooper's explanations that she was not being arrested held no weight with my hysterical mother who was in the throes of a classic catastrophic reaction. All she seemed able to get out was our name and phone number. We went to my mother's rescue teetering between annoyance and humor. But we never viewed this as a sign of a significant problem until years after the fact.

Years later, my sister told me our mother, when on the highway, would stay in the lane under the sign that said where she was going. If the sign moved to another lane, so did she, probably without a blinker. As my husband had said when my sister first talked to us about my mother's declining memory, "Puppy's been a space shot since I met her fifteen years ago, it's no surprise that she becomes more spacey as she gets older."

Of course none of the decisions for Alzheimer's patients are simple. They are always made in the context of loss and also, hopefully, love and caring. They are surrounded by ambiguities, ambivalence, confusing changes in behavior, and denial. I went back to the support group and shared my friends' clearly stated concerns and comments. The man took his father's license away shortly thereafter. The decision was painful. His father's response was no more gracious or accepting than my own mother's response. Nor is it likely to be any easier for the next person who faces the removal of a loved ones' independence.

As the wife of an early stage Alzheimer's patient wrote:

> I do worry about him driving alone when he decides it's time for the mountains. I can't always take off and go with him; so I just bless him and send him on his way. He needs to feel that he can still do things on his own. So what if he gets lost now and then? His truck is well equipped with communication and identification devices, and he is well identified with Safe-Return. Why not allow him this luxury? Soon enough this will cease.[1]

But at some point in time, hopefully before someone gets seriously injured, the issue of safety in driving must be faced. Often, the doctor holds more weight with the patient so he can be a "better" choice for "delivering the bad news" than a family member. I recently heard a doctor say that a police officer can notify the Registry of Motor Vehicles. The Callahans were lucky, no one was injured by our mother as her abilities were declining. I would not want to face those decisions again, but if I had to, I would be more aware of the rights of others' safety.

Taking an Alzheimer's patient's license away, or removing the car does not always prevent them from driving. A story told by a support group member clearly illustrates this. The woman's parents were in the city where the mother pulled over to the curb and hopped out of the car to do an errand. During the few minutes she was occupied, her husband, who had not driven in many years left in the car. He showed up at home, fifteen miles from where his wife had left him, several hours later with no idea where he had been or where the car was. They found the car, in a church parking lot, locked up tight. The church was thirty miles away and the car was found a week later. The man had not driven for many years prior to the incident. What happened will never be known.

Traveling

During the years immediately preceding and following my father's death, my parents, and then my mother, lived part-time in Florida and part time in Massachusetts. I remember going to pick up my mother in Boston one year and wondering where she was when the plane was clearly empty. Although at first I figured she was simply slow about gathering her belongings, I really started to worry when the flight crew came down the ramp. As I wondered if I had gotten the flight information wrong, my mother, cheerful as a lark, came down the ramp with her arm through a young woman's she had met on the plane.

After a warm hug and radiant smile, my mother introduced me to "her new friend," who had so thoughtfully "bought her lunch." I was so relieved and happy to see my mother, I gave little thought to her strange introduction and obvious confusion about being the woman's guest at lunch in a paying establishment. Perhaps it was denial kicking in again or just naiveté. Again, who was I to question the woman who raised me? Why spoil a happy reunion when she was so clearly well and happy to be home?

My mother looked great, I was thrilled to hear her voice and gaze into her clear blue eyes. So I didn't bother myself with those pieces of the puzzle that didn't quite fit as well as they once had. After all, Mom was getting on in years, and it was no small feat to close up a house, pack for several months and get home all by herself. Having lost my father, I was particularly sensitive to my mother's presence.

It was usually my sister who put our mother on the plane. She remembers our mother leaving her belongings, pocketbook included, in the security x-ray machine. The first time around, Mother realized it before she boarded the plane. The second time it was my sister who discovered the problem. A compassionate security guard allowed my sister to bring my mother's things onto the plane.

Traveling with the Alzheimer's patient can be exhausting. One woman in a support group told of a momentary lapse during which her husband left the train that they were on in Lisbon. With amazing luck, she was reunited with her husband after several frightening hours of not knowing where he was. This is not to say that Alzheimer's patients should not travel, but caregivers should know that it can be exhausting and some mishaps might end in tragedy. Having more than one person to share the responsibility of keeping track of the Alzheimer's patient can certainly reduce such risks. Some airlines are now very helpful in flagging reservations on their computer systems to note a memory-impaired person. This can make solitary travel for the early Alzheimer's-affected person safer and less costly.

Death, Euthanasia, and Suicide

It is not unusual for Alzheimer's patients to talk about death, their own death. And many raise the issue of suicide. I suspect this phenomenon happens more than professionals like to admit. All too often, when these issues arise there is an immediate change of subject. A swift and sure raising of the proverbial rug and employment of the largest, quickest broom ensues. But in real life, lived by real people in real families, it is not inconceivable that the issues of death, euthanasia and even suicide will be raised. At the risk of offending or frightening readers, since my mother raised the issues, I must too.

To ignore the expressed feelings of Alzheimer's patients, or any terminally ill persons for that matter, who raise the subject of death, and even suicide is to ignore their feelings. The taboo around such expressions makes them bigger than life in some ways. For some people, such thoughts are the logical extension of quality of life issues. It is an understandable expression of their need and wish to maintain control over their own lives, including taking charge of the end of their lives. Some are quite clear that they do not want their loved ones or themselves to suffer the crushing emotional torment that Alzheimer's brings to so many. I find it understandable that people wish to take charge and admirable that they are courageous enough to speak of and perhaps face what it means not to have their mind.

The gravity and complexity of the issues raised when a person talks about maintaining or wresting such control is frightening. And there are many levels to such thoughts, feelings and discussions. Some speak of handling the end of their lives themselves, even to the point of taking their own lives (suicide). Some ask family or friends to "help" when they themselves are incapable of taking their own life. If patients and their families had a way to explore these issues, and understand what it means to ask others for assistance (active euthanasia), perhaps it would lessen the burden for patients of not being allowed to talk about this and for families in being supportive to their patients. It seems unlikely to me that it will ever be a comfortable topic. Perhaps that is as it should be for great caution must be used in discussing the issues of death, assisted death and suicide.

Clear distinctions must be made between active and passive measures. For instance, letting nature take its course is different than actively ending a life. But letting nature take its course means different things to different people as could actively ending a life. Legal issues and consequences must be considered as well as patient wishes and directives. Ignorance of legal realities can cause great difficulties.

Tacit agreements regarding the end of a person's life can be made between and among people. Some, I am sure, make decisions based on their own code of ethics that would not be viewed by others as ethical or moral decisions. The consequences of such discussions and actions must be understood clearly by all involved.

Clear definitions are critical when discussing end of life issues. The term "comfort measures," for instance, is open to a variety of interpretations by different people and different organizations. The use of morphine, for example, to ease pain may hasten death in an actively dying person. (This is known as the double effect.) This definition of "comfort measure" should be understood by all, preferably before the situation arises.

Apparently, few AIDS or cancer patients act on expressed wishes to kill themselves. Although my own mother expressed such wishes, she did not act on them. Whether she did not act because she chose life over death "when push came to shove" or because she was incapable of acting will never be known.

❤

So who draws the line? What should be the reaction to an Alzheimer's patient who expresses a wish to kill herself? I don't know what is right for others but I will share two events that occurred in our journey as well as some quotes to provide food for thought.

The first event was early on, after our first attempt at a family meeting. The meeting was emotionally charged and extremely difficult. At the end, we agreed that three of us would drive to our mother's home to discuss our concerns about the changes we saw in her. After a one hundred mile drive in three separate cars, we opened her door.

Our mother came out and, after a moment of clear pleasure at our unexpected arrival, demanded, "OK, what home are you putting me in?"

Clearly our mother was more aware of her difficulties than we knew. And her instinct was, as usual, right on target. But our visit was not to discuss nursing homes. In fact, we were too upset and too early in our journey to have formulated any clear thoughts, let alone decisions about anything.

I remember little of the specifics of that difficult visit. But what I will never forget are her words spoken in rage and determination, "I will not leave my home. I will kill myself first. I will throw myself down those goddamn stairs. I'll get hit walking across Route 28. I'll die before I'll give up my independence." The words were shouted in the clear, determined voice of a mother who had always been clear about her wishes, and she was our mother, we her children. She was feisty, independent, and formidable.

The second incident happened six months prior to my mother's death while I was representing the family perspective to a group of professional caregivers. The topic was ethics. At some point in the discussion, I mentioned my mother's threats to take her life. In response, two social workers immediately offered a loud and vociferous response. Their words and my response are emblazoned in my memory.

They said, "We cannot allow the legacy of suicide to be left for families."

My response was "What kind of legacy has been left to Rita Callahan's children and their children? Is lying in a bed for years a better legacy? Is it less painful? And what gives you or anyone else the right to make decisions of such import for others?"

Clearly my response was an emotional one. But the social workers' quick words, spoken with an authority that allowed no room for the thoughts and values of others, frightened me for they were a direct threat to the concept of self-determination. I had not yet, and in fact still haven't, resolved my own ambivalence about my mother's statements to take her own life. The morality of such an act aside, I knew what was important was how my mother had thought and what she had declared as her rights and wishes for as long as I could remember.

At the end of the presentation on ethics, many people came up to me. I remember two particularly clearly. The first, a young woman whose emotional responses to the discussion had caught my eye more than once, whispered, "Keep presenting—your perspective is not being heard and it is critical. Write a book!" She disappeared as quickly as she had come. The other was a woman whose husband had stopped eating. She was working with a wonderfully sensitive and enlightened physician who had much experience with Alzheimer's. Her son, however, who admitted that his father would not want to be tube fed, was insisting that a feeding tube be inserted. He simply was unable to accept his father's not eating. She too encouraged me to continue sharing my experience, thoughts and feelings with others.

Diana Friel McGowin, an early stage dementia patient, might have reacted the same way I did to the social workers as the following passage shows:

> I could well understand the desperation of those with serious illnesses who had ended their lives out of fear and uncertainty about the future. As the news announced the indictment of a Michigan physician who had assisted terminally ill individuals to commit suicide, I listened in despair. Despite all my fears about the future, I could not consider suicide as an option.
>
> Nonetheless, I felt it should be a matter of choice for those living with chronic illnesses. The choice to float

gently from this life as opposed to becoming a forced victim of pain should be theirs. Whenever I got on my soapbox about this moral minefield, others gazed at me in all too revealing concern. Let them think what they want I sighed.

We are guaranteed the right to live, not the right to die. We are guaranteed only the pursuit of happiness, not its achievement. There are associations to prevent the pro-longing of an animal's suffering, but our charitable kind-ness to pets does not extend to our fellow beings. Instead, a multitude of legal and religious barriers raise their heads, howling in outrage. I knew what my pastor would say if he could hear my philosophy. His voice would be low-key but firm in its indictment of such a thought. Christian and Jewish martyrs would be held before me by this man of the cloth as an example. I do not know if I am of the caliber of a martyr.[2]

Larry Rose, another early stage Alzheimer's patient wrote:

... I have time to think now. Believe me, I think about dying a lot. There has to be a line drawn somewhere ... when it is time to go, when life is not quality. I would rather die six months too early than six months too late. I hope, when my time comes, that I can find some-one, like Dr. Jack Kevorkian. If I can't, I'll do it myself. The 'do-good' groups and the government have to get over their love affair with terminally ill people. Unless they are in my shoes and those of millions of others like me, they have absolutely no idea what they are talking about. I want to live as much as the next man ... but not lying in some nursing home, not knowing who the hell I am.[3]

❤

It was the story of the woman who died on her first night in the nursing home, that forced me to face in no uncertain terms what my mother's reaction would have been to being bed-bound, toothless, fed, incontinent, uncommunicative—totally dependent. I came to the conclusion that she would not want to be alive, under those cir-cumstances. I wondered whether she would want, and in fact even expect, me to take her life (active euthanasia). I found when I went to the core of my being that I was not capable of doing so. However,

I went the whole route mentally—considering how I might do it, when and under what circumstances.

Three things prevented me. The first was the fact that we had already arranged for a full autopsy, which I was afraid would reveal my intervention. The second was that I did not feel I had the right to play God. This was strange since I wasn't sure there even was a God for what God would allow the pain and suffering I witnessed each day I lived with the tragedy and grief of my mother's Alzheimer's?

The third, the one that offered me peace were the words of a friend over dinner. Her training as a lawyer and empathy as a woman combined to offer just the right words from a perspective I couldn't ignore. Her words touched me deeply. They had the ring of truth. I could imagine my well mother saying them. My friend said, "Do you really think that after all the pain and joy, after all the effort and love your mother showered upon you she would want you to spend the next seven years in jail? That is the sentence for manslaughter which is how such an act would be viewed by the courts." ❤

Table 1: Behavioral Log

BEHAVIORAL LOG Name:		Short Term Objective			Date Log Started	
Exact Time	Specific location	Precipitating circumstances (and who was there)	Behavior	Inter-ventions	Outcome	Staff Initials
Signature:						

Of Two Minds, *A Guide to the Care of People with the Dual Diagnosis of Alzheimer's Disease and Mental Retardation*, Judith M. Antonangeli, RN, BSN, Printed by Fidelity Press, 1995, p. 115..

1. Larry Rose, *Show Me The Way To Go Home*, Elder Books, Forest Knolls, CA. 1996, p.136.

2. Diana Friel Mc Gowin, *Living In The Labyrinth, A Personal Journey Through The Maze of Alzheimer's*, Delta Publishing, New York, NY, 1994, p. 105-6.

3. Larry Rose, *Show Me The Way To Go Home*, Elder Books, Forest Knolls, CA. 1996, p.76.

Chapter 4:
Legal and Financial Decisions

Alzheimer's eventually impairs the patient's ability to handle money and make reasonable decisions. On the way to those losses, many things must be managed. It is likely that additional care to that provided by family members will be needed. Whether it is in the home, in an institution, or both, there is cost involved. Therefore, the preservation of assets must be addressed and planned for.

Although some people "put their house in order" prior to the onset of a serious illness, many do not. The job is difficult and requires an admission that someday they will no longer be able to handle their own affairs. Even for Alzheimer's patients who have done this, some lose the ability to remember the reason for these choices and disassemble the very vehicles and organization they have put in place as the disease progresses. My mother was one of these people.

The complexity of laws and legal and financial instruments is considerable. There are few laymen who have the knowledge or time to acquire it when the mantle of the surrogate is laid upon their shoulders. Often, they must hire specialists to educate, advise and prepare the patient's estate. For those dealing with more than one State, this is particularly important. (Unfortunately, the meaning of

83

some of the terms I had so dutifully mastered in Massachusetts were different in Florida.)

Legal and financial advice and services can be expensive, but not having them can be even more expensive. Due to fast-changing laws and practices it is important to find legal and financial advisors who specialize in elder care for those with dementia. The increased need for Medicaid funds, a federal program that subsidizes medical costs for the indigent, makes estate planning particularly tricky.

Some Alzheimer's patients have spouses to consider, and the fear of impoverishment is real. Some simply wish to have their assets protected for their own care. Some want to hide their assets, thereby protecting them from the State and leaving them to heirs. Each of these things has become more difficult to accomplish over the past decade.

Setting Goals

The first step of the decision-making process with legal and financial matters is to formulate and clearly state goals and objectives. Planning strategies with professional advisors is a critical component of this process. Although I have been known to laugh at lawyer jokes, I could not have done right by my mother without the counsel and advice of attorneys.

It was important for me, and the people who would help me, to understand where my mother had come from. She was a child of the Depression. She and my father had raised themselves above the Depression, and they had a strong work ethic. Above all else, they did not want to be a burden to their family or to society.

Terminology

Terminology was a source of confusion for me, and it is for others. Over the years, I have found myself in the uncomfortable position of defining terms such as proxys, power of attorney, conservatorship and guardianship to other lay people. It is not unusual for people in support groups to look to other members of the group to define these terms. I cannot stress strongly enough the importance of getting legal and financial advice from professionals. States use terms differently and this can compound an overwhelming and confusing plethora of issues and decisions. Well-meaning support group members and leaders may not be knowledgeable enough to protect your patient's hard-earned assets.

Having said that, I must point out that I have learned first-hand that a little bit of knowledge can be dangerous. Because of this, and because of the confusion I felt when I realized that terms I clearly understood in Massachusetts meant something entirely different in Florida, I will not define terms except in context and in the most general way.

I also must point out that the issues I describe in this chapter, like all other chapters are those of which I am aware and with which I have experience. My parents were middle class people who owned real estate and had a small amount of savings. I did not deal with other situations and am not qualified to talk about or give advice about them. Again I must stress the need to seek competent professional advice before making decisions in legal and financial matters. Finally, the issues are presented in the order in which they presented themselves but that order may vary for others.

Advanced Directives

Advanced directives are documents in which persons identify their wishes and name a person or persons to speak for them. Such documents can deal with medical issues, financial issues, or both. To add to the confusion there are many variations on the theme. For instance, there are many types of power of attorney. Some are for a single transaction, some take effect only after the person is incapable of handling her own affairs, and some cover medical matters, while others only cover financial matters. Some of these documents can be used only after the persons are unable to speak for themselves and some while they are still able to speak for themselves.

Testamentary Capacity

One of the tricky dilemmas faced by those dealing with Alzheimer's is something called testamentary capacity. It is a person's ability to understand, at the time she is deciding and signing, what she is doing. Also called legal competence, it becomes very important if legal documents are ever questioned.

In order to include the patient, or better still, have the patient drive the process and decide on the legal vehicles that will best serve and protect her, legal planning should begin as early as possible. Deliberating about issues of durable power of attorney, health care proxy, trusts and guardianship takes time and, ideally, involves the person with the disease. For her to have the best chance of under-

standing them and making appropriate choices, they should be discussed at the earliest possible moment.

Financial Proxies and Wills

A will determines the distribution of a person's estate after death,
as administered by an executor (male) or executrix (female). Powers of attorney name someone to deal with assets, and sometimes
decisions about the person's body while the person is still alive.

Our situation began with a single document, a durable family
power of attorney prepared and executed in Florida, my mother's
state of legal residence. For a time, we went to a different document—a co-conservatorship prepared and executed in Massachusetts. Once my mother's financial assets had been depleted, the
need for the conservatorship was gone, and we went back to the
durable power of attorney.

Despite the fact that I had the legal power to make decisions all
along, I felt strongly that my brothers and sisters had an equal right
to input. A complex family dynamic, coupled with my mother's decision to name me as her sole substituted voice, made life in general,
and decision-making in particular, quite volatile and difficult.
Despite this, my consideration of the opinions and feelings of my siblings provided many voices and perspectives to be considered by me,
the decision-maker, as well as the opportunity for all of my mother's
children to offer input.

Medical Proxies and Living Wills

When my mother started this journey, there was no such thing as
a health care proxy in Florida or Massachusetts. Although living
wills were not (and still are not, in Massachusetts) legal documents
that bind medical personnel or family members making decisions for
patients, many were aware of the Brophy court case, which raised
the issue of an individual's right to determine her own fate after the
ability to communicate was gone.

One crisp, clear, cold February afternoon, Pete, our mother's Massachusetts attorney, advised my sister and me to prepare a living will
for her. He explained that while living wills were not legal in the
state of Massachusetts, they were helpful in notifying professional
caregivers of my mother's wishes and could help her children to
carry out her wishes with less guilt. Since I had difficulty seeing

myself trying to get my mother to write these things down, my sister said she would handle it while I was away on vacation.

So over Sunday dinner, my two sisters had the same conversation with my mother that had been repeated over the years about her wishes not to be kept alive should her quality of life be compromised.

When they asked if she would sign a paper to that effect, she agreed, but when my sister's neighbor arrived to witness her signature, my mother looked around and said, "Where's Sally?" She refused to sign the paper until I was present.

Being the dutiful daughter, I raised the issue with my mother upon my return.

When I said her attorney had advised us that her signature on a living will would ensure that her wishes would be followed, she said, "Fine, you get my attorney. Then I'll sign the papers. What's his name again?" With that I made an appointment for him to come to my home.

One of my sisters, my husband and I were there. When Pete, the attorney first arrived, he asked my mother how she felt about extraordinary and heroic measures. She clearly stated her lifelong beliefs on the subject, which did not vary one iota from what she had always said. He explained to her the importance of signing a statement to that effect, which she agreed to do.

Pete began by reading the statement my sisters had prepared during their discussion with my mother. My mother said that while she agreed with the spirit of it, those were not her words. Pete patiently reworded the statement (which I retyped at my computer four times in all) until my mother was comfortable with the non-specific living will that guided us from that point forward.

There are a number of reasons why a living will is not as good as a health-care proxy in protecting patient rights.

Living wills:

- ❤ Are applicable only when the patient is "terminally ill"
- ❤ Limit the type of treatment that can be refused, usually to "artificial" or "extraordinary" measures
- ❤ Require that the patient accurately predict his or her final illness and what medical technology or interventions might be available to treat or postpone death or to withhold.

❤   Do not name a particular person to make decisions on
     the patient's behalf
❤   Do not define guidelines for making such decisions
❤   Do not require health care professionals to honor them
❤   Are not legal in all states

Health care proxies, on the other hand:
❤   Are in effect all the time
❤   Are legally binding
❤   Can be specific or general
❤   Assign responsibility to a person or persons chosen by
     the patient who will evaluate each situation
❤   Are legal in most states

Despite the fact that living wills are not as effective as proxies,
some advise that a living will be attached to a health care proxy.

❤

I offer a caution about health care proxies, which name a surrogate to make medical decisions. If my mother had made a detailed
health care proxy or living will during the time she was able, it would
not have been applicable to the situations I faced as her surrogate.
She thought and spoke in terms of cancer, not a long-term degenerative dementia. Additionally, medicine changed. Death-defying technology was not available when my mother would have prepared a
health care proxy in 1981.

The potential difficulties that arise, particularly during the end
stages, can be greatly eased by planning and executing surrogate declarations by the patient. However, the sad truth is that most people
do not take these steps to declare and formalize their wishes. Even
those who do so may not be specific, or the laws may have changed
from the time their surrogates were named. The laws and legal vehicles for naming and defining the extent of control that surrogates
have are in a state of flux.

When my mother executed the durable family power of attorney
in 1981 in Florida, there was no such thing as a health care proxy or
medical power of attorney. When the money was gone and we closed
out the conservatorship, we considered a Massachusetts Guardianship that would empower the guardian to handle money, as well as to
make medical decisions. Because I was so exhausted from my husband's illness, the lawyers suggested that I consider giving responsi-

bility for decision-making to one of my siblings. We discussed this within the family and agreed on who it could be. When I explained, however, that to do this we would have to petition the Massachusetts Courts and there was no money to hire an attorney, the issue was dropped and we went back to the durable family power of attorney.

There was a time when I questioned whether or not that document actually gave me the right to make medical decisions, and whether or not my mother had intended that I make them on her behalf. It was a conversation with my husband, from whom I was already separated, that put this question to rest.

He said, "I'm not sure of much these days, but I'm absolutely sure that your mother intended for you to make all decisions if and when she became unable. I know this from conversations we had with her and from what she said to you about the durable family power of attorney in the first place. She said, 'You're in charge. You'll pull it out in a hospital and tell the others then that I've left you in charge.'" His vehemence and clarity on this issue put my mind to rest.

Later, in a meeting of four of my mother's children with hospice, the first question asked was, "Do each of you agree that Sally makes decisions for your mother?"

Each responded in the affirmative.

As a practical matter, someone had to speak for my mother, and I was that someone. Although my mother never executed a health care proxy, her chart was stamped as though she had, and I was identified as her proxy.

Helping Professionals

We were fortunate to have three attorneys who were sharp, ethical, skilled, and well versed in the issues of care and planning for dementia patients. They were painstakingly clear and unwaveringly consistent in reminding me of my responsibilities to make decisions in my mother's best interest, but always based on her wishes.

The first was Bill, the Florida attorney who had prepared the durable power of attorney in 1981. I had heard my mother speak of him over the years and knew she trusted him. Despite her repeated intentions to introduce us, I never met him in person until long after things were settled.

Pete, the Massachusetts attorney, was recommended to us by the large city hospital's Memory Disorders Unit. Because I already had the durable family power of attorney, it was my husband and I who met Pete first. We spent two or three hours that first evening describing the situation and sharing our concerns. Pete was clear and sensitive, and we left with a feeling of comfort and trust. The considerations and decisions to be made were overwhelming. We knew we needed help but we were leery. That night, in addition to evaluating our own ability to work with this man, we tried to gauge his chance of success in dealing with my mother, who was becoming more and more upset and suspicious.

The night before my mother was to meet Pete, my husband and I talked things over with her. He began by pointing out that she had always been smart about such things. He explained that we had met with a Massachusetts attorney who wanted to discuss things with her and told her of Pete's advice that some changes should be considered. She became defensive and difficult, but her basic trust in our concern for her well being won out in the end and she reluctantly agreed to meet Pete.

The first time my mother actually met Pete was the day she was told of the probable diagnosis of Alzheimer's. She had already stormed out of the hospital and was angry and uncooperative. By the time she had climbed three steep flights of stairs to get to Pete's office she was livid and met his gentle, cordial greeting with stony silence and a nasty look. His invitation to my mother to sit and get acquainted was flatly refused. She said she was there only because she had promised to meet him. Now that she had met him she was leaving. She complained none too diplomatically about the stairs. As my sister and I held our breath, Pete gallantly offered to carry her down assuring her that all future meetings would be held on the first floor. With great reluctance, she allowed us to make another appointment which she made very clear she would probably not keep.

The first document that was executed under Pete's tutelage was the co-conservatorship. My husband and I had discussed it with Pete, later with my mother, and finally with my sister. Although none of my mother's family were in the room when it was executed, she was clearly comfortable and in fact seemed relieved when it was done. I don't know to this day what Pete said to my mother during their first meeting but she came away praising him to the skies. And long after she could remember his name, she would refer to him with trust and affection as "my attorney— What's his name?"

Pete recommended a joint conservatorship for two reasons. The first was the enormous amount of work involved. The second was in answer to the initial anger that my brothers and sisters had over the durable power of attorney being kept from them, which had set the five of us into a difficult, draining and potentially dangerous situation. We agreed, after much discussion, that my co-conservator should be my older sister who, while not good at paperwork and details, would be supportive to me and assertive with the others. My sister and I also shared a common view of our mother's entitlement to the best, regardless of cost.

It was a strange and difficult alliance in many ways, but in others, it made perfect sense. I handled the details, kept the records and communicated with those with whom we needed to communicate. We went together to the bank, and my sister, the matriarch in training, kept the uproar from the others to a minimum.

I was aware that a conservatorship required more time, paper work, auditing, and accounting than did the durable family power of attorney. But I also understood the protection it provided for my mother, my siblings and me. When it went into force, Pete advised me to keep the durable power of attorney. Although I don't remember being clear about why at that time, it became very clear later. The conservatorship protected my mother's financial assets, but there came a point in time when those assets had been "spent down" for Medicaid making it no longer necessary. At that time, because there was no money for attorneys to do so, my husband presented the final accounting to the court and worked with a court appointed attorney to close the conservatorship. Then, the durable power of attorney, prepared several years before, was a very important document to have.

Assets

One of the first jobs of the surrogate is identifying assets. An asset is anything that holds value, such as cash, stocks, bonds, real estate, insurance policies, antiques, coin collections, baseball cards, jewelry and pensions. Some assets are liquid— they can be spent immediately—some are not liquid because time and effort are required to make them available to spend—like a house or jewelry.

I recommend listing assets early on. See the Asset/Liability Tracking List (Table 1) at the end of this chapter. It is important to note their type (liquid or non liquid), location and value. It is useful to prepare this list with the patient and attach the front page of each asset to the list, such as the front page of policies (stocks, bonds etc.) showing type, account number, amount etc. This task is easier said than done.

My mother, who understood the need for such things and had always attended well to details, lost her ability to maintain the painstaking system she had put in place. Because of my naiveté, I did not initiate and follow through on this until it was too late for her cooperative involvement. While I knew generally that all important papers were in her safe deposit box, it never occurred to me that she might lose her ability to leave them there.

The day my mother called to tell me that we had given up the local safe deposit box was an educational experience. After her call, I drove to the bank. When I presented the key, the woman led me into the vault and put in her key. She then moved aside so I could remove the box. It was about shoulder height, and I thought little about what I was doing until it almost brought me to my knees. Saying nothing, I went into the private booth and opened the box to find my mother's sterling silver, all twelve place settings. I put them in the bag I had brought and drove to my mother's.

When I showed my mother the silverware, she said, "Oh good. That's one mystery solved. Where was it?" I told her the silver was in the local safe deposit box, which she thought was gone. (The reason she thought we'd given up the local box was that she had presented the key to the Florida safe deposit box rather than the Massachusetts key.) When I asked where the important papers were, she shrugged and said they must be somewhere, they'd turn up eventually. They did, in the same safe deposit box, several months later.

Inventorying and determining the ultimate disposition of my mother's assets was an arduous process. Although my mother had often mentioned it as something she and I would do together, we never got to it. In retrospect I wonder if I tuned her out because I couldn't quite face such a concrete acknowledgment of her mortality. When it could no longer be avoided, she was unable. So I took a friend to her condo, to which she would never return, and we ended up with a 25 page listing of the contents that needed to be disposed of.

At Pete's suggestion, we did a rotating lottery. My older sister's proposal to first take back gifts we had given worked well except for my younger sister and I who disagreed on who had given what. She and I actually ended up sharing some things and still do to this day. We agreed that negotiating and dividing among the five of us would be challenging enough, so spouses and children were excluded.

On a Saturday night, we met at the house and divided things up. Some items, like clothing and jewelry, were not dealt with at that time because my mother was still using them. My husband, who was responsible for emptying the condo, set some rules about removing items within a week. We tackled the job. One sister and brother-in-law were helpful, and in spite of exhaustion and emotions, both positive and negative, that were bound to arise under such circumstances, we got the job done. The day after Puppy's five children sat together to distribute her belongings, four of us met to distribute what had not been claimed the night before.

The Cost of Privacy

Although my mother had taken steps to legally name me as her surrogate, she insisted on keeping her decision confidential. But when her difficulties began to manifest themselves, my understandably concerned brothers and sisters started asking questions. When they started asking, I called the neurologist (who had seen my mother) to discuss my dilemma and ask his advice. He said that although he would not leave my mother in charge of his bills if he were to go away for the summer, my obligation was to honor her wishes for confidentiality until I thought she was no longer competent. I'm not sure what my take was on her competency at the time I broke her confidence, but I knew that the others were becoming more and more concerned and the likelihood of permanent damage to our relationships was lurking in the wings.

So in a treacherous balancing act between my mother's right to privacy and confidentiality and the need for the rest of her children to know that she had made decisions and taken steps to protect herself, my husband and I finally told my sister and her husband. Although upset, they understood my predicament and agreed to tell the others. Their responses ranged from rage that I had not told them to hesitant and wavering support.

Despite this difficult time, we managed to avoid the horror of the legal divide and conquer game that is so costly to pocketbooks and disastrous to families.

Planning for the Future

Because Alzheimer's patients can live so long, it is important to evaluate their assets and plan for the future. There will come a time when it is no longer safe for an Alzheimer's patient to be alone in her own home. Many options can be considered: moving in with a relative or friend, bringing in a companion, community based services or some sort of institutional care. These all have some cost associated with them. Since so many senior citizens are on fixed incomes, planning becomes more important. As of this writing, the Federal Medicaid system is still in place and is employed by most institutionalized Alzheimer's patients (all but the very wealthy) sooner or later.

Long-term care ranges from twenty to seventy thousand dollars a year. When Medicaid kicks in, all of the patient's assets must go toward care, except for a monthly personal-needs allowance, assets under two thousand dollars, and pre-paid burial funds.

Regardless of the final use of funds, it is important to get a sense of what will be needed and plan ahead. Since my mother's largest asset was her condominium in Florida, we began the process of selling it several months before we needed the money. We did this none too soon. Although stocks and bonds are more liquid than real estate, the transformation of these instruments into cash requires planning too. While these were major decisions that overwhelmed me as a fledgling surrogate, strong support from professionals and my husband made it possible.

Selling the single sizable asset my mother had, her condo, was a lesson in many things. The first was in cutting losses. The sale occurred at a time when Florida real estate had taken a serious turn for the worse. Due to its location in the building and condominium complex, a man was interested because it offered easy access for his disabled wife. We sold it at a time when less than one-tenth of one percent of the condominiums in the city were selling. Hiring the same attorney who had prepared the original durable family power of attorney to represent my mother's interests in the transaction was one of the best decisions I made. Although we did not meet face to face until years after the sale, he was scrupulously honest, obviously fond of my mother and clear and cogent with advice.

Since it was important to save my mother's assets for her care, her Florida attorney, Bill, advised me to allow people in Florida to handle the details of packing up her belongings. I called a handyman whom I had met on my visits there who agreed to pack up what we wanted in exchange for transportation fees and a color television.

Bill called me during the packing to say that the real estate broker, who had been sleazy from the beginning, had somehow lost track of some of the contents of the house. It was the attorney's guess that the realtor and second-hand furniture dealer were in cahoots. Despite this, he advised me to accept the loss, which represented almost fifteen hundred dollars, and go through with passing papers on the property. My rage was barely contained, but the attorney understood and acknowledged it, and he advised me in my mother's best interest. The sale went through, and the attorney transferred the money. I know now how lucky we were, and how little we lost, despite my lack of perspective at the time.

All of my mother's assets, and some of her children's, were used for her care. Using her own assets, we bought her into the best place we could afford when we could no longer provide home care. "Buying someone in" is not formal or official, it is just that when beds are scarce, those with money somehow seem to get available beds more quickly than those without money. The Massachusetts Executive Office of Elder Affairs advised us that her assets and the fact that she was not a behavior management problem would serve as an enticement to a nursing home. This proved to be true.

Independence and Patient Control

In our situation, my father was dead and all of my parents' children were grown. So the issues that I faced were less complex than those faced by others. I was urged by my brothers and sisters to use the durable family power of attorney to move all of my mother's assets out of her name within a single day in order to preserve them. I felt that doing so would be tantamount to taking a gun and shooting her. It became clear to me quite early on that whatever money my mother had would go toward her care, but I was very leery of removing or "protecting" things from her control while she still understood what was happening and was able, to some degree at least, to manage her own affairs.

Had I done what my brothers and sisters suggested, it would have broken my mother's spirit and quite likely destroyed her trust in me. I have since found out that it also would have been illegal. As I shed my denial and became more able to accept the advice of the professionals, I became more vigilant about what was happening to her assets, and on occasion, tried to explain things to her. But my explanations were rarely effective, except in building trust between us.

In retrospect, I would do things the same way, leaving my mother as much control as possible. I would choose to risk the loss of some assets rather than remove control before it was absolutely necessary. The importance of allowing my mother to keep as much control as she was capable of handling, and respecting how tough it was for her to lose control, was very much on my mind. Yet I guess I was a bit slow in finally taking things over, and I know I continued discussions and full disclosure with my mother long past the point where they were productive for either of us. I'm not sure if this was a problem of my resistance to role reversal, my denial, or both. I know however, that it was affected by my mother's intense insistence on maintaining control.

However, it was not only my own difficulty in role reversal. Another element in my hesitancy to take control was my difficulty in grasping the fact that my mother was actually becoming less capable. She had always seemed so much more capable than I that I had particular difficulty imagining it to be true. Also, I paid less attention than I might have initially.

Finally, I think the main factor was my inability to lie to my mother. While many in the field call it "creative thinking," to me, at the beginning, it was lying. I always had trouble lying to my mother. I was always the kid who could never get away with it, even years afterwards. But I now know it would have been in everyone's best interest to learn much earlier to simplify answers, to substitute incomplete information and "fiblets" for complete disclosure.

Acceptable Risk

The surrogate faces many situations that must be evaluated for risk. Two that come to mind are the use of electronic transfers and allowing the patient to maintain control over checkbooks. My first experience with electronic transfers was during the second month my mother was in the nursing home. When I realized that the checkbook did not have funds sufficient to cover the next month's nursing home bill, I agreed to a wire of funds from a money market account. Though hesitant, I was assured that electronic transfers were done all the time with no problem.

Believing what I had been told, I sent off the check by mail. Needless to say, I was stunned when the nursing home called to tell me the check had bounced. After almost a week, the problem was identified as the funds having gone to an account in Connecticut which had the same account number. In addition to being embarrassed, I was livid. I guess I was just unfortunate to be caught by a small glitch in the early days of the technology of the electronic transfer of funds.

The other issue that comes to mind is my mother's insistence on keeping her checkbook in the nursing home. This was of great concern to the nursing home but my mother threatened to follow her checkbook out the door if they insisted she not have it. I fought for her right to keep it, limiting the risk by keeping a minimum amount of money in it. This worked well until she demanded more. I remember clearly her fierce eyes and angry voice as she threatened to take all control back if I refused to write the deposit she demanded. Moved to almost incapacity, I watched in amazement as she picked up a pencil and added 500 dollars to her seven hundred-dollar balance. Immensely pleased with herself, she looked at me and said, "Now who's boss?!" It was not until I was in the car, crying my way home that I fully realized that she had no idea that the money she had added to her checkbook was not real.

Handling Day-to-Day Finances

Initially, my mother and I "shared" the job of handling her finances. What this really meant was that periodically I would look things over to be sure everything was going well. What "going well" meant to me and to her were sometimes at odds. I did not get involved in how she handled cash or money machines until fairly late in the game. It was clear that some cash was lost, but her resistance to discuss it or relinquish control kept me at bay.

I did however find that some service people were taking advantage. My mother would pay them with cash, which was very unlike her, then she would pay them again by check, when a bill arrived in the mail. There were also some problems with services and repairs that were unnecessary and it became clear that she was being taken advantage of. Examples of this were TV repairs, automobile stickers and VCR's.

It was my brother who caught the problem with the TV and VCR's. My mother had lost the ability to make the TV work properly. She did not understand the cable box, and had no idea how to use the clicker so she bought a VCR, which was as mysterious to her as the cable box and clicker. (But of course who among us can say a

VCR has not brought us to our knees?) My brother would no sooner bring the VCR back to the store than she would buy another. She actually purchased five VCR's over a one month period.

My review of my mother's bills and records showed that there had been missed payments on some bills and duplicate payments on others. These reviews also underlined a problem we had been aware of for some time. My mother had great difficulty regulating her electric heat. She had forgotten the fact that it came up quickly so she should shut it off when not needed. The result was astronomical electric bills that were rivaling the national debt.

The issue of dealing with people who were taking advantage was a tough one. If we were to "take the bastard by the throat" (the person who was changing the registration sticker on our mother's car weekly), as my brother-in-law who articulated our dilemma suggested, what would happen to our mother when she next went into his place of business? How would that work in a small town? Finally, I spoke to a policeman I knew to alert him to the situation. None of us went to confront the business people directly. There are agencies like consumer affairs and ombudsmen that can assist in such matters, but my mother was not capable of describing what happened and we were too overwhelmed or naive to bring the problems to those who might have helped.

Getting Organized

One weekend, at my request, my husband accompanied me to my mother's house to "get organized and clean out her papers." She had not only agreed to this but actually initiated the event. This made sense to me since my pre-Alzheimer's mother was organized almost to perfection. When we arrived, she did not resist until he started to throw old checks, some dating back more than twenty years, into a large black trash bag. In order to placate her, he stopped until she left the room. After eight grueling hours of reviewing her filing system, which looked as though it had been hit by a tornado, we left her with folders neatly marked, and carefully and logically organized in a milk crate.

The day had been long and arduous for all of us. My husband stumbled under the weight of the old papers that he wisely insisted on putting into the dumpster himself. We left with my mother's praise and gratitude ringing in our ears. The following week we found folders missing, and the papers we had so carefully filed, misfiled. Chaos worse than before was firmly entrenched.

It was during that season that my mother's taxes got lost. My sister, who had agreed to handle the taxes with her own accountant, was having regular and upsetting conversations with the IRS who hadn't, apparently, heard of Alzheimer's. My sister was telling the IRS that the taxes were signed and mailed, which was what my mother had told her. The mysteriously missing taxes showed up a couple of months later when my brother lifted the pads on the dining room table. There lay the envelope, stamped and ready to go to the IRS.

Once I assumed complete control of my mother's finances, I began sending her a monthly accounting. This worked well for a while, but eventually became a source of conflict between us. I also sent a copy of these "reports" to my brothers and sisters but did not tell my mother for fear she'd have told me it was none of their business. This was an uncomfortable compromise I had made after much soul searching and advice from the attorney.

In retrospect, what my mother didn't know didn't hurt her, and reporting regularly with an attitude of full disclosure provided some protection for me in my role as her surrogate. Being a person who tends to be direct and up front, I also thought it appropriate that my brothers and sisters know what was happening to our mother's money. (I had no intention of stealing anything. It simply never crossed my mind.)

I don't know whether the others read the "reports" or paid much attention, but I felt it was important as I'd have wanted to know that my mother's money was being spent for her as well as what was happening "to my inheritance." I found automating such reports an advantage. Doing so in a way that didn't add to the increasing responsibilities of being my mother's surrogate voice was important. A sample Monthly Inflow and Outflow Report is presented in Table 2 at the end of this chapter. The data I captured and the reports generated from those data were helpful both within the family and when I had to report to the courts. My facility with computing tools was definitely a time saver.

Taking Notes

Notetaking for phone, mail and in person communications can greatly ease things for the surrogate. One thing I wish I had begun earlier was carrying a notebook. I found it more difficult to go back over conversations and keep things straight before I began to write things down as they were occurring. Although the idea of a notebook can put some people off (myself included at that point in time), it is a reasonable way to be sure you are capturing the range of often confusing information, and a tool to understanding it in the best interest of your patient. A format for note-taking is presented in Table 3 at the end of the chapter. In the back of the notebook, I included pertinent phone numbers, addresses and my mother's identifying information such as her Social Security Number, Medicare Number, Medicaid Number and Insurance Provider(s). See Table 4 at the end of this chapter.

Interstate Complexities

Because my mother was a legal resident of Florida but lived half the year in Massachusetts, where her family was, identifying, tracking and managing her legal and financial affairs was more complicated. Even something as simple as mail became difficult. She was no longer able to be sure things were sent to the proper address and I had trouble finding some things.

Bill, my mother's attorney in Florida, made things infinitely easier. I trusted Bill because my mother did, both my well mother and my failing mother. But doing business long distance, especially prior to the conveniences of fax and conference calling, was more difficult. However, doing business long distance was a reality I had to deal with since her financial and legal life was spread across two states fifteen hundred miles apart. One of the first things Bill told me was that I should not come to Florida since that would deplete my mother's assets which must be saved for her care. We instituted the low-tech conference call which was accomplished by my being on two phones in the house (a business and a personal) with a different attorney on each line. Given my churning stomach, I did quite well indeed.

Another difficulty of being in different states was knowing where important documents were and being sure there weren't conflicting documents. When we began working with Pete, the Massachusetts attorney, he not only set up the co-conservatorship but also drew up a new will.

Notifying Others

I did not know that I should notify businesses, banks, attorneys, accountants and others with whom my mother did business about her power of attorney. Had I done so, much work and grief would have been saved for my mother, those with whom she dealt and me.

It was only through the kind, well meaning, albeit questionable, actions of a man who handled some investments for both my mother and my husband and me that we learned of her suspiciously dwindling funds. Since his relationship of confidentiality with my mother prevented him from being direct about the situation (he didn't know about the power of attorney), he subtly asked some pointed questions and told some generalized stories of people who were having trouble managing their funds prudently.

The difficulty in the fellow's making us aware of my mother's apparent difficulty is whether or not he broke some type of law or crossed some ethical boundary. In this case, because he was acting out of concern and his actions were to protect my mother, things worked out for the best. But it is certainly possible that such a scenario could result in less than proper actions by the investment counselor and/or family member. I am grateful for the risk he took on my mother's behalf.

The investment counselor's cloaked warning was enough to catch my eye in time to move some substantial assets "out of harm's way." After doing so, I spent some time trying to get the problem on a single piece of paper in a way that my mother could understand. One bright morning I showed her the difficulty. She was very attentive, but clearly unable to grasp the true significance of the discussion. However, her diligent attention and subsequent response marked a turning point for me.

After I had made my pitch, my mother looked me in the eye and said, "You're doing fine keeping an eye on things for me and I hope I had a good time spending the money. Now let's go to lunch, my treat."

❤

When I shared the durable power of attorney with businesses, I found that most required an additional paper to be signed indicating that I, in fact, had my mother's power of attorney. The fact that the power of attorney was from Florida complicated things in Massachusetts and other states nearby. Although this request for another statement of her intention that I handle her affairs was sometimes confusing to my mother, it protected both of us, as well as my siblings, the businesses, banks, and others with whom she did business.

Preserving my mother's dignity and being aware and respectful of how things were discussed in front of her was important, however, it was not easy to learn. In fact, I usually handled things myself first, then told my mother about them. As her disease progressed, under direction of the attorneys, I began handling things and not telling her. While this was difficult for me to do, it was clearly in my mother's best interest because trying to explain things she couldn't understand was frustrating and at times even cruel. Unfortunately, it took me a bit too long to learn these lessons and comfortably accept the advice of professionals.

❤

The issue of banks and notifying them of the power of attorney is important. This was particularly painful for me because I thought I had things fairly well under control. I had accepted the power of attorney and reluctantly accepted the terms of confidentiality under which it was given. Despite the difficulties caused by my mother's insistence on confidentiality regarding the power of attorney, my siblings and I seemed to be beyond them. My sister and I visited my mother's bank where we were told of numerous incidents where our mother had come in or left the bank in tears. We listened with horror to tales of difficult phone conversations during which bank personnel tried to explain to our mother the dangers of taking balances that did not reflect uncashed checks. Our mother was no longer capable of understanding such things.

The bank's frustration at not having anywhere to turn as they saw our mother move deeper and deeper into confusion was difficult for them. They did not know of the Power of Attorney and I did not know I should share it. While it was clearly a last ditch attempt on the part of my mother to safeguard her privacy and independence, which she valued more than life itself, it caused much difficulty for her and for those who had to deal with her.

❤

One sunny Saturday morning stands out clearly in my mind. I had been directed by Pete to go back to the Massachusetts safe deposit box, copy all documents and replace the originals, without my mother's knowledge. My husband drove me to the bank and said he was going for a cup of coffee. When I asked him to "stand guard" at the door, he reluctantly agreed though he thought I was crazy. About a half-hour into my task, stomach churning with guilt, I heard him loudly greeting my mother as she walked purposefully into the bank, the copy machine at which I was busy, directly in her path.

My husband put a loving arm around my mother and stepped between us just in time to prevent her from seeing what I was doing. She gave me a kiss and accepted my explanation that I had several more things to do before we could go to her house for coffee. Still under his protective wing, she completed her business at the bank and was lovingly escorted to her car.

That evening, over dinner with friends, I once again wondered at my mother's uncanny ability to zone in on what was going on and show up at the damnedest of places at the worst times. Who knows, perhaps my discomfort, which bordered on guilt, at copying the documents was "heard" a mile away by my ever more vigilant mother. Could this have been the beginning of Heartspeak or was it the ESP of which she had spoken occasionally with fear?

Insurance

I dealt with two basic types of insurance, medical insurance and life insurance. Two types of medical insurance subsidized by the government are Medicare and Medicaid. Within Medicare there are different supplements and in the future these may change. The maze of paper work involved with medical insurance can be daunting, to say the least. There are also two types of life insurance, term and whole life.

Until my mother's money ran out and she entered the Medicaid system, my sister handled private medical insurance. This fixed amount of insurance was a spousal benefit of my father's pension. When I first took over my mother's affairs, it was a total amount of forty thousand dollars to be spent during the remaining years of my mother's life. During the process, the amount was raised to one hundred thousand dollars. While these sums sound large, they are a mere drop in the bucket if serious medical problems arise. My mother had to pay a small annual fee to keep this insurance in force.

The problem that arose for us was the fact that neither the company for which my father had worked nor the insurance company billed the annual fee. This obviously becomes a problem for a person with Alzheimer's. Also, there was no way for me to know of this benefit and the unbilled annual fee, so the insurance went out of force. When I called to find out what had happened, I was told it was too late, the benefit was forfeited by the lack of timely payment of the fifty dollars. A stern letter from the attorney reinstated the insurance.

Because I had been a member of an HMO that has little paper-work, I was unfamiliar with the work that can be involved in han-dling insurance. One of my sisters agreed to handle medical insurance. Though younger than I, she was more than familiar with the ins and outs of such systems due to the serious illness of her first son. She is an organized person who pays close attention to detail. Her contribution to my mother's care and her sharing of the tasks placed on me was significant. I do not know that I could have han-dled the time consuming insurance tasks along with everything else.

❤

Due to the number of issues and the weight of the caregiving role, it is helpful and even desirable to have assistance. However, the assistance must be productive and supportive. If people offer to help but then do things their own way, or simply refuse to complete tasks because they don't agree with the methods or rules, this adds to rather than lightens the surrogate's burden. I found that having to argue the situation or explain the reasons for doing things in a partic-ular way was more exhausting than doing the tasks myself.

My sister who did the insurance understood the inflexible requirements of the bureaucracies with which we were dealing. Her assurance that she would dot the I's and cross the T's was something I knew she would do so I willingly and completely turned certain tasks over to her with the comfort of knowing that if we had to explain something, we'd have the data and her clear approach on our side. My husband's willingness to do the support tasks of copying and collating, and endlessly review the more difficult processes, was invaluable. His clearer and more objective mind was an asset with-out which I could not have done what I did. There were other times, unfortunately, when offers of help ended up inadvertently complicat-ing a situation.

The moral here is to seek help but make sure the people you ask are fitted to the particular task. Don't try to force square pegs into round holes.

❤

When my mother's assets began dwindling close to the two thou-sand dollar mark that makes a person eligible for Medicaid, my true education began. Although social workers in nursing homes will often assist in the Medicaid application process, I did not have a good relationship with the social worker in my mother's nursing home. I did it alone. The only person who assisted in this task was my husband. Pete had already explained that this was a monumental task that required painstaking preparation and cautious monitoring.

The nursing home bill was forty-five hundred dollars a month (it began at $123/day and ended at $154/day—fourteen months later). I began the process early in 1987. It involved gathering documentation of all assets three years back. I had been repeatedly warned that I should never send an original and should always keep complete copies of correspondence. My husband and I spent over one hundred hours gathering, copying and preparing the application, which was submitted so that Medicaid would take over in August.

In May of that year, my husband was offered a job out of state. After much agonizing, I decided I would go if he wanted to take the job. He decided against it. In early September, while still waiting to hear from Medicaid, he became critically ill. He was hospitalized for three weeks and returned home with a tube in his chest through which large doses of antibiotics were pumped round the clock. By December, the Medicaid application had been denied three times, and the nursing home was sending red-letter bills that climbed to over thirteen thousand dollars before the case was settled.

I remember one particularly difficult day just after my husband had been released from the hospital. In an attempt to get away from the enormity of what we'd been through, we headed out to the western part of the state for the day. During that day, I stopped three times at a phone booth to talk to the caseworker, who was rude and nasty. But I was stuck, for he had the power to recommend approval or denial of our case.

I can't help but wonder if the problems and weird demands we experienced later were a retribution for our repeated appeals. The last appeal was won on a hardship after a note from the doctor detailed how ill my husband had been. This one required communication between Maria, Pete's associate who handled such things, and Washington, DC. It was settled a full ten months after Medicaid should have been instituted.

After my husband became well enough to pay attention, he asked the attorney about "due process." (Due process prevents a person from going in front of the same judge or jury on an appeal in the court systems.) She explained that the Medicaid system was not part of the judicial system and it was not uncommon, though it clearly was unfair, for the same case to come before the same person repeatedly. In May of 1988, I went with Maria, to the Medicaid office for our final hearing. After sitting for five minutes with a Medicaid supervisor, who said that we clearly had things under control and correct, we went for the final time in front of "judge and jury." In a few minutes, the case was approved.

During these particularly stressful months, I found out that we could drop the private medical insurance. Since my sister, who was working full time and had two young sons said she could no longer handle it, we dropped it. In retrospect, I see that it costs the Medicaid system when this happens, but at the time, we were all so exhausted that there was no way we could have managed to keep it. One would think that once into the Medicaid system, the difficulties are over. That however is not the case.

For most of the seven-plus years we were involved with Medicaid, I had to report to them every six months. This took the form of filling out a questionnaire that changed format and questions frequently. At times, I would receive seemingly random requests for bank statements from several years before that had been sent already. Despite my ability to be organized, attentive to details and play bureaucratic games, I almost lost it on more than one occasion. It seemed that just as I got to my wit's end, I would be assigned a new caseworker.

During the ten-month period we were navigating the Medicaid maze, the nursing home went without the majority of their money. They also started talking about moving my mother from the single room, for which we had been previously paying, to a triple room. After much discussion and many meetings between my sister and the nursing home, Attorney Maria finally accompanied me to the nursing home. The nursing home had apparently been cited for similar activity in the past. Maria, in no uncertain terms, put the nursing home administrator on notice that she was aware of their pending difficulties and that she would be watching them closely. She pointed out that the Callahan family had been through enough without another battle, but that she would fight it for us if the nursing home pushed the issue. Maria's intervention was effective. The move did not happen until several months later, when my mother was unaware of it.

Despite our difficulties with the Medicaid system, many have a much easier time of it. I strongly recommend using the nursing home staff if they are available to assist in the application process. Due to exhaustion, and in an attempt to ease things for everyone involved, I arranged for the pension and social security checks to be sent directly to the nursing home. The nursing home then put the monthly personal-need allowance in my mother's personal needs account. This amount fluctuated over the years between fifty and seventy five dollars a month. That was what was left of my mother's combined income of approximately a thousand dollars a month after the nursing home had been paid. It was used for clothing, incidentals, hair care and gifts.

While social workers in nursing homes routinely help with Medicaid applications, social workers in the home health setting teach and advise but Medicare will not pay for them to assist in the preparation of the application. SHINE (Senior Health Information Needs of Elders) volunteers can help however.

❤

Another particularly painful situation regarding Medicaid occurred while my sister and I were having lunch with our mother. Our conversation moved to medical care and I mentioned Medicaid.

My mother became hysterically angry and started shouting that I did not know what I was talking about and she was never going on the "welly."

My shock and the fact that I thought I might have had my terms mixed up led me to apologize and back off. With great difficulty, my sister distracted my mother with one of the kids.

When I checked my facts later, I found that I was correct and faced the fact that such discussions could not recur. The anger and upset to my mother was not worth it for any of us. Things would happen as they would, and by the time her money was gone, she would be unaware, so in some ways her dignity would be spared.

❤

Until hospice entered the picture, Medicaid and Medicare paid for all medical needs. Medicare is a federally funded medical insurance. Social Security is available at age sixty five (or younger for a disabled person). I dealt primarily with Medicare B. Occasionally, I would get a notice from them describing a service and detailing what was an acceptable payment to the provider (nursing home, doctor, and hospital). Sometimes it was nothing, other times it was less than had been billed. Infrequently, I had to pay a portion. My biggest memory of and impression of Medicare is the notification on their statements THIS IS NOT A BILL.

I found Medicare persons to be courteous and helpful without exception. Even during a major change of location, this remained the case. In the early nineties, I began receiving red letter dunning notices of past due balances from a podiatrist. After a couple of phone conversations with her office staff, I called the State's Regional Nursing Home Ombudsman with whom I had dealt on a few previous occasions. She suggested that I pay the bill, which was under $30.00, to "get them off my back." I did so and forgot about it.

A couple of years later, I received a notification from Medicare that they had paid the doctor for the visit. When I told my Uncle about this, he bristled and said this was not uncommon. Acknowledging my exhaustion, he encouraged me to follow up on this. A while later, I finally wrote a letter to Medicare, including all the numbers and identification codes of which they are so fond. I sent a copy to the doctor. In time that seemed less than possible, the amount I had paid directly was refunded to me by mail.

A year or so later, when sitting with the nursing home social worker to discuss hospice, she asked if my mother had ever had Dr. X. When I said yes, she explained that she was bringing a class action suit against the doctor on behalf of residents and families, some of whom were already deceased. It seems that the intimidating tactics used to threaten me were a standard operating procedure for this doctor. I readily agreed to sign permission for my mother's case to be used in the suit. I also called Medicare and was directed to a person who had been watching this doctor for four years. She was sure something was amiss although she had been unable to prove it thus far; the doctor had toed the line in terms of procedures, so had yet to be prosecuted.

♥

My mother had a single life insurance policy which had been purchased in the early nineteen fifties. It was a whole life policy with a face value of one thousand dollars. Due to dividends, it had accumulated a death benefit of substantially more than the face value. In 1981 she borrowed against the policy but the paperwork was nowhere to be found. When I first called the company, I was told that it was better to let the dividends pay the interest and principal so that is what I did.

As my mother became more and more infirm, my uncle urged me to call again and check things out. By this time, I was more leery and much wiser. I had also begun keeping track of whom I had spoken to and what was said. I realized that the conversations over the years were contradictory. Finally, after having been passed from person to person, which is a good strategy to get people to give up, I called a lawyer. By that time, my mother's assets were gone and I called the lawyer provided by Medicaid. He said it sounded like I knew more than he did about such things, so he suggested that I send a letter, clarifying what I had been told, and asking for answers in writing. I had been told that since I couldn't find the policy, and the bank at which it had been purchased was no longer in existence, they could not provide one. They also stated that they did not have a copy of the loan taken in 1981 and did not know what the amount was. Neither of these things turned out to be true.

Once I put things in writing, copying the attorney at his suggestion, the company became much more clear and cooperative. It became evident at that point that it was definitely in our best interest to pay the loan down since there would come a point when the policy would cease to exist when the loan amount surpassed some other amount. The terms and rules by which this policy was governed were confusing to say the least. In fact I am still not completely clear on the details, but I had learned enough to protect the policy which defrayed last minute funeral expenses and provided each of my mother's five children with an inheritance, albeit quite small. Again it was my Uncle who alerted me to the difficulties seniors were having with savings bank life insurance policies.

Prepaying the Funeral

Since we did not prepay the funeral, when the money was almost gone the most we could do was set aside $2500.00 in a burial account. The rest would have to be paid by my mother's children.

Although unable early on in the journey, like so many other things, I developed the emotional strength to handle making the funeral arrangements. Later, after discussing it with my younger sister who thought we should do it quickly, before we both lost our nerve, I called the Funeral Director and made an appointment for the following week, which happened to be Thanksgiving Week.

We met with him, and in an evening filled with slapstick foolishness, planned our mother's funeral.

At Thanksgiving, my sister told the others that the dirty deed had been done at last, and the "Kids Emergency" Saving's Bank Account to which we had been contributing for the past several months was almost completely wiped out.

Long Lost Relatives

At a time when I thought things were fairly well under control I was awakened one morning by attorney Maria. She told me that I would be receiving a note from her with a letter from a person in Vermont claiming to be an heir. This was in response to the probate notice the lawyers had filed on my mother's behalf regarding the conservatorship. At first I thought it was a joke, but soon realized it was not. According to Maria, this was not unheard of since there is a certain segment of the population who preys upon those in our situation. She suggested I not tell my siblings for a while.

The woman, who we called Gloria, spoke of one of my brothers by name, accusing him of preventing her from sharing in her true inheritance. She seemed to think our mother was dead since she mentioned his refusal to tell her where she was buried. As ludicrous as this seemed at the time, it was real. And it could have caused difficulties for us. Fortunately, she never pursued anything, and if the lawyers did anything to respond to her, I was not aware of it. On the bright side, a bit of family folklore was spawned which has grown into a pretty good story over the years. I have come to think of this long lost sibling as my Uncle dubbed her at the time, Gloria in excelsius Deo.

Circulating Credit Cards

Another strange and unexpected event happened years after my mother's credit cards were cut up and returned to the companies. I received a bill for $124.00 for dinner at a restaurant where my mother used to live. Since my mother hadn't been out of the nursing home in two years, and was certainly not capable of using a credit card, I called American Express. I expected that they would simply remove the charge from the bill when I explained the situation. Just to see if I had any extra energy I guess, they made a big deal about saying that the meal had been charged and I was responsible.

To make a long story short, it took months and several phone calls and letters to get this situation resolved. When I insisted upon seeing a copy of the charge slip, I found that a card was not run through the machine. The account number was written in and the signature wasn't even close to my mother's. That, I think, more than the copies of the cut card, and my notification to them that the account was closed, is what finally convinced them that Rita Callahan had not charged a meal on Cape Cod in 1990.

Mother Checks In and the Almighty Buck

It was a Monday night when my mother said to me, "Come in here young lady. Sit down." She promptly began, "This is a nursing home. I want to know why I'm here. I'm not sick. I certainly do not need care and furthermore, I'm sick and tired of working my fingers to the bone around here and never getting paid."

My mother was serious and furious. Finally, the fact that she was in a nursing home had dawned on her, perhaps for the first time, but at least for the first time she could express it to me. She wanted an explanation. Through the whole visit I was between tears and laughter. By the end of the visit she asked about her money, "Do I have any? How about a car, can I have a car, just a small one, OK honey?" I gave her a hug as she told me she was glad we'd had this little chat. I cried all the way home.

A short time later, my mother started hassling me about money every time I saw her. The only way to get by this was to call in my husband, a male who represented authority to her; whom she thought was judge and lawyer who sat at the right hand of God. (None of this was true.) They had a conversation resulting in his dictating a letter to me "I Rita Callahan have 35K which I have put in conservatorship with my two daughters. I receive regular accountings of my funds. It was my choice to do this and I believe it was the correct choice." She signed it, I signed it, he witnessed and notarized it, and as promised, sent a copy to her.

I carried the letter in my wallet for two years, long after my mother was able to raise the issue. On the two times she did raise it, I brought it out and she looked at it, her face becoming stern and said "Obviously I signed this and apparently we're not supposed to discuss it so I guess we won't." This is an example of the creative thinking I mentioned before, something that I wish I had learned much earlier in the disease process.

The cost of Alzheimer's

A financial aspect of Alzheimer's Disease that I have not discussed is spousal impoverishment. Estates are destroyed as families pay out a lifetime of savings for care. We were lucky that Medicaid never ended or imposed limits which would have prevented my mother's care. Long term care insurance is an option that was not available when my mother was planning for her future. Those planning now should at least consider it because at some point Alzheimer's may "break the bank" of the wealthiest nation on earth.

The total U.S. national cost for Alzheimer's care is estimated to be above $100 billion per year. These staggering costs further endanger dependent and cognitively impaired people in a society that so highly values cognitive abilities and independence. As the coffers dwindle and more of the population ages and more become ill to the extent and in the ways my mother did, who will pay for their care, particularly in the final years? Will economic realities replace compassion? Will there come a time when demented individuals are determined to be unworthy of the cost of care for them?

During my mother's journey through Alzheimer's, we did not face the issue of refusal of treatment due to lack of funds. I suppose that someone could have said that the money used to "maintain" her was wasted. While vaguely aware of that issue, I certainly wasn't going to be the one to raise it. However, I know that my mother would not have hesitated to give her life to save a person with a chance to get well and live a life with quality. ❤

Table 1: Asset and Liability Tracking List

Document	Location	Date	Value	Non or Liquid	Beneficiary	Asset Type
SBLI Life Insurance Policy	Safe Dep. Box	6/8/83	1,000 face death benefit value— 2300, cash value, less 1300 borrowed 3/81	Could be liquidated— But owed some $$?	Daddy	Whole Life Life Insurance Policy
Mortgage Note	MA Safe Dep. Box	7/9/83	Balance 23K	Owed to BayBank— will have to sell	NA	Mortgage
Deed to FL Condo	FL Safe Dep. Box	2/16/81	41K	None	None	Real estate
Daddy's Death Cert.	MA Safe Dep. Box	8/4/82	NA	NA	NA	Legal— Need for Medicaid filing
Cemetery Deed	MA Safe Dep. Box	8/4/82	Own— 1 spot left	Must have for burial— give to Digga' if prepay?	NA	NA
Stock Certificates	MA Safe Dep. Box	8/4/82	See separate list	Easy to sell but will lose if soon	None — add beneficiary	Stock

Table 2: Monthly Inflow and Outflow Report

April 1987   Worksheet for Cape Cod Five......20-APR-87

April 1987 Inflows:

Source		Date	Amount	Ck #/Bank
Social Security		4/1	$506.00	dd/Cape Cod Five
Dad's Pension		4/1	432.06	dd/ Cape Cod Five
Misc.		4/20	7500.00	from Real
Total In			**$8438.06**	

Outflows:

Insurance	Paid to/for	Date	Amount	Ck #/Bank/Signer
	AARP	4/10	21.95	309/CCF/SC
	Life	2/28	_____	Pete says leave alone
Subtotal Out			**$ 21.95**	

Misc:	Paid to/for	Date	Amount	Ck #/Bank/Signer
	Dr. K/PierceEars	4/10	$75.00	308/ Cape Cod Five/sc
	P.Sullivan(2/3)	4/20	20.00	311/ Cape Cod Five/sc
	Shawmut Bank Burial Account	?	2500.00	?/ Cape Cod Five/rmm
	Research Mrtg. Dischrg	4/20	20.00	314/ Cape Cod Five/sc
Subtotal Out			**$2615.00**	

Nursing Home	Paid to/for	Date	Amount	Ck #/Bank/Signer
	Newspaper	4/20	25.60	313/Cape Cod Five/sc
	Phone	4/10	26.63	310/Cape Cod Five/sc
	Monthly Rm&Bd	4/20	4774.00	312/Cape Cod Five/sc
	Hair		24.00	
	Hair		12.00	
	Hair		12.00	
	Hair		18.00	
	Pharmacy		70.10	
Subtotal			**$4964.33**	
Total Out			**$7601.28**	

Table 3: Note Pages

Date	Issue	Organization	Person	Specifics
6/6/86	Florida Car		Pete	FIND IT!!
6/12/86	Label Clothes	Nursing Home	Social Worker	must be done
6/23/86	Room and Board	Nursing Home	Business Mgr.	must pay one month ahead, get $ from Money Mkt.
6/24/86	Wire Funds	Investment Hs.	Broker	Wired to Checking Acct.

Table 4: Important Numbers at the back of the Notebook

Social Security #: _____

Medicare #: _____

Medicaid #: _____

Chapter 5:
Living Arrangements

When the Alzheimer's patient can no longer function independently, a very different set of issues must be faced head on. Financial resources and alternate living arrangements must be evaluated. Emotional issues must also be faced. Good decision making includes realistic assessment and a willingness to examine options, motivation, goals and consequences. Discussion, careful analysis of options and planning prior to the need for making a change are the best ways to avoid crisis decision making.

Getting a person with Alzheimer's to understand and accept that a change is necessary is not easy. Even families find it difficult to accept the fact that independent living will end, for doing so requires major decisions and changes to be made. It also requires the release of denial. However, the end of living independently must be faced at some point in time. Issues of safety, nutrition, health, caregiver burnout and isolation are usually the deciding factors. In the beginning, there is a tendency for families to minimize the level of their patient's impairment, thus complicating the consideration, timing and process of reaching such decisions.

Home Care

Home care is the introduction of people and services into the patient's home. It is designed to maintain the Alzheimer's patient in her current environment. There are a variety of city and state programs. These agencies are private, for profit and non-profit. Sometimes voluntary services are available through a variety of agencies and churches.

There are many ways to find home care services in your area; doctors, social service and discharge planners in hospitals, and agencies dedicated to servicing the elderly. The Yellow Pages is a good place to begin. Look under "AARP," "Alzheimer's Association," "home health," "elderly," "medical," and "nurses."

There are also agencies designed especially for finding care options for elders. Eldercare Locator links anyone in the United States with information about services. Providing the elder's zip code and a brief description of the problem helps to identify appropriate resources. This can be particularly helpful for out-of-state family caregivers.

Some expenses for home care services may be reimbursable through Medicare (specifically if skilled nursing at home is required), Medicaid and a growing number of private insurance plans. To determine eligibility for such coverage, individuals should check with their home care provider or with their local social services agency or Area Agency on Aging.

A recent change to the Medicare rules has made it easier for Alzheimer's patients to receive services in the home. If properly documented, Medicare now accepts Alzheimer's as a primary diagnosis that can qualify a patient for services. Use of this requires careful and voluminous documentation but the benefits to patient and at home caregivers are worth the effort. Even more recent changes have put this much needed help in the home in jeopardy.

The use of Medicare funds for help in the home is possible because Alzheimer's is considered a diagnosis of a psychiatric nature. Many, myself included, object to considering Alzheimer's a psychiatric disorder. While Alzheimer's can manifest itself in psychiatric symptoms such as hallucinations and depression, when these symptoms are treated successfully in the psychiatric patient they are, for all intents and purposes, cured. The same is not true of Alzheimer's patients for the deterioration of their brain continues despite the successful management of their psychiatric symptoms.

Activities of Daily Living (ADLs)

Activities of daily living are those things we do to care for ourselves. They include dressing, bathing, taking medications, cooking, eating, toileting and transporting ourselves to where we should be. ADL's are intrinsically related to a person's dignity. Depending on the person's definition of quality of life, assistance with bathing, dressing, and eating can be a joy for the afflicted person or they may signal complete loss of dignity. Knowing how the person feels about dignity and quality of life and respecting those feelings, looking for ways to ease the adjustments are ways for Alzheimer's caregivers to be supportive and helpful. Evaluating an individual's ability to live alone is based, at least in part, on her ability to handle Activities of Daily Living.

Bathing

People who develop Alzheimer's often become resistant to bathing—even people who were previously fastidiously clean. Bathing is a tough issue which involves more than health considerations. Often, outsiders must assist in this difficult area. While we faced far fewer of these types of issues than many, I remember gaining insight during an incident when my mother was firmly entrenched in the early stages of the disease.

My mother was staying with me at the time and excited about our imminent "night on the town." Yet she was anxious too. She became fixated on what she would wear and was impatient for the evening to begin. Not fully realizing her current state of abilities, I sent her into the bathroom to shower. Annoyed to realize that she was not showering, I went in to see what the problem was.

Much to my surprise, my mother was not sure of what she was supposed to be doing. When I repeated the direction to shower, it became clear that she did not know how. The hand held shower wand was beyond her ability to fathom. Additionally, this once avid swimmer was fearful of the water. Once I realized the problems, with a sinking heart I "showered Mom." We got through it with a minimum of disasters as we cloaked our breaking hearts in banal conversation. If she was uncomfortable about this blatant demonstration of our role reversal she kept her thoughts to herself and, with great concentration, assisted me in showering her. Once more, Mom was showing me the way through this confusing, heartbreaking labyrinth we seemed to be entering into further and further.

Beverly Bigtree Murphy, in *he Used to be Somebody: A Journey into Alzheimer's Disease Through the Eyes of a Caregiver*, describes how she imagines an Alzheimer's patient experiencing a shower:

I tried to imagine how an Alzheimer's person interprets the noise that happens in the bathroom with hard tile walls and floors and the shower running full blast and a caregiver talking loudly in order to be heard over the running water.

They interpret the caregiver's raised voice as shouting. Their clothes are being taken off and they interpret being moved under the shower as being shoved and manhandled. On top of that they are suddenly sprayed with water which may or may not be the temperature they can tolerate because sense of touch and temperature is also impaired. Strangers are crowded into the room with them and they can't tell if they're being observed or threatened or ridiculed. They have no way of knowing those aren't other people at all but reflections in the mirror on the bathroom wall. They must feel terribly violated. They are bombarded with so many variables that it must at times seem like hell, and we wonder why bath time is traumatic. Better yet, we complain that the patient is combative.[1]

Through her assistance in bathing, my mother also showed me the importance of providing ways for her to "Save Face." We learned together as I hesitantly grasped the feathery pointers she threw out for me. Together we strengthened them with shared love. "It may not be something to look forward to," I thought to myself, "and I may be frightened, but if Mom can hang in there and 'make the best of it,' surely I had better try too." I tried. I learned. We made it.

Dressing

Dressing is another difficult issue. Dressing and dressing appropriately become more difficult for the Alzheimer's patient. They forget the order in which clothes are put on. They are unaware of the effect of seasons on choosing clothing. Sometimes they simply forget certain articles of clothing altogether.

My mother was one of those women who was always dressed to the nines. She bought beautiful clothes and had a wonderful sense of style, which made her losses in this area particularly painful. We managed, or rather my sisters managed, to put this particular loss off long beyond what is typical. But, as with all else, Alzheimer's had its way.

I remember a deal my mother had made with a dear friend that the surviving one of them would be sure that the other's nails were perfectly manicured while she lay in her casket. It was but a small reminder of how important her grooming was to her. That, perhaps more than anything else, is what really changed my mother from "herself" to "the shell" she became throughout this devastation. When my mother no longer looked like a woman who walked off the cover of a magazine, I truly knew she was being taken from me. I could no longer deny this while her physical beauty was being stripped away layer by layer, day by day.

I recently heard a wonderful story about Gillian, an Alzheimer's patient in her late eighties who had loved line dancing. She entered the living room dressed for her hundred and two-year-old sister's funeral in her cowgirl outfit, complete with long fringes and cowgirl boots, her daughter sent her back to change into something more appropriate. Next Gillian emerged in a full-length red sequined gown. Finally, her daughter assisted her in choosing appropriate funeral attire.

Cooking, ironing and smoking

Cooking is frequently cited as a safety concern. Cooking a muffin on a paper plate in the oven is disastrous. Leaving the stove on can clearly be a danger, which can threaten the well being of the patient as well as that of many others. Depending on the living situation, fire can become a single or a multiple tragedy. A burner on a gas stove that is not turned on enough to ignite is a danger that can be alleviated by having the gas company install a hidden shut-off mechanism. Electric stoves could have a "safety" switch mounted out of sight that would need to be on for the stove to work.

Other concerns that are rarely mentioned are power tools and hunting implements, ironing and smoking. Power tools and hunting implements can obviously be dangerous. The person who has used these tools for most of their lives may not understand the potential hazards. The family caregiver must identify such hazards and take steps to "move them out of harm's way."

Ironing, while not as common now as it once was, is an activity that many women of my mother's generation found soothing. Years of necessity made it a common activity that calmed some people down. As an Alzheimer's patient loses the ability to evaluate safety situations yet returns to behaviors that have been with them for a lifetime, it is not unreasonable for them to take to ironing. Leaving the iron on, wandering away, and burning clothes can be the results.

Smoking is obviously of concern for Alzheimer's patients. Despite their initial intuition and understanding about safety issues, they eventually lose their comprehension of such risks. Smokers who develop Alzheimer's become a safety concern. While some people may simply be able to stop smoking when told that they must, others never agree to give it up, or forget they have stopped, and smoking becomes more and more of a hazard.

Wandering

Wandering is a particularly difficult issue for the Alzheimer's caregiver. We were only aware of my mother's wandering a few times, but I believe it is likely that she was lost more often. I have since been told that between fifty and sixty percent of early and middle stage Alzheimer's patients wander.

Families are often convinced that their loved one won't wander. But the story that was related by a support group member shows how dangerous holding onto this particular hope can be. Jason had moved his wife and seven children into his mother's house two years earlier. At the last appointment with their neurologist, the doctor warned Jason that wandering was still a danger although his mother had never wandered. An unbelieving Jason reported to the support group one week later that his mother had wandered out of the house that very night, sometime between 11 and midnight. A passing motorist, who was on his way home from work offered her a ride. It took well over three hours for Jason's mother to remember what street she lived on, even though she had moved into the house more than forty years earlier.

Jason and his family were lucky—the motorist had just lost his grandmother to Alzheimer's so he recognized what was happening and knew what to do. Others are not so lucky. I once worked with a woman whose aunt wandered off and was never found. Recently, in my community two gentlemen wandered off. They were not found alive.

With assistance from a local police officer assigned as the community liaison, the Patient & Family Services Committee of the local Alzheimer's Association is preparing a three pronged approach to protect people at risk for wandering. Community Awareness about the problem is the first prong. This includes police, fire departments, taxi services and others as well as Alzheimer's families and the community at large. Registration of Alzheimer's patients with local police is recommended in conjunction with joining the Safe Return Program. The need for both is not always understood, but quite simply, local registration is designed to familiarize police personnel with potential wanderers so they can intervene before the person becomes irrevocably lost or confused. The Safe Return program is nation-wide. Upon registering, the Alzheimer's patient is entered into a computerized database that alerts police in other communities to be on the lookout for the wanderer. Many families, mine included, encountered patient resistance to wearing the safe return bracelet. Obtaining a caregiver bracelet also helps. Having a favorite child or grandchild present the jewelry to the patient and caregiver is usually successful.

For the patient who is home and mobile, securing doors can be helpful. Most large hardware stores have plastic "knob caps" (similar to a child proof medicine cap) that spin unless pressed in particular spots. This prevents the patient from opening the door. Removing locks from bathroom doors and installing safety locks or moving existing locks on outside doors can also increase safety and prohibit wandering.

Much research has been done on what Alzheimer's victims do when they wander off. A recent local wanderer, who was found frightened but OK, was asked by his daughter whether he had heard the police calling his name. He said he heard them but was too scared to answer. This man had, quite literally, gone to ground. He had burrowed himself into the woods within a mile of his home. He got so confused he felt the need for safety. Local Alzheimer's Associations should be active in educating families, police and the community at large about the fact that normal search protocols are not effective when searching for an Alzheimer's patient and how a search should be conducted. After the first day, the odds of finding the wanderer alive decrease alarmingly, so prompt, appropriate search protocols are critical. It is important that the caregiver call the police after looking for fifteen minutes.

Incontinence

Incontinence refers to the loss of bladder control or the loss of bowel control. Urinary stress incontinence is related to a weakness in the lining of the bladder wall and can be triggered by laughter, coughing, sneezing, lifting or any sudden exertion.

Many family caregivers cite incontinence as one of the thornier issues they face. This is particularly true for children caring for parents. I have heard some enterprising attempts on the part of the patient to address this issue. Some caregivers report that their patients get the hair dryer to handle clothing that is wet due to "accidents."

Some caregivers are less upset by this problem than others. One patient used his bathroom heater to dry his pajamas. He resisted his wife's efforts to change him unless he had come to want it. Once he said to her "You're taking me apart." His wife learned to go slowly and negotiate and not to flip out about sharing a bed with someone "clad in dried pee."

Toileting ourselves is one of our most personal skills and tests of independence. It is a private experience. To not be able to control our bodies in this manner is a major loss of self-control, and understandably embarrassing. Adults with a lifetime of experience go back to baby diapers.

All struggle with incontinence at one point or another. It is an issue that is directly tied to dignity. Regardless of how it is handled, the patient's feelings must be considered.

Incontinence can be particularly difficult for spouses when it comes to accompanying their mate into a public, gender specific toilet. I recommend that the destination be chosen ahead of time based on the availability of a gender-less handicapped toilet. Women who accompany a woman with Alzheimer's into a rest room must be sure to maintain voice contact while the patient is out of sight to avoid the patient wandering away.

While incontinence is inevitable, it sometimes can be delayed. Bringing the Alzheimer's patient to the bathroom on a regular schedule can delay incontinence until the disease process has taken control of this function from them.

Constipation and bowel impaction can be avoided with careful attention to diet, exercise and products like milk of magnesia. Keeping a regular toileting schedule is very important. The Toileting Schedule presented in Figure 5 at the end of the chapter may be of help.

Neighborhood Dilemmas

As my mother's descent into Alzheimer's progressed, we began hearing more instances of her difficulties. She had given a key to a couple of neighbors but would still tell us occasionally of being "locked out." It wasn't until things really started going downhill that the neighbors opened up about how often that was happening and how upset my mother was becoming. These are tricky relationships.

It is difficult for a neighbor or friend to know when to voice concern to a person's family. Neighbors may have no way of knowing which, if any, of the person's children should be told of apparent difficulties. They may be in the bind of breaking confidences and embarrassing the patient. For these reasons, it would be helpful for family members to approach them. Once this is done, it is not uncommon for families to find out that things are considerably worse than they themselves are observing. They may also find that an unfair burden has been placed on a neighbor or friend who is uncomfortable about speaking up.

Medication and Nutrition

As the Alzheimer's patient declines, medications can cause great difficulty. The patient may not know if she needs medication or may not be able to keep track of what she has taken. Missing or doubling doses can have serious effects and consequences. The same is true for nutrition. Her ability to buy, prepare and eat nutritious food will be compromised with progression of the disease.

Support Options

A variety of services and options to living transitions are available. They range from home-based assistance to community-based programs to long term residential care. Most geographical areas have an Elder Service Agency, usually run by the state, and Visiting Nurse Associations (VNAs). Home-based care includes Homemaker Services, Home Health Care Services and hospice programs. Community-based programs include Adult Day Health Programs, Adult Foster Care Programs and Respite Care.

Supportive housing options include Congregate Housing Facilities, Continuing Care Retirement Communities (CCRCs), Assisted Living Residences and Rest Homes. Foster home care in properly supervised homes is another option. Traditional models of some of the above are inappropriate for the person with Alzheimer's.

Long term care, which many Alzheimer's families face eventually, occurs in nursing homes and in assisted living facilities. Thankfully, some congregate and assisted living facilities are opening which specialize in Alzheimer's. As with other decisions, one must carefully check into services and be sure that staff are bonafide Alzheimer's professionals, rather than those who are so quick to hop on the bandwagons that indicate a new market.

Many things must be evaluated when considering the use of such services and options. First is a realization that change is difficult for Alzheimer's patients. It increases confusion, agitation and decreases feelings of security. For these reasons, planning and executing well thought out transitions are in the best interest of the patient. (That is not to suggest that a situation that is not working should be continued, but rather that informed, well planned, intentional changes work best.) Licensing by state and federal agencies, cost, Alzheimer's appropriateness and Alzheimer's trained staff are but a few of the things you should investigate. Regardless of the options considered and eventually used, such transitions are difficult for families as well as for patients.

Most family caregivers wait too long to seek help. Because of the variations due to locale, the following discussion will be fairly generic, but there are a few resources that can quickly point families in the right direction. They are state or local Elder Affairs and Protective Services, the local chapter of the Alzheimer's Association, and Visiting Nurses Associations. Alzheimer's diagnostic centers are also usually prepared to make referrals and may be able to explain the types and costs of appropriate services. Whether a family chooses to keep their loved one at home or use long term care or some combination of home and community services, they need support. The rigors of caregiving are significant and can become all-consuming. As one caregiver said:

> The hard truth is that this illness made both of us prisoners and each of us was the other's jailer. There were days when I wondered which of us had the keys.[2]

Help in the Home

Resistance from the Alzheimer's patient about leaving her home is to be expected. Is it any wonder? Would any of us relinquish our independence without a fight? But sooner or later, things must change. The question becomes when and how. One option is for someone to assist in the home. This can range from an hour or two of help once or twice a week from a home health aide to someone living full time in the Alzheimer's patient's home. Full time help in the home can range from a series of professional and paraprofessionals working in shifts, to a full time companion or family member(s) to some combination of these.

Homemaker services provide help with shopping, cooking, light housekeeping, bathing, dressing, grooming, and toileting. Home health care services manage health and medical conditions that can be treated at home.

There are two types of Community Based Care. The first, respite, is short-term and can be provided in the home or in a long term care facility. It's purpose is to provide a break for family caregivers from their caregiving responsibilities. Many local chapters of the Alzheimer's Association have programs to support periodic respite for caregivers. The second is Adult Day Care.

Adult Day Care

Adult Day Care is a structured environment in which adults with specific difficulties and needs are supervised by professionals. It offers socialization and appropriate activities. My mother flatly refused to attend Day Care. It was hard for us to push the issue when we agreed with her protestations of not wanting to be treated as a child. We were advised poorly by the person who ran the Adult Day Health Program that full disclosure about the nature of day care was needed. While reality orientation used to be considered appropriate, it no longer is, and the cold, methodical approach of this woman did not work with our mother, or for that matter, with us. A bit of honey and sugar coating might have served us all better.

Despite our family's lack of success with day care, it is a viable alternative for many, providing much needed relief to home caregivers. The use of day care can lengthen the time an Alzheimer's patient can be at home. Day care can also improve the quality of the patient's daily life through socialization and activities that are appropriate, and at which she can be successful. A day care specializing in Alzheimer's is desirable. It is important not to confuse senior centers with day care, which are designed with specific goals in mind. There are two types of Adult Day Care; social and medical. The latter accepts people with medical needs such as the management of medications and incontinence. Medical Adult Day Programs have a nurse on staff. Social Day Care Programs do not accept people with medical needs and do not have medical personnel. Transportation is usually available for a fee.

Day care for the Alzheimer's patient is well worth considering and patient resistance is to be expected. Some find that although, according to day care workers, their patient is actively involved and happy, the family hears nothing but how awful it is at that day care. It may not be appropriate or viable in all circumstances and while most patients adjust reasonably well, some do not. It is sometimes difficult to differentiate between an inappropriate setting, reluctance on the part of the patient, and caregiver reluctance.

My heart broke, yet one more time, at a support group where I heard a caregiver relay the conversation with his Alzheimer's afflicted wife on their way to day care.

"You always complain about going but you have a good time once you're there," he said.

"That may be, Jonathan," she replied, "But it's still a place for the 'throw away ladies.' It's awful being a throw away lady." This caregiving husband was doing the best he could. The day care provided him with much needed respite and his wife with social stimulation that was appropriate and non-threatening. Her heartbreaking words were a clear indication that she understood her situation, at least at some level.

Living with a Child

Some Alzheimer's patients end up living with their children either in the child's or the parent's home. Many of the concerns over activities of daily living are lessened by moving someone in with the Alzheimer's patient, but all concerns are not alleviated. Such a choice represents tremendous changes that may require difficult adjustments for all involved. Safety must always be considered.

Of prime importance is the motivation of the child who is to become the primary hands-on caregiver. Guilt, lack of or not enough money, and sheer helplessness and hopelessness lead some to take on a task for which they may be neither prepared, nor suited or truly willing. Since the well being of the patient is the primary concern of the surrogate, the motivation of those who may offer alternative living arrangements is important. That said, it is also important to be realistic. All too often, families face the decision to change a living arrangement in crisis. We did.

Crisis decision-making is to be avoided at all costs. The best way to avoid crisis decision-making is to plan. Planning means to learn about and consider the issues and factors affecting choices as unemotionally as possible, before being faced with making a decision. This is easier said than done, on both counts, but critical.

Essentially, what is needed is a safety net for the patient. A place and people who are able, willing and committed to allowing the patient to do as much as she is able while ensuring that her needs are met emotionally, physically and spiritually. As Habilitation therapy states, it means providing a supportive environment. But all too often, nothing is considered except an inexpensive solution. NOW.

When the situation with my aunt at my mother's house and then my mother at my aunt's house had to end, my older sister said she would take our mother into her home. I was very much against it at the time. We replayed old battles around this issue which didn't serve any of us. But they were unavoidable given our grief, fear and unfinished business with each other, and with our mother.

I wasn't able to see, let alone understand, the pressures on my sister as the oldest daughter. My mother had taken in her mother. That put enormous pressure on my sister to follow in her footsteps, to provide a home for our mother. The only time my sister ever articulated this to me, was after my mother had left her house. All she said was, "I had to do it for me." Perhaps she did not recognize these pressures as they were exerting such influence on her.

My husband offered to have my mother come to our home for a maximum of six months; but he also predicted that if she did, I would end up in a hospital within one month. It was my sister who took me off the hook saying, "You've worked too hard, finished your degree at great cost and have a job offer you simply can't refuse. It would be a sin."

The deciding factor was that my sister was more available as a primary, in-home caregiver since she could better afford to adjust her hectic, but less monetarily driven schedule than the rest of us. Or so it seemed at the time. One condition my sister put on the move was that my mother's funds build a room in the basement for my nephew, thus freeing up two rooms upstairs. The second room was occupied by a "live-in helper" who my sister literally met and hired at a bus stop one day. She knew nothing about the woman, except that she needed a place to stay; so in exchange for room and board, this stranger's job was to become Puppy's keeper.

The stress created by this move was enormous. My sister's house is over three thousand square feet. It is an unstructured, highly active environment full of confusion. The house is always open and it is lots of fun for those of us who live a quieter, more subdued life. But it was not a supportive environment for an Alzheimer's patient. And the pressures that arose when my sister's child developed an infection following surgery were almost too much to bear. When I asked my brother-in-law why he hadn't said "no" before my mother moved in, he said he would have ended up in divorce court. My other sister and I agreed that my mother would have to leave as soon as possible.

Two other incidents forced us to begin our search for an alternate living arrangement. The first incident was a night when my mother went downstairs after everyone else was in bed. My brother-in-law found her warming milk on a burner which also had the daily newspaper on it. The second was when my mother got into the liquor, (she no longer drank alcohol) and emptied what was left in a bottle of some unusual cordial which she never would have drunk since she had never liked the taste. It is not unheard of for Alzheimer's patients to drink alcohol although they have stopped drinking or never did drink. My sister called me at 4:30 am to tell me to come over. She and her husband had found my mother passed out at the top of the stairs.

Ultimately, it was my mother who chose the nursing home over a live-in companion in my sister's house. This was not necessarily bad, since change is so disrupting to Alzheimer's patients. In 1985 assisted living was virtually non-existent and the only Continuing Care Retirement Community had a six year waiting list.

Assisted Living Communities that are designed and run by Alzheimer's professionals are just beginning to appear. Since each change causes difficulties for the Alzheimer's patient, it is important to carefully assess the facility being considered for its Alzheimer's appropriateness. Alzheimer's patients who try to "sneak into" an assisted living arrangement that is not geared for their needs will deplete precious resources only to find they will have to make another move.

Alzheimer's caregivers must carefully evaluate all options for changes in living arrangements in light of the ability of each to meet the needs of the Alzheimer's patient. For some, institutional care becomes the only viable option. Remember, in an effort to increase their share of the market, many are jumping on the Alzheimer's bandwagon who are ignorant or unscrupulous. ❤

Table 1: Toileting Schedule

| TOILETING SCHEDULE   Date Schedule Started_____ | | | | | | | | | |
| Name_____ | | | | | | | | | |
Date	Hours awake	1st	2nd	3rd	4th	5th	Additional times	Assistance required	Staff Initials
Signature:									

Of Two Minds, A Guide to the Care of People with the Dual Diagnosis of Alzheimer's Disease and Mental Retardation, Judith M. Antonangeli, RN, BSN, Fidelity Press, 1995, p. 141.

1. Beverly Bigtree Murphy, *he Used to be Somebody: A Journey into Alzheimer's Disease Through the Eyes of a Caregiver*, Gibbs Associates, Boulder CO, 1995, p.310.

2. Beverly Bigtree Murphy, *he Used to be Somebody: A Journey into Alzheimer's Disease Through the Eyes of a Caregiver*, Gibbs Associates, Boulder CO, 1995, p.219.

Chapter 6:
Long-term Care

There may come a time when home care is no longer feasible. It is then that another set of issues and problems arise and a new set of adjustments must be made, as support systems are changed to include new people in different roles and different environments.

Since Alzheimer's patients cannot change behaviors or learn new ones, caregiving must revolve around patient needs. The commitment to follow the patient into her new world is more likely to result in quality of life, preservation of self esteem and peace, at least for the patient.

Looking for a Suitable Facility

For many families, the decision to place their loved one in a nursing home or other long term care facility must eventually be faced. We were one of those families. Because each of my mother's children had significant responsibilities, it was not possible for any of us to accept the role of full time, hands on caregiver indefinitely.

For all families it is a difficult decision. It is a turning point, for it redefines the relationship between the patient and the caregiver. Everyone, including the person with Alzheimer's, knows the patient will spend the rest of their lives in this place. Regardless of the final choice, many intervening options should be considered before the placement of an Alzheimer's patient in an institutional setting.

Institutionalization seems to raise guilt even in those who recognize that they are unable to even consider continuation of the home care they have been struggling to maintain. Perhaps the most common cause for guilt is the consideration or actualization of nursing home care. But guilt is not justified unless placement in the nursing home translates into abandonment; abandonment in the guise of withdrawing supports for the caregiver or the patient. Even if your patient is in a facility, you are still a caregiver. Placement in a facility can relieve you of the stresses of everyday care, so you will have more time and energy to spend quality time with your loved one.

Once the decision was made to move her to a nursing home, my mother showed the same determination to make institutionalization work as she had shown in preventing it from happening. Ultimately, it was my mother who decided to go to a nursing home and she was involved in deciding which nursing home.

We knew enough to make sure that the nursing home we chose would accept Medicaid and have all levels of care, (see Table 1 at the end of this chapter). This was essential to avoid another change when my mother got worse. Different states use the same terms differently.

When the issue of nursing home placement was raised, I realized that I would not be able to handle the search along with the legal and financial matters I found so overwhelming. Time was part of the issue, but my emotions were as much or more of a factor. I simply couldn't face going into nursing homes as though I were out to buy a couch. Fortunately I was not alone; others were able to handle that task. If you are not lucky enough to have others to help, start with a deep breath and trust yourself. Promise yourself that you will look those with whom you might work in the eyes, take notes, and think of how you'll work with these people. You are your loved one's advocate and protector. You can and will do this well. Be sure to assess whether her prospective caregivers can join you *as you enter her world.*

It was agreed that my two sisters would do the initial nursing home search. My younger sister said that after looking at several homes she was finally able to go in and really look with a critical eye at what services were offered. She was so upset at the first several that she felt she had to revisit them, once she felt able to focus on the issues. These issues were very important indeed. Quality of care, staff attitudes as well as physical amenities were to define our mother's home and our relationship with her for her remaining years.

Finally, the dreaded day arrived when my older sister said it was time for me to join the search. Despite my tears, she insisted that I accompany her to a place that she and our younger sister were fairly happy with. I cried the whole time, finding little solace in the on-site "ice cream parlor," hairdresser, and attractive chapel. I don't know how my sisters faced this most difficult of tasks when they did, but I am eternally grateful that they were able to and had the courage to do so.

After my sisters had looked at more than thirty facilities between them, and insisted on my participation, it was decided that my mother had to look too. By the time she and I went together, I had moved beyond my tears. Having looked at several homes with my husband, some of which my sisters were strongly favoring, I was able to be somewhat objective.

But try as I might, I can't erase the images of that first experience of going to a nursing home with my mother. It was one of many owned by a reputable company, and one of two in our area that had an Alzheimer's Unit. As we walked toward the unit, an Alzheimer's patient zoned in on us. She took my mother's face in her hands and looked deeply into her eyes. Both my mother and I were badly shaken. I did not resist when my mother grabbed my arm and said, "We are out of here!" Also difficult was the fact that my mother looked so good that the nursing home staff did not realize she was the patient.

The first three rules of real estate are "location, location, location." For different reasons, location is a prime consideration in choosing a nursing home. We chose one that was ten minutes from my older sister because her schedule was the most flexible. At the time, it seemed perfectly reasonable that she would pop in on a regular basis.

My living arrangement was split between the city and the shore. Although one of my brothers lived at the shore full time, the shore was deemed an unreasonable choice due to the fact that three of the five of us were rarely there. This decision had a silver lining for me because it reserved my home at the shore as a haven from Alzheimer's. Although it made it more difficult to get to my mother's side when things were really bad, there were others close enough to manage things and protect her until I could be there in person.

Another thing that occurs to me in retrospect is the location of the nursing home close to a major highway. This made it easier for those who were at a greater distance. The choice of a home in the suburbs avoided the problem of parking and walking alone in the city, which is where the "runner up" nursing home was located. As my life situation changed, this would have become a monumental issue.

Alzheimer's units

At the time we were looking there were few Alzheimer's units available. Of the two places that had such a unit, one was not available when we required placement. The other was in a poor location for our family. So my mother entered a nursing home that did not have a unit that specialized in Alzheimer's. We made the best decision we could at the time. But, if I had it to do over again, and when I am asked, I say, "Look for an Alzheimer's unit." I say this for many reasons.

Alzheimer's units tend to have better staff-to-patient ratios. Also, the staff on Alzheimer's units understand the disease and are specially trained to provide appropriate, failure-free activities and handle difficult behaviors. Staff at Alzheimer's units tend to be better equipped to deal with the difficult transitions patients and families face. Alzheimer's units frequently have more and better-suited support structures in place.

The people who work in Alzheimer's units are constantly learning. Finally, though I have no personal experience with a family member in such a unit, I have had considerable exposure to professionals who work in them and family caregivers whose loved one is in an Alzheimer's unit. I find them to be more aware of the end of life and patient rights issues than staff in a facility without a designated Alzheimer's unit.

As of 1995, specialized care units were available in only 10 percent of the nursing homes nationwide. Table 2 at the end of this chapter sums up my reasons for finding them desirable. Table 3 can help in comparing Alzheimer's units. But sometimes a home with an Alzheimer's unit is not available. Although my mother was not in an Alzheimer's unit, she received consistently high quality, loving care for almost nine years.

There may be many reasons for considering a long term care facility that does not have an Alzheimer's unit; proximity to family, cost, and availability are but a few.

Those who will be considering long term care facilities that do not have special care units dedicated to dementia patients should refer to Table 4 at the end of this chapter.

Finally, the six theoretical concepts for special care units are instructive for those who wish to find a unit in a long term care facility designed to meet the needs of Alzheimer's patients. These concepts, which were developed for a report produced by the United States Congress Office of Technology Assessment, are presented in Table 5 at the end of this chapter. The mission statement of an Alzheimer's unit should reflect an understanding of and a commitment to these theoretical concepts.

As is true in so many other areas of Alzheimer's care, the term *Alzheimer's* is being used by some as a marketing tool and money making ploy. Some of these people are unscrupulous while others are merely ignorant. Since it is the task of the Alzheimer's family or surrogate decision-maker to find a suitable living alternative, which in many cases is an institutional setting, they must be very careful when selecting alternative living in a nursing home.

Family/Patient vs. Professional Opinions

When Alzheimer's-affected persons enter a long-term care facility, their direct care is transferred to professional caregivers. This brings with it a plethora of potential problems.

The appropriate role for professional caregivers is to advise and guide, then to implement decisions. Loving, caring, thoughtful decisions made with full information and adequate emotional and spiritual support are the goal. Somehow a balance must be struck between compassion, respect of patient wishes, and the needs of the family, within the milieu of traditional medicine. It is imperative to remember that even when the patient is powerless to do and speak for herself, *her rights to have her wishes followed must still be paramount.* Furthermore, to maximize her powerlessness by not respecting her wishes is wrong. In traditional, patriarchal medical systems and in the hurry and flurry of life in an institution, that is easy to do. *The power of position, the power to speak for a patient who cannot speak for herself, do not make the morals of a medical professional or family member or anyone else more right for a patient than the wishes and morals of that patient.*

The nature and importance of medical decisions is complicated. A strong team of decision-makers, family members and the expertise of medical people can combine to find the best solutions for each Alzheimer's patient. The fact that Alzheimer's patients go through similar changes and progress through a series of stages should not lead anyone to group them into a category of patients who should be treated this way or that. For their life before Alzheimer's makes them unique individuals who are entitled to their right to have treatment that is consistent with, and respectful of, their personal beliefs and values.

Drugs as therapeutic interventions

Drugs for treating the symptoms of Alzheimer's disease come in and out of favor. It is important to understand the types of medications commonly used for those with Alzheimer's disease as well as when medication is appropriate. The use of drugs should not be the first tool used to manage problem behaviors. Drugs should be used in the short term and introduced only after all other attempts to change or manage the problems have been tried without success. Older people metabolize drugs differently than younger and the changes in their bodies due to the disease process also affect how drugs work and how effective they are. Some drugs actually work differently in the person with Alzheimer's than in the general population.

That said, it is important to know that there are drugs that are relatively safe and effective. While infrequent, there are times when drugs can improve the quality of life for an Alzheimer-afflicted individual. Drugs should always be used in conjunction with non-chemical interventions. A major classification of drugs used to manage difficult behaviors is *Psychotropic*. Psychotropic drugs affect mood and behavior by working on the brain.

Teamwork, Trials and Transitions

Whether or not the medical component of the team accepts the family decision-maker's ideas, the patient must always be the first and sole priority. Table 6 is presented at the end of this chapter as a tool to assist a decision-making team to define both the issues to be addressed and the underlying goals and objectives that will meet the patient's wishes. The trials and transitions faced when institutionalization occurs are many, varied and difficult.

There are many feelings to be managed and new relationships to be forged when the Alzheimer's patient enters a long term care facility. The nature and role of family caregivers fundamentally changes when the Alzheimer's patient is institutionalized. At that time, strangers become the hands-on caregivers on a daily basis. They make decisions, provide services and create environments that used to be the sole purview of the family caregiver. These changes present both losses and relief to family caregivers. They also present challenges and opportunities for the growth of patient, facility staff and family caregiver.

The relationship between long-term care facility caregivers and family caregivers is likely to be long, so getting off on the right foot is essential. A caring facility staff became my primary source of information, support and understanding. It is the responsibility of the professional caregivers to maintain boundaries while getting closer to the family caregiver. This can present problems for professional caregivers who may need forums in which to discuss issues and identify solutions. To move behind a barrier of professionalism in an attempt to avoid this issue leaves the primary caregiver without a much-needed ally who is also "human." The concept of "objective neutrality" which is taught in some schools of nursing has no place on a unit that is designed for the care of persons with Alzheimer's disease.

It is critical that professional caregivers realize that family caregivers are still and want to remain caregivers. In fact, the family is the single system involved with the patient for the entire journey. While some may be "abandoned" in nursing homes, in my experience, most are not. Abandonment should never be assumed.

When entering a new facility, the patient's loss of autonomy and independence can be startling and upsetting to the family caregiver and sometimes the patient. Once an Alzheimer's patient is institutionalized, the question immediately arises, although often is not stated, of what falls within the realm of quality care. The definition of this becomes very important to patients, families and staff. It is not uncommon for the various groups to have different views on what quality care is and how to achieve it.

For the patient, independence, dignity and self determination may be the sole criteria by which she defines quality care. While sharing that definition to varying degrees, the family may also include safety in such a definition. Professional caregivers may define quality care exclusively as health and safety and add comprehensive, unlimited medical treatments. Each group's definition of quality of life affects its definition of quality of care. These definitions may change over time. They did for us.

The decision to institutionalize changes the role and dynamics of family caregiving and raises many new issues and feelings that will need to be addressed by family and professional caregivers. The largest of these is loss of control. The family caregiver becomes an outsider rather than on the inside track. Once the patient is in an institutional setting, many decisions are simply removed from the realm of patient and family. There are many difficulties advocating for a parent or spouse when the advocate is outside the system.

Institutions have rules and regulations and certain formalities. Some are imposed by state and federal regulations, others by the administration of the facility, corporate owners and some by shift supervisors.

Many families have a difficult time understanding that rules are a necessity. They find it difficult to imagine their loved one living within such a structure and often feel angry and upset that the decisions about their loved one are no longer theirs alone. These feelings can be heightened by anger over the exorbitant rates they pay, as they watch their family's life savings disappear. Many are plagued by guilt over not being able to care for their own. People who are used to autonomy, being in control and calling the shots might have struggle after struggle with the nursing home staff.

Although placement is not supposed to be affected by the ability to private pay, our family felt it definitely was. Participants in support groups have expressed a feeling that those with money or political clout had definite advantages when it came to placement in certain facilities.

Due to limited finances and too few beds, I was advised by the Office of Elder Affairs to seek placement relatively early in the course of the disease because home care would drain the coffers leaving nothing to help a placement. It was sound advice.

❤

In the first several months of placement, we treated our mother's new home as a new apartment. This was initially established in response to her repeatedly referring to it as such. This made it easier for all of us to settle into the new routine.

On the short ride to the nursing home, my mother said to me "You get one thing straight young lady, no one's putting me anywhere. I've chosen my "new apartment."

By the time my mother and I arrived, my husband and brother had already moved her own furniture, stuffed animals, and pictures into her "new apartment."

As the four of us sat in the beautifully appointed dining room, eating a barely palatable lunch, my mother looked up and said, "Dear God, how depressing."

Holding our collective breath and with breaking hearts, one of us (I don't remember which one) got us through that little moment with a laugh and a prayer.

When the social worker said "It's time to go, don't smother mother," we left. I made it out the door and just past my mother's window before I fell apart.

❤

I remember my mother's reaction after I had spoken to a nurse about an upsetting incident.

My mother turned to me and said, "You handled that well Honey, you're doing fine."

Shortly after she entered the nursing home, she turned to me and said, "Ignore that one [another resident], she doesn't behave well. Don't let it bother you, she can't help it."

I also remember the many times she said, "Thank you, thank you. I don't know what I'd do without you," as I gave her a hug goodbye. At the time, I didn't realize how important these words would become or how my recollection of them would provide the strength to persevere when my energy was so depleted.

❤

I was reminded of the promise I made one day, before nursing home placement, when my mother pulled at her hair and cried, "I'm crazy, I'm losing my mind."

With great difficulty and a breaking heart, I pulled her hands to the table, and holding them explained that she was not going crazy, was not losing her mind, but had a disease in her brain called Alzheimer's which was causing the problem.

She asked what we were doing about it and was pleased when told of the trips to the specialists at the big city hospital, which was, as she said, "the best."

When she cried, "What will become of me, what will we do?", resisting my overwhelming urge to run, I looked my mother in the eye and said, "I don't know, but whatever it is, we will figure it out together."

Her response, "Thank you for telling me, I was so frightened, thank you for being honest," came back to comfort me in the darkest of times.

As my mother was losing her ability to guide and instruct me, others took over; doctors, nurses, aides, clergy and some family members.

❤

The advantages of institutional placement can be many. Depending on the situation and the motivation for placement, institutionalization can provide a safe haven in which the patient and her family can get back to some sense of relationship that is not overburdened with safety, independence and dignity issues.

Shifting the mantel of daily care to others freed us to interact in more familiar ways with our mother. Acts of care were more spontaneous and chosen rather than required. Our mother's reference to her room as her apartment allowed us to relax in this new setting. It eased the transition, making future decline less stark. We had many moments of love and laughter in this new "apartment."

A good adjustment is affected by the attitude of the patient, staff and family members. All must adjust at various levels. In some ways, the patient's adjustment can be the easiest. If the patient senses a positive, cooperative relationship between loved ones and facility staff, it can provide her with a comfortable and safe feeling. If distress and competition is sensed, the patient is more likely to be upset. Although time and the progression of the disease change the issues to be faced, getting off to a good start can ease what is to come.

❤

After my mother entered the nursing home, we all settled in fairly well and readily. We did what we had always done. We took our mother out and to our homes. Things were better and in many ways less stressful than they had been in a while. When the issues of safety and dignity were passed to the hands of others, we were able to get back to the business of being a family once again, at least for awhile. I would even go so far as to say that our mother's quality of life and the quality of family relationships improved upon institutionalization.

Our mother was safe, clean, well fed, and stimulated. Routine and structure combined with regular attention, as well as assistance with activities of daily living, were provided by caregivers in eight hour shifts. She had dignity, and she had friends with whom she could converse, although it often made little or no sense to those around them.

As our mother moved into her own world, her children slowly relaxed and learned to become part of a larger home, responsible to and for many mothers, those other poor lost souls wandering the corridors. There were those who gave us kisses, those who held our hands, those who understood our pain at some deeper level than our friends and associates. Some of them supported us through our transitions. Many shared pearls of wisdom. Institutional life was not a life we had chosen. It was not a life we wouldn't change if we could. But it was one with which we learned to live. The nursing home was a place in which we learned we could still love.

❤

Institutionalization brings family caregivers in touch with other demented and ill persons. The neediness of other residents can be the proverbial straw that breaks the family caregiver's back. A coping strategy that my sister dubbed "look & leave" is a way to avoid contact with other residents. Asking help from staff is one way to minimize the disruptive effects of other residents. Not only do professional caregivers know the residents, they also have skill in dealing with people who exhibit problem behaviors such as yelling, hitting and disrupting. I viewed the nursing home as a community in which I had a large investment. Until the end, I interacted with other residents regularly and was frequently mistaken by new residents and staff as a member of the staff.

❤

Handling problem behaviors is of great interest to the Alzheimer's family facing long term care placement. The goal of Alzheimer's units is to accommodate difficult behaviors without physical or pharmacological restraints. However, sometimes that is not possible. After a bonafied program of Alzheimer's appropriate behavior management techniques are applied unsuccessfully, restraints may be considered. But this should only be with input from the interdisciplinary team, including of course the primary family caregiver. If medication is used, it must be to alleviate specific symptoms. Medication must be monitored critically and should not be considered as a long term solution. Medicine should never be used to ease the professional caregiver's job.

It is the vision of drooling, drugged patients lining the walls of nursing home units that has given nursing homes such a bad reputation. Alzheimer's Special Care Units are nothing like that vision. A very reputable all-Alzheimer's facility in Massachusetts never has more than a very small percentage of its residents on pharmacological restraints at any one time. Any kind of restraint, physical or pharmacological must be used in the best interest of the patient and always considering his rights.

Staff

As in any other group of people, in the nursing home I came across professionals of great compassion, humility and sensitivity, and other professionals whose motivations and methods of operating were very definitely focused on their own aggrandizement. Although I am still angry at those who acted this way, I attribute it to their unwillingness or inability to deal with the difficult issues and resultant problems that accompany Alzheimer's.

Poor attitudes and professional immaturity build defenses and barriers, while candid communication, open listening, respect and the synergy of dedicated people seeking thoughtful, respectful, loving decisions for the patient are what is desperately needed.

There are a number of dilemmas with which facility staff must struggle. In order to do their job well, they become emotionally involved with their patients. Yet, they sometimes are faced with families who are so bereft, they speak of ending their loved one's life, or wishing "God would take her," that an unhealthy over-involvement sets in. This can result in a tug of war which is difficult for all involved.

Another dilemma is the professional caregivers' need for support. Their job is difficult. They are in some ways, second class citizens, although they do the yeoman's share of the work. Yet they are rarely supported adequately.

There is also a need for education. I was surprised to find the variation in nursing staff in terms of their training and values. This can be confusing and, in some cases, result in patient's wishes not being followed. Since I have talked about such things with those who train nurses, it is clear that the variation is even wider than I had perceived.

Countless professionals have since advised me that professionals who refused to honor decisions, either overtly or covertly, and those who challenged our decisions, sometimes confronting us directly were totally inappropriate and unprofessional. I am sad that it tainted our experience and diminished our ability to trust the other professionals, the vast majority of whom were compassionate, skilled caregivers. It would have been incredibly difficult, if in fact possible, for us as family caregivers to put aside the nagging doubt such behaviors raised as we were struggling through our journey. That fact made the whole situation more difficult not only for us, but also for the dedicated professionals who cared so lovingly and competently for our mother.

Yet professional caregivers have the right to their feelings, thoughts and values. It is important that facilities have strategies to handle situations in which the professional caregiver's personal values are in conflict with the patient's or her family's to the point where professional caregiving cannot be done well or in concert with patient values and wishes. There is, and should be, no shame in such situations. Reassignment should be viewed as a respectful strategy that ensures patient rights while respecting professional caregivers.

Values clarification should become common fare on the menu of staff development. If done well and repeated often, staff, patients and families will all be better off. The point is to protect patient values and rights, not to disrespect or deny professional caregiver values and rights. Imperative for such an approach to work are acceptable alternatives for those professionals who are uncomfortable, or whose values are challenged to the point of violating or totally disrespecting them.

Particularly difficult for me were the frequent turnover of facility administrators, social workers and directors of nursing. In my mother's almost nine years in a single nursing home, each of these positions saw upwards of 10 people. In addition, there were two medical directors. Somewhat minimizing the effect of this was the consistency of staff, supervisors, nurses and aides.

The biggest frustration with this high rate of turnover was that new people often came in with "great new ideas" about improving things. While this is understandable and in some cases reasonable, the old adage of "don't fix it if it ain't broke" certainly applies. Added to this is the fact that any change in the situation with an Alzheimer's patient is difficult, so those that can be avoided should be, for the comfort of patient and family alike.

The other exhausting element of changes in administration resulted in the replay of issues that had already been resolved, sometimes multiple times. Things like chart review and patient care review meetings were not always easy to establish, so they were particularly upsetting when changed. It takes considerable energy for family caregivers to engage in power struggles with new staff members who are invested in instituting "their" new policy. This is energy which is in dangerously short supply.

❤

One of the most difficult dilemmas that heavily-involved family caregivers face is establishing and maintaining boundaries. This becomes more difficult the longer the patient lives in an institution. In order to make accurate assessments of what is happening and to decide upon appropriate responses, it is critical for the family caregiver to maintain a certain objectivity. What can make this difficult is the fact that the professional caregivers, particularly those of long standing with the patient, become the people with whom the family caregivers interact on a regular basis. They understand the patient, and after a time, those who are particularly skilled at long term care, often come to understand the family caregiver and his problems better than anyone else. They become more like friends than friends, more like family than family. They have a vested interest in the patient, and that shared bond is very strong indeed.

In our case, the caregivers on the floor were consistent over many years. They saw my mother and I progress from mid to late to end stages. They were there through holidays and illness. They celebrated triumphs and grieved over losses. They began to know my well mother, bit by bit, as I shared what she had been like. The stories my mother's children shared were a gentle way to humanize the demented shell our mother was becoming. The professional caregiving staff and I learned to respect and trust one another.

❤

At times, after disturbing incidents, other family members questioned my ability to remain objective about professional caregivers. I questioned myself on occasion. The problem was that the staff was the first line of defense, the ones with whom I most often discussed concerns and problems. They responded to me as a human being.

They recognized and shared the Herculean task of loving and caring for my mother. My mother's professional caregivers and I became closer than family. The professional caregivers had proven themselves to be in for the long haul. That presented potential problems and clear challenges in terms of maintaining healthy boundaries.

❤

Whether family members are aware of it or not, they adopt certain coping strategies to help them navigate the halls and issues of the institutions in which their loved ones are placed. Some are "social butterflies." They flit from staff to patient to other residents, visiting, and engaging in social interaction.

Others are "look 'n leaves." They make a direct line from the elevator to the patient, as though they are in a dark tunnel, avoiding contact with staff and residents alike. Once at the patient's bed, they look then leave. This is a way to avoid interactions that can be very painful. It takes all the "look 'n leave's" energy to even walk into the nursing home. All they can manage while there is a quick, duty bound visit that is over as soon as possible.

Others envelop themselves in a suit of armor or simply don't come at all, or find seemingly strange ways to ease their grief and anger (one of my sisters ironed) while still others are "bridge builders." These "bridge builders" make a concerted effort to become part of the home. They interact with patients, other residents and staff. Many family caregivers, as I did to some extent, move from one coping mechanism to another and back over time.

❤

Although I couldn't have described it in the beginning, I learned a way of being and interacting that I came to call "nursing home mode." It was a gear into which I switched when I had to deal with the "facility." In some ways it was a defense, a shell that protected me from the reality of having institutionalized my mother. In others, it was a method of controlling my emotion, ensuring that my verbal and body language were in concert with the best interests of my mother.

Nursing home mode became a way of imposing a calm that I rarely felt in situations that were extremely difficult. It put my brain in high, my emotions in neutral and my anger and grief in reverse. My senses became heightened in a way. It was as though I moved into another state of consciousness, almost an observer of what was going on.

When in nursing home mode I became particularly aware of being supportive and courteous to those with whom I was dealing. I struggled to phrase questions and concern in language that would not make professional caregivers defensive. I sought a posture and affect that conveyed understanding coupled with seriousness.

The stakes were very high indeed. I was trying to build an environment of physical and emotional safety, dignity and respect in which my mother, who was unable to tell me what happened when I wasn't there, was going to live out the remainder of her life. I was trying to let the professional caregivers, into whose care I had entrusted her, know that I was not "dumping" her, that I was her protector first, but that being her protector was not mutually exclusive to being her professional caregivers' ally. It was a state of vigilance, at times hyper-vigilance, that was exhausting. But it was the only way I could cope with the enormity of the task and the emotions that went with it.

It wasn't until I switched into this gear when my husband was hospitalized that I started to consciously recognize it. To this day, I'm not sure that I fully understand it, but I know that with certain "old timers" at the nursing home, I lowered the throttle on nursing home mode, relaxed my guard, and became more myself. Over time, my growing trust in those whom I viewed as co-advocates for and co-protectors of my mother, allowed me to lower my shields and deflate the bubble in which I so often encased myself.

❤

As a group, my brothers and sisters and I did not establish or maintain a visiting schedule. In fact, at the first family meeting a statement was made that each of us would do what we wanted, when we wanted. While a schedule of visits would likely have been a battleground that put bigger wedges between us, such a schedule could have eased tensions, provided a structure for sharing the burden and held off or minimized burnout. For me, it could also have prevented the profound sense of loneliness and intense feelings of carrying this burden alone.

Shortly after my mother was placed, my oldest brother and I had a conversation about the importance of dealing reasonably with her professional caregivers. This meant behaving in very deliberate ways, thinking about what we said before we said it and calculating the consequences and potential costs to our mother. Being supportive and pleasant, courteous and open were strategies we adopted. We agreed to keep our emotions in check and work diligently to build a team with all who cared for our mother. Finally, we talked about the need to choose our battles.

♥

The phrase "choosing battles" indicates a defensive stance. It connotes war, conflict, and stress. While perhaps this is too strong to fairly describe the situation, it is a good description of the state of mind of the family caregiver when institutionalization is faced. Anger, grief and sometimes guilt abound. There is a level of mistrust and fear. There is a feeling of desperation and concern about the future. There is a sense of loss of control and frequently, a struggle for control that ensues. It is important for caregivers to recognize such feelings and deal with them. Talking with my brother helped each of us by validating the experience and sharing our grief. Somehow, naming the different feelings was enough to bring them to a manageable level. All family members struggle with such things, particularly at first.

Keeping track of clothes and personal possessions is difficult in an institutional setting. We made choices to accept risks that the nursing home was uncomfortable with such as allowing our mother to maintain possession of and control over her clothing, jewelry and checkbook. As described earlier, I limited the risk to the checkbook by keeping a minimal amount of money in it. I was able to change the precious stones in her necklace to synthetic when she said "have the jewelry appraised and insured, but I'm keeping it here." My sisters did my mother's laundry for more than the first year, thereby maintaining some control over her clothes.

Over the years, we struggled through many issues. Some were more difficult than others. Eventually, little by little, we let go of many things by focusing from them onto others. Our mother was a beautiful woman, impeccably groomed and very aware of her manners and dignity. It was impossible for the nursing home to keep her looking the way she always had. She was always bathed but her clothes became more and more stained. Replacing them did not remove the problem. The problem was not the nursing home's laundry. The problem was Alzheimer's.

♥

Family caregivers must adjust to the fact that inconceivable behavior might someday become the norm. I remember an incident in which my mother was injured above her eye by a bell that had been thrown by another resident. At the time, I was shocked by the

event and angry that the facility would tolerate such behavior.
Shortly after that, as I approached my mother from behind, with
great difficulty I removed a full bowl of oatmeal that she was ready to
hurl at the person across from her. That bowl of oatmeal brought
new meaning to, and appreciation and respect for the old saying
"there but for the grace of God go I." After that experience, I was
more open to and capable of objectively evaluating skin tears, alter-
cations between residents and issues of potential mishandling by
staff. It was my first glimpse of the importance of staff who are educated in Alzheimer's care and who are well supported.

A Designated Communicator

It is customary for a long-term care facility to require a single
family contact. I was that contact. The logistics of calling more than
one family member is problematic for a number of reasons. It can
become a burden on the facility whose staff have so many other
things to do, and communicating with more than one family member
leaves the facility open to disputes and disagreements as well as mis-
representations. Finally, different family members may hold differing opinions of what is appropriate and what is not.

We experienced and caused all of the above. After an incident in
which my mother choked, the Director of Nurses dealt with my older
sister as well as with me. After a particularly difficult and lengthy
phone conversation with my sister that was "unproductive and abusive" in the words of the Director of Nurses, I was informed that from
that point on she would only discuss issues with me. I remained the
designated communicator, except for a few circumstances in which I
brought one or more of my siblings with me to a meeting at the nursing home or arranged for someone else to be the primary contact
while I was away or on respite.

Incident Handling

My mother became very agitated when she was handled for personal care. Caregivers who took the time to explain who they were,
call my mother by name, and explain what they were doing usually
had an easier time of it.

It is very difficult to accept the fact that it is virtually impossible
to guarantee safety at all times. The struggle to find a reasonable balance between dignity, independence, self-determination and safety
becomes more difficult once institutionalization has occurred. Fam-

ily members may tend to forget the problems they faced in addressing these issues while the patient was at home.

But the sad fact is that the ratio of staff to patient, and the dilemmas sometimes created by patient rights affect safety. It is all too easy for a family to place blame when something happens. Sometimes, blame is deserved and must be addressed; but more often than not, in my experience, it is the disease and nature and limits of the institutions themselves rather than specific people, that should be blamed.

Policies, procedures and people must always be examined after an incident to be sure that they did not contribute. But the harsh reality is that incidents can and will happen. It is the exception, rather than the rule, for a person who is in a facility for more than a year not to have an incident.

♥

Shortly after my mother entered the nursing home she put a veal patty with which she was displeased in her drawer.

Four days later, she dropped it on the administrator's desk and said, "This is disgusting! I pay good money to be here and I don't expect to be served something like this again."

Subsequent "room searches" after that were upsetting to all. While the family understood the health issue caused by hidden food, we had trouble with the method and timing of the searches. Perhaps most difficult was our mother's reaction. At that point, she was able to use the phone and called me at 11:00 at night to complain about people going through her belongings. My brother, older sister and I met with the social worker the next morning to express our concern.

Many incidents occurred over the years, some of which have already been described. Most were minor (although few felt minor at the time). Two were major, involving serious injury. Over time, I learned to evaluate incidents in light of the facts after hearing the "whole story." But of course, hearing the whole story was a myth since I never heard my mother's side. I worked hard to preserve and strengthen relationships with staff rather than attacking. This is not to say that there were not times when I was upset and made it known. But overall, it was to everyone's advantage to pull together and solve problems rather than point fingers and place blame.

Although it is often difficult, family caregivers must keep in mind that everyone who handles their patient is a human being. People have varying degrees of skill and patience. People have good and bad days. People are human and therefore imperfect. In some ways, it is amazing that more situations which involved safety and injury did not arise. My mother was handled every two hours for over five years. This did not include contact for toileting, bathing, dressing, or feeding.

While perfection and an incident and injury-free home is the goal, it may not be an attainable goal. Perhaps more important than the incidents themselves, are the results of the incidents, the response to them, how the home and those in it are improved as a result of the incidents. Appropriate response is critical to improving long-term care facilities and ultimately care for individual patients.

Leaving the Facility

In more than eight years of dealing with the nursing home, my mother was only sent to an emergency room three times. The first was early on for an x-ray. At that time, we made it clear that non-critical transfers of this nature would be done by family. We were concerned about the use of ambulances for non-critical transports. We also felt a need to accompany our mother when she was outside of her new world.

The second transfer happened after an injury requiring stitches occurred during a transfer from my mother's bed to a cardiac chair. The nurse on duty called the doctor who sent my mother to the ER by ambulance. I arrived at the hospital thirty minutes later. I had difficulty getting into the ER, and while waiting, called a friend. My friend asked if I thought someone had mishandled my mother. My reply was an emphatic "No," but upon return to the nursing home, my mother's primary nurse informed me that my mother had, in fact, been mishandled. The incident and the stitches could have been avoided. By the time I was told this, there had been an in-service meeting for all aides on that wing and within twenty-four hours, for all facility staff. The nursing home also reported the incident to the state.

In this situation, as it always was, the response of the nursing home was total candor with me. They took swift corrective measures with the party at fault and issued a written reprimand. I asked that the aide not work with my mother for a few months. After hearing that the aide was usually very good, I asked that the reprimand be the extent of action taken with her or him in the matter.

My older sister was angry that our mother was transferred to the emergency room before the family was notified. She stated that our mother could not speak for herself and must have a family member or facility staff member with her at all times. The facility did not have the staff to provide such escorts and the nurse on the scene judged that immediate transfer was indicated. Alzheimer's units are more likely to have enough staff to provide such escorts.

I found my mother in the hospital emergency room placid, unaware and unfazed. It was like seeing an infant in the middle of the expressway during rush hour. Not having seen her outside of the few hundred square feet that had become her universe, witnessing this total dependency and inability to interact was particularly startling to me. I agreed with my older sister that a member of the family must be with our mother if she left the facility, but I did not agree that the nurse was wrong in sending her immediately. I recognized that the nursing home must make judgment calls. And while not altogether comfortable with it, I understood the decision.

At this time, much discussion ensued about the appropriateness of transferring for any reason. It was not until five months later that my mother was again transferred. This time it was for choking, projectile vomiting and cessation of breathing. She was out of the facility in under ten minutes on the order of an on-call physician.

Within thirty minutes of my mother's arrival at the ER, four family members were there, two of whom took her living will and my power of attorney with them. Once again, my older sister was adamantly opposed to the transfer. My brother and husband, who were also on the scene said that while my mother did not appear to need to be at the ER by the time they arrived, they were hesitant to judge because they were not there when the decision was made to send her.

I arranged a meeting with the Director of Nurses, my sister and myself. At that time, the Director of Nurses explained that she would not ask her nurses to sit by and watch someone choke to death. She supported the decision to transfer given the circumstances. This was a very tense time between the family and facility. While I shared my sister's concerns about our mother, I also saw the difficult position the nursing home was in. And I felt that my sister was jeopardizing years of bridge building with her accusations and unchecked anger. On the other hand my sister still believes that her visible, vocal rage was the key that was needed to unlock what some at the nursing home had managed to hold tight to—ultimate control over medical decisions for our mother.

Clearly the timing of transfers is an issue. Because Alzheimer's patients cannot fend for themselves, they need someone with them. Whether or not a patient is to be transferred must be determined and communicated before the incident initiating the transfer occurs. Even once the decision has been made not to transfer, whether or not the nursing home will act in concert with the decision depends on the nurse or supervisor in charge of that shift and/or the on-call physician. We had an agreement that the Director of Nurses would be notified immediately if transfer was being considered but the unsettling family concern lingered. It was not until hospice was involved that we trusted that the hospice nurse, who had to be called prior to treatment or transfer being initiated, would prevent the hospitalizations we had been against for years.

The next incident occurred when my mother was assaulted by another demented patient. The shift nursing supervisor immediately called me. She was very clear with the doctor who was on call that a transfer to the ER was against the wishes of the family. After she described the incident, my mother's injuries and the treatment ordered by the covering doctor, I concurred and reiterated that my mother was to be treated at the nursing home. The nurse supervisor also suggested that family members wait to go to the nursing home for a couple of days, but my sister and brother happened by. Although they hadn't spoken to one another, and they saw her twenty four hours apart, their description of our mother to me was identical in word and tone. Each of them said, "It's bad, very bad, but she seems OK, just very quiet."

It was a brutal attack in which my mother's face was badly mauled. I expressed concern about my mother's eyes. At my request over the phone, the supervisor called the doctor back to ask for a prophylactic eye ointment. The nurse had to fight with the doctor to prevent transfer. While this is a very difficult position for a nurse to be in, it was the excellent communication between the family and facility and within the facility on that day, between supervisors, staff and changing shifts that ensured that the transfer did not occur. My sister and I were so appreciative of the appropriate handling of this extremely difficult situation that we made it formally known.

There was an aura of shock for the first several days following the incident. Aides and nurses were openly crying, and trying to console each other and me. Some staff were visibly and vocally angry at the patient who attacked. It was I who asked them for understanding and compassion. Perhaps the violent nature of the attack and anticipated response by the family had the management paralyzed. But, in retrospect, it is obvious that management should have responded to the caregivers' emotional needs at that time.

Levels of Treatment

I was unaware, until little more than a year before my mother's death, that specific levels of care have been defined. Each level of care spells out treatments and withholding of treatment for individual patients. The goal of this is to minimize uncertainty about the extent of medical intervention.

I learned of this when hospice gave me an excerpt entitled "Ethical Issues in the Treatment of Advanced Alzheimer Dementia: Hospice Approach" from *Clinical Management of Alzheimer's Disease,* by Dr. Ladislav Volicer and his colleagues. My immediate reaction was "Why didn't someone show this to me ten years ago?"

The book excerpt identified several levels of care which are outlined below. I recommend the entire book chapter for those who would like more information.

1. The patient receives an aggressive diagnostic work-up, treatment of coexisting medical conditions, and transfer to an acute-care unit if necessary. In the event of a cardiopulmonary arrest, resuscitation is attempted. Tube feeding is used if normal food intake is not possible.

2. The patient receives complete care as defined above but resuscitation is not attempted in the event of cardiac or respiratory arrest ("do not resuscitate"[DNR]).

3. This level involves DNR and no transfer to an acute-care unit for medical management of intercurrent life-threatening illnesses. This eliminates use of respirators, cardiovascular support, and so on, which are available only in an acute medical setting.

4. This care level includes DNR, no transfer to acute-care unit, and no workup and antibiotic treatment of life-threatening infections (pneumonia, urinary tract infection). Only antipyretics and analgesics are used to ensure patient comfort. Partial isolation techniques are used for staff protection.

5. Supportive care is given as defined above but eliminating
    tube feeding by a nasogastric tube or gastrostomy when nor-
    mal food intake is not possible. Fluids necessary for hydra-
    tion are provided orally only if the patient is not comatose.[1]

A number of things are required to effectively use such a leveling
system.

- ❤ A multidisciplinary team approach to caregiving
- ❤ Inclusion of the family caregivers early in the process
- ❤ The commitment of professional caregivers to opening
  the discussions before crises occur
- ❤ A commitment on the part of all to openly and honestly
  assess their own motivations and
- ❤ A commitment to work toward an understanding of the
  patient's wishes
- ❤ Recognition and acceptance of the individual's right to
  self determination
- ❤ An understanding of and openness to palliative care
  because for some the later levels are strictly palliative
- ❤ The willingness and commitment to provide as much
  staff development as is needed to ensure that those who
  will be carrying out the decisions made at the level of
  care meetings will be able to do so consistently
- ❤ Finally, there must be adequate, ongoing support for all
  caregivers.

Some may choose Level 5, while others may never go beyond
Level 1. But it is the patient's wishes that should determine the
appropriate level. In our case, if we had had the opportunity to go
through a level of care process in this more formal, structured way,
my mother's wishes might have been more clearly defined to her professional caregivers earlier, and the process would likely have helped
me to look at the options in light of her Alzheimer's and accept them
more easily. Even if that had happened, I see the leveling care process as one that should occur repeatedly. There are several articles
that deal with how to effectively create teams to determine and carry
out levels of care in a responsible, respectful environment.

Outside Assistance

Over the years, I occasionally found outside assistance helpful.
On a few occasions, I made use of the state's ombudsman program.

An Ombudsman is an impartial person who visits nursing homes on a regular basis and works with patients and families to resolve issues with the nursing home. Ombudsman programs are usually under the auspices of the State Elder Affairs Office. Once, as described in a previous chapter, I was accompanied by one of my mother's attorneys to settle some issues with the facility. Additionally, I received assistance from hospice, the Alzheimer's Association and support groups. On a few occasions, the support group leader offered to come to the facility with me. In later years, clergy were involved off and on. Finally, as I progressed in the process to taking a more holistic approach to my mother's care, I found myself becoming more open to alternative and supplemental support and care structures.

Hospice programs are being introduced to more and more Alzheimer's units. Whether hospice services are out-sourced (brought into the nursing home) or provided by facility staff and resources, they are an important option for some patients and families that offer a philosophy of palliative (comfort only) care to meet their specific needs and to honor their wishes.

The introduction of outside professionals to the nursing home environment can be tricky. There were times when the staff expressed a concern that they would be displaced. They were very attached to my mother and initially defensive about involving outsiders. Because facility staff and I had an open, candid relationship, these issues were raised directly with me, and I was able to assure professional caregivers that the outsiders were adjunct rather than replacement in purpose and nature.

Over time, some of these outside relationships strengthened both groups and provided opportunities for education and the consideration of different perspectives. Hospice specifically comes to mind in terms of education and presenting different perspectives. Sensitivity to the feelings and concerns of facility staff is critical to team building. One of the first things hospice said to me was that the nursing home staff was grieving too. I don't know if the staff was aware of their grief before hospice arrived on the scene.

When involving outsiders, it is very important for all to be clear about the purpose and scope of involvement of the outsiders. Additionally, lines of communication must be clearly defined and adhered to. The involvement of others can improve the care of an Alzheimer's patient but can also complicate communication and decision making. For this reason, skill at team building, a willingness to work at developing viable alliances and an openness on the part of all caregivers, is required.

♥

In this litigious society, it is all too easy to approach problems by threatening law suits. While perhaps understandable, except under the most extreme circumstance, this is non-productive as well as costly. It sets an adversarial tone between professional and family caregivers and drains alarmingly limited energy into activity that does not necessarily benefit the patient.

If a high level of concern about the treatment in a particular facility exists, transfer to another facility should be considered. However, sometimes it is guilt or difficulty in adjusting to institutionalization that makes family members so quick to threaten suit. There are people and agencies (state elder affairs, ombudsmen) who can facilitate problem resolution.

The bottom line is that the primary caregiver must hone and then trust her instincts and judgments. She must also develop a cooperative relationship with the nursing home staff to make quality control the norm. All caregivers must remember that professional caregivers are human, and that all caregivers deal with a process that is fraught with room for error. The golden rule of "do unto others as you would have them do unto you" is applicable.

In a very real sense, the professional caregivers who dealt with my mother became an extended family to me. I came to understand that their feelings, values and beliefs deserve the same respect as those of any other loved ones. The bottom line of course was, and remained, my mother's wishes, well being and comfort. And, it was those things that drove all decisions, but the team carried them out. And despite the difficulties we encountered and the fact that I wish we had chosen a facility with an Alzheimer's unit, we were very fortunate indeed to have had the loving, consistent, highly effective staff we did.

Some of the difficulties we faced are easier to swallow knowing we left the place better than we found it. Our differences weren't for naught. Lasting changes have been made at the nursing home since our years of involvement. The skill and compassion of two of our nurses have been recognized and they have been promoted to positions of power. They now begin discussing patient wishes and treatments at admission. It is an ongoing, formal process designed to prevent most of the problems we faced.

In the final analysis, healthy teamwork created a synergy that changed the horrors of a dementing illness to a growth opportunity for all involved. There can be great satisfaction in participating in a team that values and honors the lives of Alzheimer's patients as they wind down. We were fortunate indeed to have had our mother cared for by such compassionate and skilled professionals. ❤

Table 1: Long Term Care Facility Levels of Care

Level	Description
1	Skilled nursing facility that takes both Medicaid and Medicare. Medicare coverage can be up to 100 consecutive days, the first twenty of which are paid 100% by Medicare, the remaining days are 80% Medicare with a 20% co-pay. These facilities also accept Medicaid.
2	Nursing facilities that do not take Medicare.
3	Facilities that offer supervision and assistance with activities of daily living such as dressing, bathing, toileting, meal preparation, laundry, transportation etc. These facilities do not offer nursing care.

Source: This table was developed with a Social Worker from Elder Services of Cape Cod and the Islands.

Table 2: Questions to ask when evaluating an Alzheimer's Unit

1. Who evaluates patients for appropriateness of placement? Where? At what point in time?

2. Is there a "mission statement" and "philosophy of unit" statement you can review? Does it reflect a therapeutic or passive approach?

3. Are there separate activity rooms? What hours are activities run?

4. Are activities designed for and only attended by Alzheimer's patients?

5. Are activities "failure-free"? Ask to see this month's calendar of events.

6. Do staff bring patients to activities and meals (rather than letting them get themselves to these events)?

7. What is done about patients who don't want to or refuse to participate?

8. How are the doctors, consultants and hospital and acute care facilities affiliated with the unit?

9. Are patients accompanied by a unit staff member if they leave the facility? If they go to an Emergency Room?

10. How are specialized medical needs handled such as dental, eye and ear specialist, doctors, podiatrist, physical, occupational and other types of therapists etc.?

11. How are difficult behaviors managed?

12. Who is the geriatric psychologist/psychiatrist affiliated with the unit? How often is she there? Can families request an evaluation? Can patients be given chemical restraints without family permission?

13. What is the percent of physical and chemical restraints on the unit at any one time? How are restraints decided upon and how often is their use reviewed? What if the family or patient disagrees with their use?

14. Are there any Medicare beds in the unit? What is the policy on discharge to other units and out of the facility? (hospital or acute care settings?)

15. What if the patient becomes inappropriate for the unit? How is this determined, by whom, when?

16. What happens when the patient becomes Medicaid eligible?

Table 2 (continued)

17. What role can/do families play in daily care and in treatment decisions?

18. What is the Visiting Policy?

19. What is the Admissions Policy? Is there a waiting list? Are beds filled based on the list or need?

20. What is the policy on problem resolution?

21. What is the frequency and percent of agency staff used in the unit (nurses, aides)?

22. Does the unit use color coding, dull floors, no mirrors?

23. Is there a hospice contract in place?

24. How are family supported? If through support groups, how often do they meet and who facilitates them?

25. How are staff supported? If through support groups, how often do they meet and who facilitates them?

26. What communication techniques are used with demented patients?

27. How are ADL's handled? What time is allotted for dressing, feeding, toileting etc. each resident?

28. Can I observe the unit for an hour or two during the day, early morning, at mealtimes, on the weekend?

29. Can I speak with family members of other demented patients?

30. How often are staff trained? In-house and at professional conferences? Which conferences? Which staff? Can I see the in-house curriculums? Are the trainers certified Alzheimer's Trainers?

31. How are the spiritual needs of patients met?

32. Are finger foods available? How and when are staff trained to feed patients? How long do they have to feed each patient? What techniques are used?

33. How is communication with the family handled, how often, who communicates with whom, by what method, (fax, phone, in person, e-mail etc.)

Source: This table is based, in part, on the *Patriot Ledger* article, April 23, 1996, by Sue Scheibel with Paul Raia and "How to Evaluate an Alzheimer's Special Care Unit" published by the Alzheimer's Association of Eastern Massachusetts

Table 3: Alzheimer's Unit Specifications

Alzheimer's Unit Characteristic	Home Reply	Comments
Staffing patterns:		
1 staff member to 5 residents on the 7 am to 3 pm and 3 pm to 11 pm shifts		
1 staff member to 9 residents on 11 pm to 7 am shift		
a full-time Unit Director		
a full-time Activities Specialist who works exclusively with Unit residents		
Training:		
all staff who work directly with residents have at least 12-hours of approved training in Alzheimer's Disease		
all other staff have at least 2 hours of approved training for Alzheimer's Disease		
Deterrents to Wandering:		
a security system on all doors guards against wandering and all Alzheimer's or demented residents have the required wrist or ankle band in systems that work that way		
a safe, enclosed area inside & out that is available and easily accessible for residents to pace		
Unit Features:		
there is a dining room on the Unit		
the physical design is simple and soothing and does not confuse residents		
soft bland colors		
bright but not glaring lighting		
no mirrors		
no background color		
floors that are a single, light color but not shiny		
color coding and texture to define rooms, doorways and sleeping areas, including camouflaged exits.		
a varied menu with lots of options		
finger foods are available		

Table 3: Alzheimer's Unit Specifications

there is an activities room on the Unit		
Therapeutic Activities:		
all activities are designed for AD pts. and are failure-free		
a minimum of 1.5 hours of activities per week for every resident (The best units have 250 hours/wk for 40 residents)		
activities are available for Alzheimer's residents twenty four hours a day		
Management Strategies:		
a goal of No drug restraints		
a goal of No physical restraints		
a consultant works with staff to see that drugs are the last strategy used to manage agitated residents and always in conjunction with non-chemical strategies or restraints		

Source: This table is based, in part, on the *Patriot Ledger* article, April 23, 1996, p. 1, by Sue Scheibel with Paul Raia and "How to evaluate an Alzheimer's Special Care Unit" published by the Alzheimer's Association of Eastern Massachusetts

Table 4: Non-Alzheimer's Unit Facility Questions

Non-Alzheimer's Unit Home	Home's Reply	Comments
How many other residents have AD?		
Can you interview AD resident's families?		
Are doors and windows secure?		
Does a security system prevent unsafe wandering inside and outside?		
Is there a ratio of at least 1 staff member to 9 residents on all shifts?		
Which activities include Alzheimer's residents?		
Have any staff been trained specifically in caring for people with Alzheimer's disease?		
What is the policy on the use of physical restraints?		
What is the policy on the use of drug restraints?		
What is the criteria for discharging from the unit/facility?		

Source: This table is based, in part, on the *Patriot Ledger* article, April 23, 1996, p. 1, by Sue Scheibel with Paul Raia and "How to evaluate an Alzheimer's Special Care Unit" published by the Alzheimer's Association of Eastern Massachusetts

Table 5: Theoretical Concepts

These theoretical concepts for Special Care Units are intended to bring greater uniformity of purpose into the varied SCU context:

1. Something can be done for individuals with dementia.

2. Many factors cause excess disability in individuals with dementia. Identifying and changing these factors will reduce excess disability and improve the individual's functioning and quality of life.

3. Individuals with dementia have residual strengths. Building on these strengths will improve their functioning and quality of life.

4. The behavior of individuals with dementia represents understandable feelings and needs, even if the individuals are unable to express the feelings or needs. Identifying and responding to those feelings and needs will reduce the incidence of behavioral problems.

5. Many aspects of the physical and social environment affect the functioning of individuals with dementia. Providing appropriate environments will improve their functioning and quality of life.

6. Individuals with dementia and their families constitute an integral unit. Addressing the needs of the families and involving them in the individuals' care will benefit both the individuals and the families."[2]

Source: The Six theoretical concepts for SCUs quoted above come from a report produced by the U.S. Congress Office of Technology Assessment (1992, pp. 17-22).

Table 6: Medical Objectives and Levels of Care

Date	Volicer Level of Care*	Medical Condition/ Problem	Goals /Objectives	Options	Comments
11/86	Level 2	Worsening Back Pain	•Comfort •Maintain Ambulation	•Anti-inflammatory •PT •Calcium Shots	No PT Shots not covered by Insurance
2/89	Level 3	Cellulitus on upper right arm	•Comfort	•oral antibiotic •antibiotic cream	cream only
12/90	Level 4	Unexplained fever	•Comfort	•test for UTI •X-ray Chest •Throat Culture •Broad spectrum Antibiotic •Tylenol	No tests Tylenol Oral Antibiotic
5/93	Level 5	Congestion	•Comfort •Cure Infection	•Suction Lungs •Hospitalize •Tylenol •Antibiotic	no suction no hospital
7/93	Level 5	Sizable open wound on left lower calf	•Comfort •Stop Bleeding •Avoid Infection	•ER •stitch •antibiotic cream •oral antibiotic	No Oral Antibiotic Monitor antibiotic cream for allergic reactions
9/94	Level 5	Congestion	•Comfort	•Suction Lungs •Hospitalize •Tylenol	Tylenol only

* The Levels of Care above are the same as those described on pages 157-158 with the addition of NO TUBE FEEDING for each.

1. L. Volicer, Y. Rheume, J.Brown, K.Fabixzewski, E.Brady, Chapter 10, Ethical Issues in the Treatment of Advanced Alzheimer's Disease: Hospice Approach, *Clinical Management of Alzheimer's Disease*, Aspen Press, 1988, p.170.

2. Stephen G. Post Ph.D., *The Moral Challenge of Alzheimer Disease*, The Johns Hopkins University Press, Baltimore, MD, 1995, p.11.

Chapter 7:
Medical Decisions

As Alzheimer's disease progresses, its all-encompassing devastation creates medical situations that require thoughtful treatment or thoughtful withholding of treatment. People with Alzheimer's still may have symptoms and processes going on that require medical attention, but they may have lost the ability to ask for help. Along the way, we faced many medical decisions: whether or not to remove my mother from the nursing home to an acute medical center such as a hospital emergency room, how to treat injuries, and the use of tests to determine the source and/or cause of a particular problem or condition. It is in the area of medical decision-making, more than any other, that the need for a fully functioning, multidisciplinary team is most important.

I remember a strange discussion at one of the first support group meetings I attended. It was about an attendee's husband who was at death's door with cancer and a kidney disease; but as his Alzheimer's progressed, both of these preexisting conditions improved. My mother was being treated for hypertension, arthritis and osteoporosis when we received the diagnosis of probable Alzheimer's disease. She also had recurring skin cancer. But aside from those conditions, she was quite healthy. As time went on, her hypertension was kept under control without medication. One of my brothers and I have wondered if this was due to the fact that entering the nursing home had removed the stress of having to "hold herself together."

It seems that more professionals, like more families, are seeing Alzheimer's disease as a terminal disease rather than simply as a chronic, degenerative one. A person's perspective affects how she approaches and makes decisions about medical issues. Because the disease process can be so long, and it is often a secondary event that causes death, it is critical that family caregivers and surrogate decision-makers are clear on the progression and ultimate end of the disease process. Without such information and understanding, it is almost impossible to make appropriate medical decisions.

But of more importance than the perspective of families and medical professionals are the wishes of the patient. Family caregivers who make decisions out of ignorance, neither acknowledging nor understanding the true nature of the disease and the consequences of their decisions, may act in ways that are contrary to patient wishes.

Diagnosis, which is the first critical medical decision has already been covered in depth at the end of Chapter 2.

Garden Variety Illnesses and Conditions

Like all human beings, Alzheimer patients get sick. Unfortunately, their illnesses can be more insidious and devastating than in persons who do not have Alzheimer's. Physical deterioration is part of Alzheimer's disease. In addition to the common colds and flus that most of us get, Alzheimer patients are also more susceptible to other, more serious conditions as their disease progresses. As with other aspects of the disease, everyone does not experience every complication, and the rate and specifics of progression of the disease cannot be predicted except in the most general ways.

There are a number of common problems faced by most patients with Alzheimer's, some of which persist into the later stages of the disease.

Incontinence

If they live long enough, all Alzheimer's patients become incontinent. Incontinence can cause other problems that must be monitored and sometimes treated. It is also something that some family members identify as the point in time at which they must stop certain things, such as taking the patient home for holidays, or being a hands-on caregiver.

If incontinence is the result of the disease process rather than another medical condition, such as a urinary tract infection, it must be managed since it can't be cured. There are many products available for managing incontinence. Gaining patient cooperation, at least initially, can be tricky and for some, it is never acquired. We went through a number of issues with my mother's incontinence. The choice of cloth vs. paper or plastic diapers and finally, not using diapers at all was faced. Diaper rash can become a serious problem and cause significant discomfort. Shortly after my mother became bedridden, the use of diapers for those in the nursing home that were bedridden was stopped.

Gender specific illnesses

Since Alzheimer's does not prevent the onset of other diseases and medical conditions, men might still develop prostate problems and women gynecological problems. The handling of these—from identifying illnesses to testing for and treating them—raise issues that those who do not have Alzheimer's don't face. Prostate problems, for example, may lead to frequent night time trips to the toilet where the patient and caregiver may not get back to sleep, resulting in the patient becoming agitated and confused and both becoming sleep deprived.

Testing

If a person has had regular medical care the decisions of whether or not to keep up with customary schedules of testing such as PSA (prostate antigen) readings, pap smears and mammograms must be evaluated. Additionally, pre- or co-existing conditions must be reviewed such as heart or kidney disease, breast cancer, prolapsed uterus, and prostate cancer.

In a support group, a caregiver told of her shock at finding her mother's prolapsed uterus hanging out of her body when she went into the bathroom to assist her. Because her mother had always been so private and hadn't been to a doctor in almost thirty years, it was the first time Alice had been in the position to learn of the problem. The doctor informed Alice that her mother's uterus had been out of her body for at least a year. The treatment options were an office procedure in which a pesory (ring) would be inserted vaginally to keep her mother's uterus in place, or surgery to remove the uterus. Alice opted for the pesory but found that each six-month visit to replace it became more difficult. However, as her mother's

Alzheimer's worsened, Alice was more and more adamant about avoiding surgery. The staff at the nursing home insisted that the risk of infections was too high to do nothing. Professional caregivers advised sedating the patient and sending her with an aide to the hospital via ambulance. After much thought and a conference with the doctor, Alice decided not to accompany her mom. The pesory was removed and not reinserted since the medical staff and family believed that to be in the best interest of her mom. Surgery was avoided. The nursing staff was able to handle the prolapsed uterus once the patient was no longer ambulatory.

Another support group member told of her mother's recurring breast cancer. The daughter was upset that the doctor's attitude was not to do any testing or treatment given the patient's age and dementia. This daughter found another doctor who was willing to do a lumpectomy. The patient responded very well to the surgery which was done in the doctor's office under a local anesthetic. The daughter, who was nervous about being present during the surgery also did well. As she told the group how wonderful this "miracle" doctor was, someone suggested that she let the local Alzheimer's Association know that he is "Alzheimer's friendly."

Still another support group member told of her decision not to do any more testing to monitor her sister's breast cancer and aneurysm. They had agreed years before not to use any extraordinary measures and not to treat life threatening illnesses. The caregiver was very comfortable with this until a doctor in a hospital wanted to insert a feeding tube. This suggestion forced the sister caregiver to reevaluate the situation. She chose hospice over any aggressive testing, treatment or feeding measures.

Anesthesia

Anesthesia can be difficult for anyone, but with a dementia patient it can worsen their already compromised situation. The benefits and risks of surgery must be weighed even more carefully for the Alzheimer's patient than for others. And it is critical that the surgeon or referring doctor understands Alzheimer's.

Marty, a regular support group attendee, agonized for months over whether or not to treat her husband's prostate cancer. He was in his early sixties and had been in the nursing home for almost a year when the cancer was discovered. After listening to her lamenting about what to do for many weeks, another group member finally asked her what her husband would have decided for himself had he been able. The idea of considering his input was clearly foreign to her. Marty couldn't imagine the answer. She decided to proceed with the surgery, which was performed as day surgery. The results were positive but her husband reacted badly to the anesthesia and began a downward slide.

Marybeth was struggling with a different situation. Her sister Hester had broken her hip in three places. Three pins were inserted and she recuperated at a nursing home for five weeks during which time she had daily physical therapy. Upon her discharge back into Marybeth's care, Hester refused to avoid the stairs since she felt no pain and could not remember the injury or surgery.

Flu shots

In the earlier stages of institutional care, when patients are still ambulating and interacting, withholding treatment (flu shots, antibiotics; topical, oral, IV) may not be an option because the facility must take reasonable measures to protect the greater good. This means that the interests of the individual may be sacrificed to a certain degree. Once my mother became a hospice patient, no flu shot was given.

Teeth

Teeth affect speech and nutrition as well as appearance. My mother had had dentures for many years before she entered the nursing home. Once there, she lost her dentures, which had been getting looser and looser as her gums receded. Because her eating seemed to be affected, a dentist was called in. Shortly after the dentist's visit a set of dentures was made that made her look like a horse. Needless to say her children were horrified. When I raised the problem with the dentist he informed me that my mother had not "cooperated" with him in any way. When I asked if he knew that she had Alzheimer's, he said of course, then complained again. I couldn't help but wish that my mother had managed to bite him with the teeth in.

The fact that my mother no longer had teeth meant nothing to her. The problem in this case was her children seeing the unmistakable evidence of the destruction going on within. We gave up on the teeth, deciding that it was not worth it to put her through another fitting, particularly with someone who was not "Alzheimer's-friendly."

Eyes

The nursing home employed the services of a mobile optometric team. Since my mother had stopped reading years before, we were not particularly concerned about her sight as she had always had the "eyes of a hawk," including the set in the back of her head which her children were convinced were real. She had only worn reading glasses. One day I got a call from the optometrist who told me my mother had an unusually high reading on a glaucoma test. When I called my mother's doctor he said it would not be appropriate to take her out of the facility to an opthamologist and he knew of no one who would come to her. When I expressed concern about the glaucoma reading he said he did not feel competent to prescribe the recommended drops.

In the meantime, I had spoken with the Alzheimer's Association who urged me to pursue treatment since glaucoma can cause loss of vision, and, if the ocular pressure becomes too high, pain. My concern about this situation was exacerbated by a significant maternal history of glaucoma. After a long, pleading conversation with the optometrist, she finally agreed to see what she could do. Within a few weeks the optometrist found an opthamologist who was willing to prescribe the drops based on the optometrist's findings.

Since my mother always had a problem when people went near her eyes, I made it a point to explain the situation to her and to be present a few times when the drops were administered. She still wasn't good when people approached her eyes and the drops were clearly uncomfortable but despite this discomfort, I couldn't withhold them. Her dependence on her sight seemed to grow as her ability to move decreased. I simply couldn't stand the thought of her going blind. At their request, I called the local Alzheimer's Association back to give them the names of the "Alzheimer's friendly" doctors.

♥

An unfortunate incident a few years before the glaucoma was discovered is worth noting. At a support group, I found out about a local neuro-opthamologist who was conducting a study on the optic nerve and Alzheimer's. When I contacted him, he offered to conduct, free of charge, a full exam and provide whatever corrective and medical measures were appropriate if we would agree to his using my mother's case in his study. He also needed two other Alzheimer's patients that my mother's medical doctor found immediately. However, the Director of Nurses failed to arrange the exams as promised and we lost out on a complete eye exam and the opportunity to help with research. I am not sure whether the Director of Nurses did not agree with the research, did not want the extra work it might entail, or simply didn't understand how important it was to me, but to this day I am still angry at her lack of follow-through, despite her continued reassurances that she would handle it.

Nutrition/feeding

If the Alzheimer's patient lives long enough, she will eventually lose the ability to feed herself, and ultimately the ability to swallow. But as we all know, good nutrition is a requisite to good health, so it must be addressed. It is not uncommon for Alzheimer's patients to fall into situations where good nutrition wanes and their health suffers. Changes in living arrangements usually address this issue. In the later stages of the disease, however, more serious and difficult nutrition and feeding issues arise (see Chapters 10 and 11). Until that point, finger foods can solve difficulties with handling utensils thus maintaining the socialization that comes with meals.

Podiatry

My mother had gone to the podiatrist for many years before the onset of her Alzheimer's. This continued in the nursing home, although by the end, it was simply to cut her toenails. There were times when this benefit was questioned by her insurance, but one look at the nasty ulcerations caused by uncut toenails to her ever more fragile skin was enough to convince me that it had to continue. The doctor agreed and rewrote the order in a way that would ensure insurance coverage.

Walking

About a year and a half after entering the nursing home, my mother started to fall for no apparent reason. This led us into a difficult period of evaluating whether or not to use a wheelchair. The nursing home was insisting on a wheelchair but my sister was saying we would take our chances. After I brought the issue to the support group, I began to support the use of the wheelchair because I could not face the pain my mother would be in if she broke her hip. Within a few months she was wheelchair-bound all the time. The use of the wheelchair caused some injuries to her hands, which were getting caught in the wheels. She never quite mastered its use so we

were particularly upset by these injuries. Better communication
among staff or a simple sign that her hand was weak and tended to
slip into the wheel when the chair was moved might have prevented
this recurring, painful oversight.

From the wheelchair, my mother moved to a cardiac chair. Cardiac chairs are like recliners on wheels that allow changes in position
to many different parts of the body. This was something that I had
dreaded for a long time. It was also one of those situations that I was
more than ready for when the time finally came. My mother was
ready too; in fact, she had been ready for a while and once I saw how
much more comfortable she was in the cardiac chair I started to
wonder and finally asked why it had taken so long. It was explained
that they had been waiting for one. This meant that she was at the
top of the list but couldn't move up until someone died, releasing the
chair. If I had not been so afraid of this inevitable next step and been
able to address the issue directly, we would have bought the chair
ourselves, months earlier.

Seizures

One spring morning, a nurse's aide found my mother in the
throes of a grand mal seizure. None of the family was present until
later that day by which time our mother was subdued due to the
administration of a sedative. The doctor started her on a course of
anti-seizure medicine called Dilantin. During subsequent phone
conversations with the doctor, I learned new things about Alzheimer's and seizures.

Seizures are not uncommon in patients with Alzheimer's. But
because a patient has one seizure does not mean she will necessarily
have another. The use of the Dilantin continued for a year after
which time the doctor told me he was more concerned about the
side effects of the medicine than another seizure. He pointed out
that a seizure does not actually cause any damage or changes in the
brain. Rather it is an indication that that has already happened. He
also said that although terrifying to witness, people who had seizures
were unaware of them while they were occurring.

My mother didn't have another seizure and we stopped the Dilantin shortly after my conversation with the doctor. She did however
begin to have seizure-like activity during the last two years of her
life. During these episodes, which were never adequately explained
to me by anyone, her limbs and torso would start to move uncontrol-
lably. The most severe event that I witnessed was when her body

folded in half, from a slightly reclining position and then returned. She laughed when it was over. Relieved that it was apparently not uncomfortable and certainly not of concern to her, I tucked my astonishment and fear away and laughed with her.

At one point, the use of clonopin was suggested to control the trembling and jerking of my mother's body. But I was on respite and my mother's primary nurse refused to disturb me. The nurse also voiced my strong resistance to the use of any drugs. When I returned, we discussed it and decided against using the clonopin.

As is the case with many situations in Alzheimer's assessment, logging and critical review is helpful. If the patient has seizures or the types of trembling and jerking exhibited by my mother, a log might have helped identify the cause. A seizure log is included at the end of this chapter to assist in doing this. However, there may also be things that will not be explained, and while this is difficult, it may in fact be the case. Acceptance that no explanation is to be offered can be eased by the assessment and logging process.

Bed sores, cellulitus

My mother was bedridden and unable to move on her own for the last several years of her life. Occasionally, she developed a skin tear that became infected. On a few of those occasions, it progressed to cellulitus. During the later years, transparent op-site bandages were helpful to all of her caregivers, myself included, since we could see the problem area and monitor its healing without having to remove the bandage.

Bed sores are a source of concern for all bedridden patients. As they decline, their bones become more protruded and certain spots on their bodies bear their full weight. Bed sores, referred to as *decubitis* by the medical people, can be uncomfortable and a source of infection.

My mother had wonderful skin all of her life and her nutrition was maintained by the supplement she got daily, but it was the consistently skilled care she received at the nursing home that prevented painful bed sores. A loving and vigilant staff repositioned my mother every two hours for several years. When the second hospice team came to the nursing home fourteen months prior to her passing, they were astounded at the integrity of her skin and the lack of decubitis incidents.

Infections

The two most common fatal events in Alzheimer's patients are sepsis and congestion. Sepsis, an invasive infection that runs throughout the body, can be caused by urinary tract or other infections. Congestion can be caused by fluid in the lungs, pneumonia, and by congestive heart failure. Perhaps in these areas more than any others, the confusion around comfort vs. curative abounds. With urinary tract infections, even if the decision is made not to medicate, hydrating with cranberry juice can provide comfort.

The old folks friend

While I have heard many lay and medical people refer to antibiotics as comfort measures, they are by the very nature of their chemical makeup curative. While a secondary result of the antibiotic may be a reduced fever, which in turn may make the patient more comfortable, antibiotics were not developed as comfort drugs. Their use, while questionable in terms of preventing death, indicates a desire to cure. There may be other more appropriate drugs and treatment modalities for providing comfort. Tylenol, cold compresses at the base of the brain (neck) and alcohol rubs are at least as effective in bringing fevers down, thus providing comfort.

There are two reasons why I make this distinction. The first is that the technological tools available to medical providers today make it possible to sustain "life" almost indefinitely. With consistently good care, warm loving touch and the technological and pharmacological tools of the trade, people can be kept alive long after they would have died only ten or more years ago. This raises uncomfortable but critical issues for those making decisions for Alzheimer patients. The saying "pneumonia is the old folks friend" was repeated to me many times over the years. While it may seem crass, it was a way for others, some of whom were medically trained, to provide another perspective to help me evaluate potential treatments in light of my mother's wishes. We did, eventually, decide to withhold all curative treatments.

Communicating Medical Decisions

The doctor is the key professional caregiver in any Alzheimer's care team. It is she or he who will provide or prevent treatment and interventions, educate the patient and her family to the issues, and speak to the families when their patients become ill. We were blessed with two remarkably intelligent, clear thinking, compassionate doctors. Although their styles and bedside manner were as different as night and day, each was able to hear and understand my mother's wishes and always willing to reflect them back to me when I was faced with heart-rending decisions. Both doctors were available, supportive, and clear throughout our journey. Particularly in light of the high turnover of nursing home administrators, social workers and directors of nursing, we were fortunate to have had only two doctors.

I chose the first when my mother entered the nursing home. He was the medical director, a wise old timer who was terrific with my mother. I had the advantage of getting to know him at the nursing home during mutual visits. During these chats, he made it clear that he understood my mother's wishes and was perfectly willing and able to see that they were followed. He described her wishes as meaning "kind, compassionate care liberally laced with common sense." His gregarious nature and almost flirtatious manner with my mother made both of us extremely comfortable with him almost immediately. He told me that he had also discussed issues of care directly with my mother.

After more than five years of dealing with this wonderful man, I asked if he would discuss with my siblings the difficult decisions he and I had so often reviewed. He said he never agreed to family meetings but since we had been working together for so long, and he was so fond of my mother, he would make an exception. My four brothers and sisters agreed to come to his office. After an hour and a half visit, during which the doctor did most of the talking, my mother's five children left in complete agreement that Doctor D understood our mother's wishes and that he would ensure they were respected. For the first and only time, we were in complete agreement. We agreed to accept his advice in all situations. However, when actually faced with acceptance of Dr. D's choice of treatment for our mother (stitches in the ER) it did not meet with unanimous approval. Despite this, we were crushed when he retired shortly thereafter.

The next doctor, who also became the medical director of the nursing home, had a different approach. Although very willing to hear and abide by my mother's wishes, he was clear that at no time would he make decisions. He said he'd always abide by my decisions, and would discuss the issues but stressed that the decisions were mine.

As I did with all other new people, I introduced the new doctor to my mother. By that time, she was end-stage and showed little reaction to him. I clearly remember him taking me into the hallway where I cried as I tried to tell him of her wishes and maintain enough composure to assess his willingness to understand and act accordingly. Dr. N was incredibly compassionate, listening and helping me through the difficult instructions to him regarding my mother's wishes. I had been told by the director of nurses that this doctor and his associates would abide by family decisions ranging from "going the whole nine yards" to "doing nothing." It was not until almost the end of our association that he confided to me that his attitude was moving more toward "doing nothing". This doctor's compassion and candor were enormously helpful throughout those last agonizing years.

♥

Strategies must be sought for keeping family members informed. In our case, communication with family changed over time. Initially, my older sister and I went to doctors with our mother. One or both of us then called the others. Although at times there were problems in how the others heard our message, or how we conveyed it, the family seemed to at least have a similar understanding of how our mother was at any given point in time. We all spent enough time with her so we probably, to some extent at least, made our own judgments about her progression into Alzheimer's. But our levels of frustration, anger and fear seemed to be less in sync. Some of this was of course attributable to whatever else was happening in our lives. And some, I am sure, was our own unique reaction to the changes in our mother, and for the last several years, her institutional home and professional caregivers.

In the early days of my mother's stay in the nursing home it was not unusual for two or three of us to meet with nursing home staff together. On two occasions, I asked the doctor to meet with at least two of my siblings and me. And on one occasion, four of the five of us met with the hospice and nursing home team. The meetings with the doctor were quite helpful in that all of us heard the doctor's input directly and at the same point in time. Each of the doctors was candid and direct about the state of our mother's health and the progression of her disease. While what each of us heard and took away from those meetings varied a bit, for the most part, we all seemed to be on the same page. No spouses were included in our meetings with medical professionals.

For some reason, the question of whether or not to tell patients about their Alzheimer's diagnosis is frequently raised. I understand the hesitation and debate about whether or not to tell the patient, but in the final analysis, it seems to me that the person has a right to know what is happening within her own body.

Also, I have yet to meet or hear of an Alzheimer's patient who doesn't, at some point in time, know that something is seriously wrong. However, this does not make telling them of their diagnosis easy. The courage to have such a conversation with my mother never seemed to be there at all. The times that I had conversations with her about her diagnosis were infrequent and difficult, but difficult as they were, on each occasion I realized the importance of being honest with her, regardless of the outcome.

One obvious problem is the patient's inability to retain the information. So the agony leading up to and during such conversations is likely to be short-lived for the patient. Yet naming the problem can offer comfort and a sense of control to the patient, at least for the moment. Caregivers also need Alzheimer's out of the closet. Naming and feeling free to talk about Alzheimer's can significantly reduce the isolation so painful to caregivers.

My mother had told a friend of her suspicions about having Alzheimer's on more than one occasion. We heard this from her friend. Occasionally, she would also drop hints to us. I clearly remember her insistence on attending my graduation for my Master's degree. The graduation was only six weeks prior to her entering the nursing home. What amazed me was her ability to remember the graduation. My parents had missed my high school graduation and we had made a family decision to skip my college graduation due to my father's ill health. So perhaps it was something she simply felt she had to do, but by that time I wasn't particularly interested in attending. At my mother's insistence we went. Due to her difficulties, I walked off the stage and we left directly for dinner. After dinner, my mother confided her biggest fear—"losing her mind." On that occasion, I did not remind her of her diagnosis.

Chart review

If professional caregivers are involved in daily care, decisions must be communicated to them once they are made. This may involve many people who work different shifts. A patient's chart is one way to communicate with professional caregivers. Since Alzheimer patients are unable to remember what happens during their day, and eventually become unable to verbalize their thoughts, keeping up with what is happening to and around them becomes difficult.

For many years, daily notes in my mother's chart were made by each shift. This later changed to notes of exception which tracked only problems or significant changes. I found reviewing my mother's chart extremely helpful for many reasons. First it kept me up to date with what was happening. Second it allowed me to discuss with her what had been going on. Third, it kept me at an informational level similar to that of her professional caregivers. Finally, it ensured that the notes that had been guaranteed as being communicated to all of her professional caregivers were in fact there and that they were clear. This became more and more important as the end neared. It was very rare indeed (I only remember one occasion in almost nine years) that I took issue with what I saw written in her chart. On that occasion I discussed the issue with a supervisory nurse, the social worker and the administrator.

It is important to note that the chart is a legal document and the rights of the patient must be protected. Changes to the chart were crossed out and initialed rather than removed or covered over with a liquid eraser. For the most part, reviewing my mother's chart allowed me to see the high quality of care she was receiving. Patients and their surrogates have the right to review medical charts.

As helpful as chart review became for me, on more than one occasion my right to review my mother's chart was challenged. The worst was early on, when my mother was still walking and talking. The situation became so ridiculous that I went to the State Ombudsman who accompanied me to a meeting with the administrator. When he pulled down a manual the size of Rhode Island that outlined the rules and regulations, the Ombudsman told him to put it away. She pointed out that my mother was obviously incapable of reviewing or understanding her own chart and that I was her daughter and legal surrogate. Therefore, she expected him and his staff to cooperate fully and make my job of advocating and protecting my mother easier rather than harder. Although not pleased, he backed off and I didn't have another problem until the next changing of the guard.

The nursing home had a rule that all chart reviews must happen in the presence of a nurse. I understood the reasoning behind this, and always told the nurse that I was going to look at my mother's chart. The nursing staff very quickly made it clear that I could look whenever I wished. They trusted I would come to them with any questions I might have. This worked well for all of us until another new administrator or director of nurses or social worker rocked the boat, already in dangerously rough seas, again. Over our tenure at the nursing home, this happened six or seven times.

Medications

The primary use of medications in the treatment of Alzheimer's is to alleviate symptoms of the dementia, including agitation, wandering, violent outbursts and other difficult behaviors. However, many Alzheimer's patients can avoid the need for medication *if they are in a supportive environment that understands their needs, deficits and functionality.*

The use of medication is an area where it is imperative that family caregivers work with professionals who understand and deal with Alzheimer patients on a regular basis. And drugs should never be used to manage "problem behaviors." Often, such behaviors result from unmet needs rather than the disease itself.

While it is not fair to say that no one but a specialist can be effective in providing appropriate care, it is true that Alzheimer professionals are more experienced at working with such patients. Furthermore, their experience better positions them to make accurate assessments and find effective strategies more quickly for relieving difficult behaviors.

Recently, some drugs and vitamins that are typically used for other purposes have been introduced as treatments for, or potential preventers of, Alzheimer's. The jury is still out on the most recent of these—ibuprofen, Vitamin E and estrogen, although a recent study shows great promise for the latter. A well respected researcher recommended the use of each of them at a recent conference. As the daughter of an Alzheimer's patient, I often joke about taking all of these and doubling the dose. The temptation to start using these, or to increase the dosage, should be discussed with a physician. I have yet to meet the daughter or son of an Alzheimer's patient who is not terrified of having their minds stolen too, becoming patients themselves.

The use of drugs for any reason must be carefully monitored. I think of the decision-making process regarding the use of medications as cyclical—identify options, cautions, side effects, and the expected or hoped for outcome of using the drug up front. Once the patient has begun taking the medication, the cycle should continue by monitoring and periodic reassessment. It is never advisable to start a drug and simply forget about it.

Some drugs have side effects that are worse than the benefit derived from using them. In the case of clonopin, which was suggested for my mother to ease "seizure-like activity," I chose not to use the drug. I had two reasons for this decision. The first was that although watching the strange gyrations her limbs and torso went through was difficult for those of us with bedside seats, it did not seem to bother my mother in the least. The second was that the drug would have a sedative effect which would have taken my mother further from me.

The only behavior-altering drug given to my mother was Ativan. This was used during her early days in the nursing home to ease agitation. It was also used during the last twenty four hours of her life for the same reason. At that time, Ativan, a mild psychotropic sedative was prescribed on a PRN basis. PRN means that nursing staff assesses the need for the medication and administer it accordingly. We monitored its use carefully. When my mother's agitation decreased as she moved further into her strange new reality, the need for Ativan ended.

❤

I was shocked recently to hear a horror story that I thought was a thing of the past. A woman and her nephew came into a support group describing a sad, debilitating scenario. They had worked with their patient, the nephew's father, for two years to find solutions that would accommodate his dementia while maintaining his dignity. They had agreed that they would do whatever they could to prolong his independence. The patient came to a decision to join an assisted living community and did reasonably well there for several months. When that was no longer appropriate, his sister and son found a nursing home whose administration assured them they handled dementia patients.

According to nursing home staff, the patient became "unmanageable" so drugs were prescribed. After a period of weeks, the nursing home sent him out for a "psychiatric" evaluation. He was bounced from one psychiatric unit to the next across the state for several weeks, becoming increasingly agitated despite the increased dosages of drugs. During this debacle, in an attempt to figure out what to do, his son was talking to an Alzheimer's Association psychologist while the patient's sister was working with a local nursing home Alzheimer's unit director. Due to the intervention of both of these Alzheimer's professionals, the patient was temporarily placed in an Alzheimer's facility many miles from his family until a bed could be made available at the Alzheimer's unit near his son.

By the time the patient's son and sister came to the support group they were exhausted, angry and mistrustful of all professional caregivers. As their story unfolded, amidst tears and expressions of rage, they told of a sweet loving man who had walked into a nursing home under his own power, able to speak, being transformed into a non-verbal, non-ambulatory zombie who had aged years in a few short months.

When they returned to the support group the following month, they were transformed. Their patient was walking with the aid of a walker, was speaking again and was almost off all drugs. The Alzheimer's Unit Director was correct, there was nothing wrong with the man other than the fact that he had Alzheimer's. This patient's unmanageable behaviors were symptomatic of an inappropriate and unsupportive environment.

The woman and her nephew are now deciding whether to expend energy, which is understandably in short supply, pursuing the irresponsible treatment their patient had received or just go forward, with the sweet man they recognized as their loved one. Their grief and rage over the ignorant, irresponsible treatment he received is slowly healing as they interact with people who understand their family's battle with Alzheimer's. ❤

Table 1: Seizure Log

Date Log Started: Name:						
Exact Time	Specific Location	Time of last dose of anti-seizure medication	Description of Seizure	Duration of seizure	Behavior following seizure	Staff initials
Signature:						

Source: *Of Two Minds, A Guide to the Care of People with the Dual Diagnosis of Alzheimer's Disease and Mental Retardation*, Judith M. Antonangeli, RN, BSN, Fidelity Press, 1995, page 137.

Chapter 8:
Caring for the Caregiver

I was much better at caring for my mother than I was at caring for myself. Fortunately, by the end of my caregiving years, I had finally put together systems that supported me. While it is true that it was often too little too late, I am hopeful that others can do better for themselves in this area.

So please, learn from my mistakes—it is why I share them. Seek and accept support. You will need it. You deserve it. It can and will help you and your patient. If caring for yourself represents turning over a new leaf for you, what better time to begin than now? Your conscious decision and careful choices to care for yourself will pay great rewards. This may just be the thing that gets you through the challenges of caregiving in one piece.

There are two types of caregivers, family and professional. I include friends who are caregiving in the family caregiver category. Caregiving is a challenging task which requires support systems to bolster caregiver efforts and prevent burnout. Effective systems are not easy to find and are rarely adequate as is pointed out in so much of the literature on Alzheimer's caregiving. However, the task of caregiving can be gratifying, and can be a source of growth and satisfaction if caregivers are supported well.

Although the majority of family caregivers are women, adult caregiving daughters being second in number only to spouse caregivers, there are also many men caregivers. Men may be even more at risk than women because they tend to have the attitude that they can "tough it out" and it is usually more difficult for them to ask for help or share their feelings.

Caregiving for an Alzheimer's patient is a long, exhausting, extremely challenging process. Primary caregiving can overwhelm even the strongest and most dedicated of people.

The first thing caregivers should be told, again and again, until they understand it as something necessary to survive, is that the need to care for themselves must be primary. Clearly it is in the best interest of the patient as well as the caregiver to keep the caregiver healthy. Dr. Ann Hurley tells her nursing students that caregivers are not unlike an automobile that racks up many miles over tough terrain. They must be greased, oiled and cared for. The ability to provide service and stay on the job is directly related to how they maintain themselves.

The long, risky road of Alzheimer's caregiving often creates multiple victims. Obviously the patient is victim to the disease, but so can the caregiver and his or her family be victims. This needn't happen. There are ways to be a caregiver for an Alzheimer's patient that allow the caregiver and his family to remain intact.

In order for this to happen, problems must be recognized and faced. However, there is so little time left at the end of a caregiver's seemingly endless day that identifying and facing problems other than those that are constantly "in one's face" is particularly hard to do.

Caregivers are unlikely to have adequate coping mechanisms to deal *unassisted* with the magnitude of the caregiving task. Alzheimer's caregiving exacts a toll on the emotional, physical, psychological, social and spiritual health of all involved.

The length of my caregiving role certainly added to the problems I faced. The fact that I moved from one stressful situation to the next without time to recover from the first left me with a cumulative effect that became devastating at points. While I had always thought of synergy (more than the sum of its parts) as a positive thing, synergy changed its character as the challenges of caregiving and the blows of Alzheimer's combined to sap my ever-waning strength. Caregiving severely tested my love and commitment.

Looking back, I wish I had known enough to take a break at the first signs of burnout that set in for it is much easier to deal with before it sets roots in place. Prevention is so much easier than treatment when it comes to caregiver burnout.

It took years for me to even begin to find appropriate support systems. In the meantime, my husband and friends were burning out as I exhausted myself and them with my need to discuss every situation, agonize over every decision. They were no better equipped than I to place limits, construct healthy boundaries, or put this disease in a place that would be manageable. They did not know how to help. None of us understood the emotional toll, although we saw its ravages. We were racing down a path that led to the edge of a cliff but none of us knew it.

Self Care vs. Selfishness

Although the decisions I made for my mother were right all along the way, the decisions I made for myself, by not acting on my own behalf, were costly indeed. But my upbringing did not prepare me to care for myself. Much healthier for Alzheimer's caregivers is Jennifer Louden's view:

> Self-care is not selfish or self-indulgent. We cannot nurture others from a dry well. We need to take care of our own needs first, then we can give from our surplus, our abundance. When we nurture others from a place of fullness, we feel renewed instead of taken advantage of. And they feel renewed too, instead of guilty. We have something precious to give others when we have been comforting and caring for ourselves, and building up self-love.[1]

Like most women raised in an Irish Catholic family in the nineteen-fifties, sixties and seventies, I was taught to serve, to be selfless, and to define myself and my success by my relationships. When carried to extreme as it was with most people I know, this theory became a poor game-plan indeed, especially for the primary caregiver of an Alzheimer's patient.

One of the problems for caregivers is that they become more and more vulnerable, losing whatever resiliency they might have had at the beginning of caregiving or when they were younger, as the caregiving role moves from months to years. The importance of pacing is often overlooked by the caregiver. I began this role when I was thirty, although I wasn't really aware of actively caregiving until three years later. My youth and the belief that I could and would do anything it took, was both a blessing and a curse.

These beliefs combined with societal messages and expectations that women should care for everyone else first, before we even think of self care. In fact, self care is often synonymous with selfishness. For some, myself included, selfishness is considered a sin. Being trained to value every one else before ourselves makes it hard to focus on self care. It is by habit, if nothing else, that we think of ourselves last. And although expert nurturers, our nurturing skills are directed at everyone but ourselves until we have nothing left *for ourselves*.

I simply did not have the life experience to understand what a long term commitment of this magnitude meant. I couldn't imagine the costs it would exact on my mental, spiritual and physical health and on the health of my relationships.

Human Needs

All human beings have needs. We have needs for our well being, like food, sunlight, contact with other humans. Our needs are non-negotiable—they are things we cannot do without.

Both Alzheimer's caregivers and patients have needs; regardless of what else happens in primary caregivers' lives, their afflicted loved ones will not stop needing them. Becoming an Alzheimer's caregiver does not negate the caregiver's needs. In fact, if anything, caregiving makes meeting personal needs more important. Caregiving also makes one less able to meet ones own needs because energy is being depleted by the role of caregiving.

Although it is long, the move from one loss and crisis to another often happens in ways that don't allow primary caregivers to catch their breath, attend to personal relationships, and perhaps most important, develop and maintain a sustaining relationship with themselves. It is common to hear primary family caregivers say, "If I can only get through a, I'll be fine." Then a changes to b and b to c. Years later, primary caregivers look back and say, "What happened? Where is everyone? Where am I?"

Table 1 at the end of this chapter is a needs assessment tool designed to help you define and monitor your own needs. Fill in each of the four columns and review it often. (For example, the minimum number of hours of sleep you may need to function is six, while eight and a half hours is reasonable for you but ten hours optimum, with a mid-day nap twice a week.) In this way, you can identify problems in meeting your own needs before they become disasters that are costly to you and your patient. Unfortunately, I have heard the specifics noted in the "Current Status" column in Table 4 at the end of this chapter all too often in support groups.

Medical care

It is essential to establish and maintain regular medical care— both preventive and reactive. Unfortunately, it is not unusual for the caregiver to put personal needs on the back burner. This can have serious consequences if it happens too often or for too long. In order to be our BEST (Body, Emotions, Spirit, Thoughts) we must strive for balance.

Keeping in touch with one's primary care physician can be critical to the general and specific health of caregivers. But some physicians are not cognizant of what Alzheimer's means to caregivers. Education is imperative, for if the caregiver's physician is to be aware and supportive, there must be an understanding of what the caregiver is living with—the stress, the grief, and the weight of the physical and emotional burdens their caregiving patients carry.

When my journey began, I was young and I had an even younger physician. I remember her wondering out loud, as I described my plight as a caregiver, why I was so upset since my mother hadn't died. This was upsetting to me and had me wondering if there was something wrong with me or the way I approached caregiving. Neither of these things was true.

This happened many years before the disease had the visibility it has now. I was simply too young to know enough and did not have adequate information to set her straight.

My primary-care physician's seemingly insensitive reactions were born of ignorance rather than malice. She is a wonderful, caring woman who obviously picked up a better understanding of Alzheimer's disease somewhere along the way, perhaps in part from me. By the end of my journey, she played an important role in helping me keep my mother's wishes in the forefront. She was wise enough in the earlier stages to direct me to my mother's physician when I had questions and concerns about alternative treatments for my mother. My comfort with my physician as a trusted and supportive person allowed me to call when I needed her.

Exercise

Exercise is important if for no other reason than to relieve stress. Gentle exercise, that takes into account the general physical condition of the caregiver, is appropriate. Unfortunately, caregivers, who are highly stressed by definition, can be more prone to injury. The strong emotions that accompany caregiving can push a caregiver to limits that might otherwise be avoided.

During my years of caregiving I tried cycling, walking, swimming and gardening. At one point or another with each of these exercises, I injured myself. This was very discouraging. Despite how well I knew exercise served me, and how important it was, injuries made me less willing and less able to try again. So while exercise is important, it must be exercise that is not too taxing on a body and mind that are already severely taxed.

For the caregiver who is with the patient day in and day out, finding a way to exercise with the patient is usually most successful although it may be of less benefit to the caregiver. Lack of time and energy present problems for all caregivers in carrying out exercise regimens.

Nutrition

Nutrition is important for everyone but taking the time to buy and prepare healthy foods is one more thing that sometimes slides to the bottom of the caregiver's priority list. Perhaps this is an area where less involved friends and family members can assist. My husband was in charge of nutrition in our household, but this had been the case long before my mother's disease. Although I grew more interested in sharing this responsibility as the years passed, the stress of caregiving left me less willing to do something that was not on the top ten of my list of priorities.

Rest

Of prime importance, and in great jeopardy for the primary caregiver, is adequate rest. When patients do not sleep, or the home caregiver is unable to sleep because of being afraid of what will happen while doing so, a dangerous cycle of exhaustion can begin. Some families take turns staying with the patient in her own home, thus sharing the risks that come with lack of sleep.

I never slept a whole night when my mother was in my home. Although I rarely had trouble sleeping, and have always been blessed with the ability to sleep regardless of what is going on, I was always waiting for the other shoe to drop when my mother was with us. The same was true for at least one of my sisters and her husband.

While more of an issue for those who are caregiving at home, lack of sleep is a problem for most caregivers, including those who are not hands-on daily caregivers. Inadequate rest affects all aspects of the caregiver's health and life and makes the person less able to cope with the challenges of caregiving. Adult children are often concerned about the risks to their caregiving parent and with good reason. Sometimes it is the caregiver's inability to sleep that eventually leads to serious consideration of nursing home placement. If lack of sleep is a problem, it should be addressed immediately with the caregiver's physician.

Since lack of caregiver sleep is directly related to sleeping problems for the patient, logging sleeping problems is helpful. There are many things that can cause the Alzheimer's patient to awaken or not go to sleep. The temperature in the room, noise, and lights can all affect sleeping. Finally, be sure they have gone to the bathroom prior to going to bed. Not giving the patient any liquid for a few hours before bed is a strategy that many find useful. The sleep log at the end of this chapter can assist the caregiver in identifying issues that contribute to sleeplessness.

Respite

It is critical to periodically get out from under the overwhelming swamp of loss, emotion, bureaucracies and too little support. One way to offset the strains of long term caregiving is by finding and taking advantage of appropriate respite care.

Respite is a short-term alternative care arrangement designed to give the caregiver a break from the tasks of caregiving. Respite should not be confused with a vacation. Respite is a break from caregiving, not from the rest of your life's routine.

Family, friends or professionals can provide respite. The fact that caregivers go so long without a break makes it particularly difficult to take one when it is available. There can be many reasons for waiting too long but the primary ones seem to be the lack of availability of respite and the caregiver's discomfort with the respite options available.

When the demands of caregiving become greater than the caregiver's emotional, spiritual or physical resources, the word stress is understood as never before, viscerally—at the core. This is when burnout begins to take hold.

Dedicated as I was to my mother, there were periods of time when I accepted respite. Usually, this was suggested or strongly urged by others who were more objective. The support group leader convinced me to allow my husband to "cover for me" for two weeks. After two weeks, I had great difficulty going back to my role as caregiver, and in fact did not return for five more weeks. I struggled with guilt and exhaustion. In retrospect my respite was healthy for all of us. Approximately once a year, I took a short respite. For me, respite meant not visiting my mother and not checking in with nursing home staff and in later years, hospice.

A common feeling engendered by respite is guilt. Some allow guilt to stop them from availing themselves of appropriate respite while others accept the respite but feel guilty. Jamey, whose mother is in a local long term care facility, is the only family member around. Jamey has been involved in her mom's care from the beginning and is at the nursing home two or three times a week. Once a year, her aunt comes for two months. During that time, Jamey's visiting becomes sporadic as she tries to pick up overtime shifts at her job and keep a side business running but she says at her support group, "Can someone please tell me how to not feel the guilt? I know I'm entitled to a break. I know I need one, and I desperately need the money. The time for these things is when my aunt is here but I just can't seem to get my feelings in tune with my logical mind!"

Perhaps feeling that no one else can care for your loved one in exactly the same way, or as well as you can, is justified. Caregiving becomes a way of life, a habit to which you must adjust in order to survive. While it may be difficult to break out of it, and even more difficult to find acceptable coverage, you *must* for if you don't care for yourself, where will your loved one be? Where will you be?

For me it was time to come down off the cross and recognize that I was not only entitled to a life and reasonable breaks, but that I *needed them.* While the respite caregiver may not be as able to meet your loved one's needs as you are, an appropriate respite can meet his needs sufficiently. The danger of burning out is very real for Alzheimer's caregivers.

A new support group member described his disillusionment with his respite choices as follows: "Shortly after my mother entered the nursing home, I asked one of my sisters to "cover" for a period of time during which I was unable to go. My sister agreed but later told me she saw no need to visit the nursing home, so she didn't. Many years later, my brother said he'd monitor my mother's fever and other problems until my wife came home to take over for me. (We had agreed that when she returned I would go away for a few days because I was so burned out.) My brother called me the first night to say that he had stayed with our mother for almost a half-hour so didn't have to go back for a month at least. Each of these revelations decreased by one my sources of respite. The first because my sister just "blew me off"—she actually lied to me. The second because my brother obviously did not 'get it' or couldn't follow through on his offer. So as a result of these situations I became less willing to take a break, even when it was abundantly clear that I desperately needed one. Thank God for my wife!"

A careful review of the following questions (adapted from *The 36-Hour Day*) will tell you if you need to make changes.

- 💜 Do I feel so sad or depressed that I am not functioning as I should?

- 💜 Am I often lying awake at night worrying?

- 💜 Am I losing weight?

- 💜 Do I feel overwhelmed most of the time?

- 💜 Do I feel terribly isolated and alone with my problem?

- 💜 Am I drinking too much?

- 💜 Is my drinking interfering with how I function with my family, or my job, or in other ways?

- 💜 Am I using pills to get me through each day? Tranquilizers and sleeping pills should be used only under the careful supervision of a physician and only for a short time. Pep pills (amphetamines) should never be used to give you an energy boost.

- 💜 Am I drinking too much coffee each day? Excessive coffee use can be hard on your body and reduce your ability to manage stress. (Caffeine is also found in tea and most soft drinks.)

- 💜 Am I screaming or crying too much? How much crying or screaming is too much? One person may feel that any crying is too much while another feels that crying is a good way to "get things out of my system." You probably know already if your moods are exceeding what's normal for you.

❤   Am I often losing my temper with the impaired person?

❤   Am I hitting him?

❤   Do I find myself more frustrated and angry after I talk with my friends or family about these problems?

❤   Do I find that I am getting irritated with a lot of people—friends, my family, the doctors, my coworkers—more than just one or two people in my life?

❤   Am I excessively angry? Anger and frustration are normal responses to caring for a person whose behavior is difficult. However, if your anger begins to spill over into many relationships or if you take your anger out on the sick person it may be helpful to find ways to manage your frustration so that you do not drive people away from you or make the impaired person's behavior worse.

❤   Am I thinking about suicide? The thought of suicide can come when a person is feeling overwhelmed, helpless and alone. When someone feels that he cannot escape an impossible situation or that he has irrevocably lost the things that make life worth living, he may consider suicide. Suicide may be considered when someone feels that the situation he faces is hopeless. When he feels there is nothing he or anyone else can do. The present can seem intolerable and the future appears bleak, dark, empty and meaningless.

❤   Do I feel I am out of control of my situation or at the end of my rope?

❤   Is my body telling me I am under too much stress?

❤   Do I often feel panicky, nervous or frightened?

❤   Would it help just to talk the whole thing over with someone who understands?

If the answer to some of these questions is "yes," it may be that you are carrying too heavy a burden without enough help.[2]

Vacations

Throughout the first several years of caregiving, my husband and I took vacations, real vacations where we left our jobs and home and went somewhere that was duty free for us. My sister and I had a saying during these early years, "If Mamma dies, put her on ice." This was no more than a signal that I needed the break. In the early years while vacationing I did talk to my mother on the phone while I was away. When she was no longer able, I had no contact with any care-givers (family or professional) until I returned. The theory here was "no news is good news." In the last several years, vacations were a luxury I could not financially afford. They were sorely missed.

Stress management

It is difficult for people who have not experienced it directly to understand the draining, exhausting, seemingly endless and hopeless nature of caring for the victim of a progressive dementia. People have different operating styles and coping mechanisms but the total-ity of the disability of dementia patients is not something generally within the realm of experience in this culture.

The high level and ongoing stress created by caregiving for an Alzheimer patient increases the caregiver's risk of succumbing to what I think of as "-isms, -holics and 'bad talkin'." These are behav-iors and mind sets that alone or in combination produce alco-hol(ism), worka(holics), exerciza(holics) and a plenitude of others. Bad talkin' about oneself or another caregiver and their lives can be a habit or a newly acquired activity that demeans and drags them down even further than the difficulties they are experiencing as care-givers. These are things to watch out for, and, if they start to creep into the caregiver's life, attend to them.

Creative artistic expression, journal writing, support groups and psychotherapy are but a few of the healthy ways caregivers can address these problems.

Maintaining Relationships

Caregivers have a minimum of two relationships to manage. They have a relationship with their patients and a relationship with themselves. Both of these relationships will change because of the introduction of Alzheimer's into their lives.

The stress and strain of caregiving cannot help but affect relation-ships. Increased communication, additional supports and a desire and commitment to preserving relationships are needed. These things are of course more difficult to manage at a time when so much energy is being expended on the physical and emotional tasks of caregiving.

My husband was unable to express the toll my mother's situation and my caregiving role was taking on him, on me and on our relationship. This left me clueless, as I wallowed in a cloud of grief and confusion, barely coping with the day-to-day losses and decisions. Neither of us had the tools to communicate about the problems caregiving presented. In fact, although we knew it wasn't fun, we didn't recognize caregiving as a problem of more or less significance than any other in our lives.

It is only with the cloudy clarity of hindsight that I am beginning to see what was constructive and what was not. The apparent willingness of my husband to support me through it all, was, literally, too good to be true. I couldn't have done what I did without him, but the toll it took on him and our marriage was high. Had I been aware of the potential and actual destruction, while I may not have made different decisions for my mother, I would have made conscious choices that were more in keeping with my husband's welfare and the welfare of our marriage. But as is true with all marriages, responsibility must lie with both spouses. I could not have made those choices given my husband's lack of communication.

Earlier involvement in an Alzheimer's Support Group, appropriate counseling and other such supports would have provided us with the language and forum to discuss the deep pain of our current situation which was dredging up old, partially unresolved losses. I am convinced that with adequate information and appropriate professional support, much of the stress on our marriage could have been relieved and, with skillful support, channeled into positive growth for us as individuals and as a couple. While my mother's Alzheimer's and my caregiving role were contributing factors, they were neither the sole nor primary reasons for the dissolution of our marriage. However, that is not the case in all caregiving marriages that end in divorce.

The complex dynamics of my family of origin contributed to the strain on my marriage. My husband was faced with a situation in which he watched his wife and mother-in-law battling a devastating disease on one front while on another, his wife was turning to face the emotional turmoil that resulted among her siblings and herself. A family who had experienced, but never effectively dealt with significant losses in the past was blowing apart as we sniped at one another in fear and panic. My husband's issues of incomplete grieving were a parallel contributing factor.

The way my siblings and I finally dealt with the complexities of caregiving and the feelings it aroused within us was *not to deal* with them. This placed my husband in the impossible role of being my solitary support. None of us were malicious, all were concerned and in pain. Sadly, our inability to be constructive in supporting one another resulted in damaged relationships. Early intervention by professionals who understood the disease and had skill with family dynamics might have helped us to avoid at least some of the damage that resulted.

Although someone you love gets Alzheimer's, the rest of the world continues to spin and your own life goes on. You may have and raise children. You may meet new friends and lose old ones. You may bury loved ones after dealing with illness. You may get married or divorced.

By the mid-nineteen-eighties, if I had taken one of those stress tests that are sometimes in magazines, I would have been way off the charts. Fourteen months after my mother went into the nursing home, my husband became critically ill. He was hospitalized with a mysterious, life threatening infection for 23 days, came home with a tube in his chest through which antibiotics were pumped round-the-clock for months, and had unexplained fevers for 11 months. A year later, a pre-cancerous condition was found and my husband began a classic "mid life crisis." Eighteen months later, my rush to an emergency room was followed by major surgery on me.

My mother did not stop needing me during that time. Her money ran out and her Medicaid application was denied three times and was appealed four times; the final hardship appeal was a process that lasted more than 10 months. During this time family relations deteriorated further. The stress of Alzheimer's alone is overwhelming. Adding other stresses can be devastating. Although we tried for four years to save it, our relationship of 25 years was a casualty. That would have broken my mother's heart. It broke mine. Still, to his credit, my husband remained my primary non-professional support throughout the course of my mother's illness.

Emotional Health

The need to experience and express difficult emotions is often denied to family members by those well meaning friends, spouses, colleagues, and professionals who simply don't know what to say or do. Many feel helpless and at some level may be afraid that the caregiver's pain may get too close to them. Offers of platitudes and overly simple solutions can make caregivers feel alienated, alone, and questioning their sanity and mental health. This is particularly true for those caregivers who have consciously chosen to face the issues and deal with their resulting emotional upheaval.

The following lists can help you identify useful information about yourself and your coping strategies.

I find it hard to:

- Ask for help
- Accept help
- Cry
- Talk about my situation
- Leave others in charge

- Admit I can't do it alone
- Feel negative feelings
- Put myself first
- Be kind/gentle with myself

I feel free to:

- Cry
- Talk
- Laugh
- Express anger
- Accept time away from caregiving

- Seek respite
- Focus on myself
- Go out with a friend
- Take a Vacation

Caregiving can also raise old issues for the caregiver. Issues of previous losses, medical situations and other life experiences can come crashing back, uninvited and sometimes unrecognized to complicate and intensify the issues raised by Alzheimer's.

Additionally, family issues can be replayed as Alzheimer's raises old, unfinished business within families of origin. Table 3, *Coping Strategies*, at the end of the chapter, is designed to help you review the strategies you use to cope with the feelings and issues you face as a caregiver.

I found two ways to address these feelings and issues. For immediate (short-term) relief I did things like take a hot bath or a walk. Sometimes I felt the need to seek more lasting relief. This required a commitment to myself that was more strenuous and costly in time, money and effort. However, it was an investment in my health and well being. It was an investment in my future. *It was a lasting investment in me.*

Compare your strategies to the following list of healthy coping strategies. Be sure to note whether they are short term coping strategies or long term lasting changes.

Healthy Short Term Coping Strategies:

- Talk with a Friend
- Talk with mate
- Hire Help
- Evening of Relaxation
- Vacation
- Slow Down
- Clergy
- Medical Help
- Respite

- More Rest
- Regular Exercise
- A Warm Bath
- Social Engagement
- Lots of Hugs
- Eat Better
- A Good Cry
- A Be Kind to Me Day
- Take a Day Off

Healthy Long Term Coping Strategies:

- Yoga
- Support Group
- Family Support
- Meditation

- Journal Writing
- Counseling
- Work with Clergy

Alzheimer caregiving is a package deal. Along with the tasks of caregiving come emotions aroused by the painful issues that must be faced. These feelings range from anger, sadness, guilt and despair to the eventual release into relief, gratitude, joy and love.

The first lesson I had to learn about feelings was that they are real entities that have an effect on me. But most importantly, I learned *that feelings are neither good nor bad, they just are*. This was tough for a woman raised in the Roman Catholic faith. Judgments were the foundation of the controlling Catholics who had such an influence on me from the beginning of my life. Feelings were not only judged as good or bad. I was also taught to repress and deny negative feelings and thoughts. Doing so takes lots of energy and was unhealthy for me. But what was I to do with these feelings? I hadn't been taught other coping strategies and the time, effort and support to learn new ones simply weren't there for me, as a caregiver.

Letting down

In order to cope and survive the demands of caregiving, a caregiver must have opportunities to let down and deal with the strong emotions that are raised by Alzheimer's and the caregiving role. This society, which is so hell bent on fun and easy-going relationships, makes this particularly difficult. For letting down, really letting down, requires a strong, supportive environment and people who provide safety, trust, faith, validation and love. Caregivers need to know and to be told that "it's OK to slow down or even stop for a bit." A safe emotional space is needed to meet this need.

If caregivers do not find safe places and people with whom they can let down, they are at greater risk in a number of areas. These include regretting their role, being less able to cope with the day to day stresses of caregiving and being less able to accept the painful realities of what is happening to their loved one. Finding safe, supportive places and people is not always easy, but it is *essential*. A place to begin such a search might be the family doctor, or an employee assistance program, a friend, or clergy. For me—the fact that my mother was far away from the shore where I spent my time on weekends coupled with my new home in which there were no memories of her provided a regular, built-in respite.

Grief

Grief is an enormous problem for the Alzheimer's caregiver. The insidious nature of the losses over such an extended period of time is devastating. Living in a society that neither acknowledges nor supports grief makes things worse. Not only is the patient changing before the caregiver's eyes, their relationship is also changing. Professional's use the term "anticipatory grieving." It is a term I strenuously object to because it seems to *lessen* the validity of the losses and grief. Another term I have heard is the "everlasting wake." While I understand the sentiment, it seems inaccurate because the person is still alive. What makes the grieving process so difficult and bizarre is—how can one complete the letting go when the person is still alive?

Grief is a process through which feelings are experienced when we lose someone in our lives (through illness, death, divorce or some other means). The process of grief is one in which the person left behind must come to terms with their relationship with the person who has left. They must face what their life will be like without this person. Grief, at its most intense and frightening stages seems to take control of the mourner's life. The feelings of sadness, despair and hopelessness are sometimes overwhelming. Anger, denial, bargaining, acceptance and sadness are the five stages of grief defined by Dr. Kubler-Ross. I do not view grief as resolvable but rather something to be experienced and embraced so it can be fully integrated and the person left behind can move on.

For a term that is so familiar to adults, grief is often misunderstood. Societal expectations can couple with family histories to compound the difficulties of grief. Add to that the fact that an adult grieving for a parent is often not validated and you have the ingredients of a Molotov cocktail, ready made.

We learn to grieve from those around us. Depending upon our cultural background and the personalities of our families, we develop our own unique histories with grief. Some of us may have lost loved ones but not been allowed to feel, or express our grief, or at least not fully. This can cause problems at the time of future losses and later. Grief is not pleasant. Grief is not easy. But grief is necessary.

Given the unusual nature of this disease and the different ways of coping with the loss of a loved one, we must be patient and understanding of the mourning process that takes place.

I remember a conversation with my sister toward the end of our journey. She expressed her anger at those who had deserted us in our plight saying, "They better not show their faces when she dies. If they turn up at the wake, I'll show them the door, post haste."

One night my mother told me very seriously and sternly "Don't you shed a tear till I die!"

I had no idea that she was asking something that would be impossible for me so I dutifully agreed. I realize now that my mother's command was a signal to me that *she would not be able to do this Alzheimer thing if we were too open about the grief of it.*

Although I saw my mother visibly sad at times, there were two times that left an indelible mark on my mind and heart.

It was evening as I walked into my mother's room in the nursing home to lights that were turned down low. As I moved toward her bed I realized there were tears streaming down her face!

Instinctively, I wrapped her in my arms and said "Oh, Mamma, what's the matter? Why are you so sad?"

I was amazed when her face lit up at my words and recognition of her sadness. Apparently, she had no recollection of whatever had transformed her beautiful face into the mask of grief I had just glimpsed. Too bad I couldn't forget too. I knew all along that my mother did what she could to protect me. Although it was very much in character for her, I was always amazed at how she managed it when so much else seemed to be gone.

The other thing I remember about that visit was how long it had been since I had even tried to hug my mother for she was rigid by then and the bars on the bed were always raised.

Another day, I arrived early one morning to find my mother again in tears. Apparently her breakfast had been left on the bed tray and she had tried to feed herself. Tears of frustration, shame and rage fell as I saw parts of a muffin caught in her armpits, hair, crotch and on her stomach. It was clear she was no longer able to feed herself. Now if only I could convince the nursing home staff of this we would be able to move on.

Over my years of caregiving I came to welcome my ability to cry. Although crying hurt my eyes and gave me a horrendous hangover, experience taught me to welcome my tears. They were unpredictable at times, and of course most often showed up when I least expected or wanted them, but they eased my grief and provided release from the burden of caregiving. Tears cleansed my pain and made way for joy. Tears are the friends of the Alzheimer's caregiver. They are critical to coming through caregiving in one piece and let the sadness out.

Humor

Our culture is addicted to positive thinking. Americans want to be happy, upbeat, energetic, and hopeful, so we slap on a veneer of positive, phony faith, behind which lurks a heart full of pain and fear. But humor is too often the only band-aid offered to the Alzheimer's caregiver who feels so much pain. For this reason I found humor to be a double-edged sword.

Although humor was critical to my survival and humor certainly made our journey more bearable, it was also sometimes used inappropriately. For some of those trying to support me, humor became their only strategy. Humor has its place. God knows I could not have survived this difficult journey without it but, at times, humor was disrespectful. In retrospect, I realize it was a way for those using it inappropriately to avoid and deny the deep pain that my mother's Alzheimer's raised in them. Sometimes my pain needed validation and healing rather than distraction. While I recognize that people have different coping strategies and some of what I just described may have been a clash of coping strategies, that did not negate my need for validation of my grief, loss and sadness. I believe there is a cultural tendency toward "happy" instead of "sad" that made my journey more difficult and more lonely.

Too often, those who show a depth of pain, which can be overwhelming to themselves and others, are made to feel invisible. Being told to lighten up, get a grip, and to look on the bright side deepened my pain. Meeting caregiver pain like this is destructive for it denies the reality that family caregivers face day in and day out.

Anger

I have yet to meet an Alzheimer's caregiver who did not feel anger. Some claim they don't, but their body language and choice and delivery of words quickly belies their often vociferous denial. There are many reasons to feel anger at Alzheimer's. The loss of a loved one in such a bizarre and difficult way is but one. A lack of understanding from others and acceptance of the caregiver's feelings produces anger. The myriad of problems and struggles that occur within caregiving families is fertile ground for growing and harvesting enormous anger. And let us not forget the condescending, insensitive, brusque treatment at the hands of some professional caregivers.

Finally, caregivers often feel anger at their patient and at themselves. This anger is perhaps the most difficult to handle. Harboring anger at the patient can seem unreasonable and unkind to the exhausted caregiver. When caregivers feel anger toward themselves, this can be the beginning of depression, which can be caused by anger turned inward. Anger turned inward can have very serious consequences indeed. Understanding the difference between sadness and grief and depression, and finding ways to validate and express anger are very important for the survival of the Alzheimer's caregiver. Identifying Alzheimer's as the culprit and the source of anger rather than blaming the patient or themselves is helpful for many.

❤

I am still struck when I think back to the day my sister and I sat in a Chili's restaurant a thousand miles from home over iced tea as she quietly, calmly asked me for "the real scoop" regarding the assault on our mother's face. I saw in my sister the rage and grief I had been holding at bay. It was evident in her tightly controlled words, and her tightly wound muscles too, but most of all in her flashing eyes. We sat as two controlled, civilized beings discussing something so out of control, so beyond civility it was previously beyond our imaginations. She had her emotions in check, but they would not be denied. She spoke of how wonderful it was to be over a thousand miles away, the relief distance brought knowing there was nothing she could do, no way she could go and face the Alzheimer's demons that gazed out at us from our mother's eyes.

But even with that distance, her rage was wild, she would have strangled someone if she could have, she would have hit someone if she could have gotten at them. And I felt the same way, but not until I too was a thousand miles away, perhaps where my rage was safe, there were no living targets in reach that could be held in any way responsible. As I look back on that day, I am grateful for my sister's ability not to spew her rage at me. Perhaps she saw the grief in me. Although she rarely mentioned it, and then only in offhand, unexpected ways, I know in many ways she understood the load I carried. I know she appreciated the toll it took on me and worked hard not to add to it.

It reminded me of other times I had seen other siblings act out what I had been feeling. Were we all somehow connected too? Was their emotion and action a reflection of my own unfelt, unacted upon emotions and actions? Might we together make a whole? How much of each of our reactions were over-reactions because we couldn't seem to be heard by one another or by others in our lives—family, professional caregivers, friends? How much of our pain was being acted out in old ways, over old, unresolved issues, as we watched in helpless horror as our mother slipped away?

❤

Wouldn't it be nice if we could meet Aristotle's challenge in *The Nicomachean Ethics*?

> Anyone can become angry—that is easy. But to be angry with the right person, to the right degree, at the right time, for the right purpose, and in the right way—this is not easy.[3]

Displacement is a way of directing emotions at people, objects and situations inappropriately. With the angers that can be generated by Alzheimer's, is it any wonder that anger will be displaced? But what is the cost of such displacement? What effect does it have on patients and their caregivers? At times, I had to work very hard to separate my pain at watching my mother's slow regression from my more general anger at the ignominy of the entire disease.

For people who are uncomfortable feeling and expressing anger, it sometimes comes out in harmful ways. My own theory of how to prevent or at least minimize displacement is by tending to the feelings, all of the feelings, engendered by Alzheimer's. This requires a commitment to feeling emotions, and to dealing with them. That is a very tall order in our busy world that is so unwelcoming to difficult feelings. It is the only way to avoid displacement and ensure lasting emotional health.

♥

And then there were "the carnivorous clichés"—hackneyed phrases that seemed to feed my anger. Like many caregivers I found these phrases, "tough it out," "let it go," "put it behind you," "accept it as God's will" trite, disrespectful and counterproductive. Yet these sayings are often offered by well-meaning friends and professionals.

♥

I believe much of the anger patients express is displaced onto their caregivers, giving new meaning to the saying, "You always hurt the ones you love." One moment the patient is off fighting the wars within her damaged mind, the next, she's back fighting—spilling her frustration and anger onto those around her who watch in helpless horror.

What are caregivers to do with such heavy burdens? How are they to survive their own and their patients anger and grief? Who is willing to share these difficult, dangerous emotions, and if no one is, what are they to do with them? Are there ways to survive this blasted disease intact? Absolutely, dear reader, absolutely!

I eventually found an outlet in writing. It was like a floodgate had broken. Although I don't understand the process, I know that it kept me sane. Writing provided a way for me to acknowledge and name my feelings, and a space in which to hold them until I was able to deal with them. Many were the mornings and nights when I would sit to pour the devastation of this disease, through keys, into a computer. Often I didn't retrieve and review these for days or months but eventually, I found I had to and it was healthy for me to do so.

Writing moved me forward on the path of my growth and healing. Writing didn't remove my anger; some things always evoked anger in me. Finding ways in which to safely feel and express it made my anger less frightening, less destructive and more manageable.

Joy

Joy may seem like a strange emotion to raise here, but it is an emotion that Alzheimer's caregivers can feel if they allow themselves to view their role and their loved one in a certain light. It requires a change in perspective, an acceptance of the changes in their patient, and the courage to venture into the world of their loved one as she slips further and further afield. Doing so can provide avenues that would otherwise be closed. The joy of a smile, or connection with the severely demented person can be enormously powerful and healing to both the patient and the caregiver.

I recently heard two wonderful stories of joyful caregiving. The first was told by an elderly man who is the primary caregiver for his wife of more than fifty years. While out in a store she was attracted to the large display of brightly colored balls. Noticing her interest, he suggested they buy one. They now play with the ball throwing it in and out of clothes baskets and a net he has rigged up in the kitchen. He pointed out that there are no rules and said both of them have a wonderful time with this new activity. A caregiving daughter then shared a story about using balloons in the same way.

A similar story is that of a caregiving husband who has taken to dancing with his wife in the late afternoons. This relieves her "sundowning," which is an agitation many Alzheimer's patients experience as the sun goes down. It also provides a way for them to enjoy and express their love for one another.

The ingenuity and openness of each of these caregivers allows them to enter into their loved ones' world and has brought joy to patient and caregiver alike.

Alzheimer's presented experiences I would have missed without it. The joy I felt as I watched my husband lay my overtired mother on the couch to rest for Christmas Eve activities, the joy we shared as our laughter echoed in the cavernous room with the old wood floor, a huge bay window and a chinese red fireplace, equaled or surpassed our earlier joys. The joy in my mother's eyes as she met my childhood friend's toddler for the first time was no less wonderful than it would have been if she were well. In fact, it may have been heightened because of the fact that though her world had shrunk to a few hundred square feet, she could still respond to a child.

Relief

Relief is an emotion that many feel at a variety of stages in the disease process. I felt relief when I heard the diagnosis of probable Alzheimer's...when my mother entered the nursing home ...when I got the call that she was on the verge of death and again when she finally died. I felt relief when the autopsy report came in the mail and I still feel relief when I realize that I am no longer carrying the weight of her dementia on my bowed shoulders. But in each of the instances in which I felt relief I also felt other emotions. Frequently these feelings were conflicting.

Toward the end, relief became something I scrutinized carefully. Relief to someone as exhausted as I was could have put my mother in jeopardy. There were times when I questioned the timing and content of my decisions because they provided relief more than anything else. At these times, trusted friends and family helped me sort through the muck and mire of my exhaustion and carefully evaluate my motivations.

Relief sometimes evoked guilt. Over time, I learned to banish the guilt, but it was not easy. Though my relief was understandable, it sometimes seemed to bring with it more trouble than it was worth. I struggled to accept feelings for what they are, just feelings and to honor and accept them. I must point out that to this day, years after my mother's passing, I periodically feel a lifting of the weight of caregiving. I recognize and welcome my old friend "relief" as my shoulders rise a bit more and my step becomes slightly lighter.

Guilt

The sticky wicket of guilt is one that most Alzheimer's caregivers experience at one point or another. Guilt can rear its ugly head when independence is lessened, the patient is placed in a nursing home and the issue of withholding treatment is faced. I think there are two types of guilt: healthy guilt and unhealthy guilt.

Healthy guilt raises questions and provides signals that something might be amiss. It is healthy guilt that allows large numbers of people to live with rules and laws. Healthy guilt is productive, initiates motive review and keeps us honest.

On the other hand, unhealthy guilt is non-productive. For me, unhealthy guilt was a waste of energy. Unhealthy guilt can stem from old, unresolved issues, from an overly strict or rigid upbringing and a general discomfort with the difficult decisions that the Alzheimer's caregiver faces. This type of guilt is an expense, a waste of energy that serves neither patient nor caregiver. I found that the best way to banish unhealthy guilt was to place responsibility for the painful decisions where it belonged, with the disease.

The questions that often plague family caregivers are what I call the "shoulda-woulda-couldas". "I shoulda been there more, if only I woulda done it this way, I coulda been or done x or y or z." Assuming caregivers are doing the best they can, these shoulda-woulda-couldas are unhealthy. Sometimes, a simple sentence from someone is all it takes to put these tendencies where they belong—out of sight, out of mind. My mother's sister, who I saw infrequently, made it a point to banish these nasty guilties by saying again and again, "You kids have nothing to feel guilty about. You've done a wonderful job for your mother." I often called upon her words even when I hadn't seen or spoken to her in a long time.

My mother would not have wanted me to "give up my life" for her or her care. She did not want to be a burden. But what about the patient who would want spouse or child to give up their lives to care for her? Although I did not face this I know there are those who do. I would suggest that those caregivers find someone who can help them to sort through the complex issues to find solutions that are respectful of everyone.

Isolation

Because Alzheimer's caregiving isolates people, the need for social support for both patients and caregivers is universal

As Alzheimer's patients go further and further into their strange new world, others may become less and less willing to expend effort in ways that allow them to stay connected.

It is not unusual for caregivers to become socially isolated. This occurs for many reasons. Time and effort to maintain relationships is in short supply. Sometimes friends do not welcome the behaviors and waning social skills of patients. This can result in lost friendships. While in some cases this represents a true loss, in others it can be viewed like cleaning the closet of those things that no longer fit. However, the feeling of loss, whether it is of a genuine or fair weather friend can add to the grief a caregiver feels.

Support structures can be formal and informal. Support can be provided by people who are most immediately available to caregivers, like family members. Friends, institutions, and a variety of professionals, and sometimes strangers, can also provide support to the Alzheimer's caregiver.

Organizations such as the Visiting Nurses Association can step in when caregivers become too exhausted to manage their patients alone. Alzheimer-friendly nurses who have had many years of experience are able to show caregivers ways to keep themselves and their patients safe. There is no need to "reinvent the wheel." As one grateful recipient said, "Why didn't I think of using a chair in the bath? It seems so logical now but I just never thought of it."

Current medical systems often do not recognize the need to support professional and family caregivers. Worse, the medical community sometimes exacerbates the problem by expecting that family caregivers be as detached, objective, impartial, and professional as they expect themselves to be. If family caregivers can begin to recognize Alzheimer's as a *process*, looking back and gaining perspective, they might find it easier to cope; but they are likely to move back and forth between objectivity (reality) and subjectivity (emotional connection). Others can assist Alzheimer's caregivers in doing this. The fact that I could be subjective *and* objective strengthened my ability to make the right decisions for my mother.

Fear

In my life, I have faced four frightening medical situations: my father's aneurysm, my husband's critical illness, the delivery of my sister's first child and my mother's Alzheimer's. My initial reaction to each was an overwhelming urge to run. In each of those situations, I was terrified and a part of me wanted to stick my head in the sand. But the truth of the matter is, I learned, over time, that the demons and monsters in my mind were worse, by far, than the reality of each of these situations. Armed with the truth, I could at least marshal my energies into constructive action rather than spin my wheels in a head full of fear, which did nothing but exhaust and further terrify me.

Alzheimer's brought many fears to the surface. One that grew as time went on was my fear of losing my memory of the mother who had raised me, forgetting the personality and voice of Puppy.

Despite my fear and exhaustion, as I grew into the caregiving role, I found the courage to face the lion, look down his throat and roar back when that was in my mother's best interest. Over time, the memories of my well mother, Puppy, are slowly returning. This is a bittersweet experience for as I remember her, I also know the depth of my loss. And I find myself grieving the well mother, which I couldn't do as I was bonding with the ill one.

Rejuvenation and Replenishment

Alzheimer's caregivers who make a commitment to rejuvenation and replenishment through rest and relaxation will fare better in both the short and long term. All caregivers need to rejuvenate and replenish themselves. But what is restful and relaxing for one person may not be for another. The three *M's* of music, meditation and massage were heavy hitters in my coping tool kit.

Music helped me to relax. It also helped me cry, and sometimes music was able to bring back happy memories as they faded more and more into the background. During the last forty eight hours of my mother's life, music helped both of us through her final transition. It helped us let go.

Meditation was difficult for me as it is for many. I needed instruction and encouragement to make it useful. It was and is still worth my time and effort. Meditation allowed my racing mind and heart to be still long enough for me to feel the grace of the "angels" being sent to help me.

Massage, although expensive, was also helpful in my journey. Sometimes, knowing that I would soon be the one being cared for made my role of caregiver bearable. It also allowed me a chance to just be, or talk, or sometimes cry with a person and in a place that was emotionally safe. I highly recommend the three *M's* as a staple in the diet of nourishment for the Alzheimer's caregiver.

Yankee ingenuity

Sometimes a little Yankee ingenuity can help turn around a potentially stressful situation.

When June, a woman in her late seventies woke one night to a sound of clanging, she went to investigate. Her husband Joe had somehow managed to get halfway down the cellar stairs. Joe outweighed June by 60 pounds and his behavior had recently become erratic. Realizing they both might end up at the bottom of the stairs if she tried to get Joe to safety herself, she called 911. The next day June prevented future problems by putting a lock high up on the door, since it was becoming increasingly clear that Joe might confuse the cellar door with the bathroom door which was next to it.

Another night Joe had fallen in the bathroom. Rather than awaken her daughter who was due at work early the next morning, June gathered blankets and pillows and told Joe they were "camping out" for the night. As June shared this particular story she ended it by saying, "I could almost imagine us back in our sleeping bags under the stars. It was the best night's sleep we'd had in weeks."

Friendship

The introduction of Alzheimer's into friendships is a challenge. Even the most compassionate and caring of people are severely taxed when trying to provide support for the primary caregivers of Alzheimer patients. They often can't understand the total immersion of their caregiving friend and become discouraged at trying to distract them. It is not uncommon for friendships not to survive the difficulties of caregiving. Our culture does not support friends staying for the long haul any more than it supports partners in a marriage struggling through the hard times. Our world is so stressful to begin with, that adding the enormous grief and burden of caregiving to a friendship can end it. Stress on friendships can be relieved by better overall support for caregivers and then friendships can be more balanced.

Friends often don't know what to do, how to help, or what to say to their newly donned Alzheimer caregiver. They can't really understand the wearing nature of caregiving. They may feel that their friend has lost perspective and the ability to enjoy life. They may be right. They may find that their own problems and joys are less welcome in the life and heart of their caregiving friend. These things may also be true. So people often just drift away. They call less, until they don't call at all. They pull away from the deep, deep pain that has become so much a fact of life for their former friend.

But some friends stay. Some friends are wise enough, and strong enough to allow the caregiver to talk about their experience, although they've heard it a hundred times already. Some friends love enough to find words and gestures that ease the caregiver's burden. Some are there through the journey and continue to be there when it is over. These strong, courageous people are true friends. They are worth their weight in gold.

One friend, who was religious about our monthly dinners always made it a point to ask about my mother. In that way, I knew that she cared. Another friend would occasionally say, "I know how hard this is." Her acknowledgment of my situation rather than avoiding it actually made it easier for me to relax and focus on other things. Just knowing these friends were not trying to sweep my mother's heart-breaking situation under the rug eased my loneliness.

Patients helping caregivers

Sometimes caregivers are fortunate enough to find that the patient can be a source of support to them in their caregiving role. I found this to be true. Perhaps it was because of the fact that my mother was my mother, and I her child. Perhaps it was an innate, instinctual reaction. I sometimes thought of my mother's support of my process through this journey as something she learned in "Mother School," the location of which no one seems willing to disclose to me though most folks seem to acknowledge its existence. Perhaps it was a cooperative effort with us. Perhaps she knew how much I needed her support, and in some way, I found a way to help her give it. Whatever happened in this regard, I know how important it was and how grateful I remain.

Jolene tells of the day that she said to her mother, "My head hurts." Since her mother rarely spoke at all, Jolene was surprised when her mother replied, "My head hurts too." When Jo told me this story eleven years after her mother's passing, she had tears in her eyes as she relived the many emotions it evoked—joy at realizing her mother was still listening to her, sadness at how long it had been since she had heard her voice, and love that they could still share, even if only a headache.

This story points out a very important point in that weird phenomenon called role reversal. Role reversal is a *process* rather than something that happens at a discrete point in time. Most caregivers I have talked to about this see it as something that seems to move back and forth between them and their loved one. What is critical here is that the person with Alzheimer's does and can realize that they are needed, they can still give, they still have the capacity to comfort and share, albeit diminished and differently. But in the context of such loss, their gifts of sharing are that much more precious.

I remember untold nights when I would say, without even thinking, "Oh Mamma, I feel so much better just having talked it out." The fact that I did all the talking didn't seem to matter since her eye hugs and other expressions of understanding, comfort and love were often there. This does not mean I was deluded into thinking she was "all there" for my eyes could clearly see she wasn't, but my heart and spirit knew her essence was still there, and her love was still being offered. I needed and accepted that with gratitude. Perhaps the writing I did, which was often in two voices, mine followed by her response, kept what she would have said, if she were able, more real and alive for me. An added benefit to writing is that I can go back now and relive some of those experiences with her responses. And with the passing of time these writings have offered a healing I would never have known.

Family

Families can be the source of support or of pain. Mine was both. Sometimes, it was family who could bring me back as others couldn't. Sometimes I could hear things from anyone but family. We helped each other through our mother's Alzheimer's, and we made it worse for each other. But I suspect the making worse was a function of old issues as much as the disease itself.

I found I loved my family more by the time the journey ended. I found I could both hate and dislike them too. It was a mixed bag to say the least. After all is said and done, I am grateful that I have been blessed with this family. With all our warts and problems, we are a unit bound by history, time, shared experience and, most importantly, love. The rents torn in the fabric of our family were not permanent. And we are stronger where these rents have been repaired. We have survived Alzheimer's intact. But some families do not.

Colleagues

According to a 1987 survey by AARP and the Travelers Foundation, sixty-three percent of caregivers are employed, either full time (53 percent) or part time (10 percent). One-third of employed caregivers report they have lost time from work as a result of their caregiving duties. Alzheimer's caregivers who also work have a balancing act that challenges them even more. I was fortunate to work for a compassionate organization and have an incredibly supportive supervisor.

Years before the family care act was even thought of, the state of Massachusetts allowed the use of employee sick time for caregiving family members. Additionally, sick time could be used in increments of two hours. This allowed me, as my mother's primary caregiver, to leave work and return. When I took the job, I hadn't a clue about how heavy the burden of caregiving would become. Nor did I know how long it would last. My employer's humane, caring policies allowed me to be there when my mother needed me, and to continue my career.

The college at which I worked through the last several years of my mother's life was a community of caring people. The countless kind and thoughtful words and gestures over the years were helpful to me at many levels. Just the acknowledgment of what was happening by those around me helped keep me connected and grounded. The willingness of people to ensure I was found if my mother needed me, or to ask about the most recent crises, made my journey that much easier. There were many who had already, or were simultaneously dealing with the same issues. Those of us who belong to the "Alzheimer's Club" have a special bond that cannot be broken.

Finally, my boss is a particularly spiritual and moral human being. He was willing to discuss the difficult issues and offer his objective, moral ideas. On more than one occasion, it was this man who steadied my faltering walk toward the end of my mother's life. He was interested enough to listen and offer constructive feedback when I needed it most. To this day, I feel a loyalty and respect for him and the organization that worked with me to allow me to complete the daunting task of primary caregiving for my demented mother.

Professional caregivers

Professional caregivers have a dual relationship with support. They both need and provide it. As with family caregivers, if they are to be supportive and nurturing, they must be supported and nurtured themselves. The need to support professional caregivers must be taken seriously if they are to be successful at caregiving. As time went on, my relationship with my mother's professional caregivers became two way as each of us gave and received support.

Professional caregivers are busy, and many are likely to have dealt with the issues over many years. Sometimes this renders them impatient with the surrogate decision-maker's need to work things through. The labeling of family caregivers as "emotionally needy," "unstable," or "incapable of making decisions" can be destructive. While occasionally this may be the case, it is difficult to describe a healthy reaction to Alzheimer's caregiving when there is so little data. What's healthy for one, may not be healthy for another. More often than not—the level of grief expressed by a family caregiver is warranted by the losses they have experienced.

It is certainly not too much to ask to have the feelings of family caregivers understood and respected and perhaps even embraced. Family caregivers should not have to justify or defend showing emotion and vulnerability, nor be subject to judgments about their decisions. Most family caregivers handle an extremely difficult situation over an extended period of time amazingly well.

An unproductive situation can result in inappropriate labels being assigned to family caregivers. Such inappropriate labels can exacerbate and increase stresses for heavily-involved family members. Furthermore, they can impede the ability of family caregivers to advocate for their patient.

I shrank in horror when I heard a psychologist refer to his Alzheimer caregiving constituency as people who were "so needy." He either did not understand the stresses they faced or was so frightened by them that he fled behind the judgmental jargon of his profession. He was taken aback when I suggested that by definition the caregiver was likely to be upset, but that did not mean they were mentally ill, unable to control their emotions or emotionally needy.

Long-term care facilities need to assess their skill in supporting families through this arduous journey. To treat the patient and disregard the family, especially the family member responsible for making decisions for the patient, can only result in less than optimum care for the patient. It can be excruciatingly painful for families to watch the progression from proud, independent, striking, vibrant loved one to unkempt, toothless, bed-bound, demented dying patient.

Supporting and caring for the Alzheimer's caregiver as well as the patient is a primary responsibility of the professional in Alzheimer's units. Alzheimer's professionals are skilled in doing this over the long haul. This support and these wonderfully dedicated people help the caregiver survive the experience and move on after it is over. They help them to process the losses and emotions throughout the journey. They encourage and when necessary teach the Alzheimer's caregiver healthy coping mechanisms. Their respect and validation of the journey make it easier, and offer more opportunities for growth.

This is an area where those who have hopped on the Alzheimer's bandwagon can cause much damage. It is why bonafide Alzheimer's professionals who truly care about Alzheimer's patients and families are the best choice for diagnosis, community, interim and institutional care. In the best of these diagnostic centers and special care units, staff and supervisors are constantly educated; those who are not fit for the task, leave.

How can the family caregiver judge the professional caregivers ability to meet patient and caregiver needs? Unfortunately, the onus is on caregivers to do just that in order to avoid dealing with people who are either unfit or unwilling, or both, to support their caregiving efforts. While this may seem like just one more task the family caregiver must assume, it's success will impact the future of both patient and caregiver. Alzheimer's is difficult enough without adding the burden of dealing with professionals who neither understand nor are willing to learn about the disease and its effects on those around them. Professionals must want to provide support, and know how to do it.

It is critical that professionals have support also. A local Alzheimer's unit has weekly sessions for staff with a neuro-psychologist as part of an ongoing education program. All caregivers, family and professional, are entitled to supportive environments that can bolster their efforts to love and care for their patients without judgment.

Support groups

Alzheimer support groups are places where people can go to talk about their experiences dealing with Alzheimer's. They are usually facilitated by a former caregiver, a professional caregiver or a mental health professional. Confidential and emotionally-supportive, they are safe places where caregivers and family members can talk openly. Support groups can be great places to find resources and to keep abreast of research and other related issues. A caution must be offered, however, for sometimes, in an effort to help, people can give incorrect or misleading information.

There are two types of Alzheimer support groups—patient and caregiver. I was unaware of patient support groups until it was too late for my mother. Some support groups run for a limited time, with a particular focus and have a fee associated with them. Others are open, ongoing groups. For me, support groups were a godsend.

If someone had asked me fifteen years ago if I considered myself the type of person who would avail of a support group, I would have answered, "Not on a bet." I didn't actually find my way to one until we were well along in our journey. I was a member of two groups over the years which were led by three different people. My husband said at one point that he wished I had found a support group long before I did. In retrospect, I agree that it would have been helpful to both of us; in fact, I wish he had joined me.

Over the years some have been disparaging about support groups, labeling them "cheap therapy," "a waste of time" and other unhelpful things. I found such remarks ridiculous then and find them even more so now. The support groups to which I belonged offered something no one else could—people who *understood what I was living with*. They too were trying to process this foreign behavior by people they love. There were times when I went because I didn't know what else to do with myself. There were times I didn't go because I just couldn't take any more Alzheimer's. But for the most part, and in the long run, support groups were the most powerful tool in my bag of tricks. When nothing else seemed to work, when no one else seemed able to listen, when my world was dangerously atilt—it was to the support group that I dragged myself.

I have noticed a problem for certain populations in small communities. Many people who, in their professional lives, are seen as helpers or people in a position of authority find it more difficult to go to support groups. These might include doctors, nurses, police, teachers, clergy and providers of services to the elderly population. Support groups seem unsafe to many of these people. When I have suggested that professions are not the topics discussed at these groups, they answer, "But what if I come in contact with someone from the support group in my work?" While I understand their hesitancy, I know that Alzheimer caregivers need all the help they can get. Perhaps small communities could find a way to hold Alzheimer support groups that are limited to those in the helping professions so they can share freely and not be worried about showing vulnerability.

Spiritual Health

Although I couldn't have heard it myself at the beginning, I urge all involved in the process of Alzheimer's to open their hearts and seek spiritual sustenance and healing. That needn't be through formalized religion. In fact, in retrospect, I realize I prayed from the outset, to my father who had been dead for many years, to my aunt, who died early in the process, as well as to the God of my childhood.

When my mother's descent into Alzheimer's began, I had already fallen away from my Catholic upbringing. I felt much anger and distrust at a church that had deeply wounded and controlled the family in which I was raised.

There were two occasions on which I sought advice from a priest. The first was during a time when my mother was in her own house with her sister. The other concerned the decision to withhold curative treatments. I spoke with a priest on both of these occasions out of respect and concern for my mother. I had much reluctance to overcome before this actually took place. In order to make the decision to stop curative treatment, I felt the need to check in with the church which had been such a central part of my mother's life. I went for her, despite my anger and distrust. Little did I know where that fateful night would lead.

Something, which I now think of as divine providence, led me to a priest with whom I could work. After my first meeting with him in the summer of 1993, we continued to meet regularly until eight months after my mother's death. He met with my husband and me and helped us pray with my mother.

Oasis

There are times when Alzheimer's caregivers need a place that is free from the stress and pain and the work of caregiving. Different people will find oases in different places. What is an oasis for one may not be for another. The commonality in oases is their universal meeting of a deep need of the Alzheimer's caregiver.

I found different places and people that served as an oasis for me. For a long, long time, my marriage was my primary oasis. Time spent in the loving emotional safety and security of that relationship was enough to recharge my batteries. My marriage was a salve to my breaking heart. But caregiving went on for so long, and so many other difficult things intervened, that my marriage could not withstand the pressures indefinitely. Eventually it lost its ability to soothe my pain, smooth my ever more creased brow, and help me to deal with the tensions that had become a primary focus in my life.

Despite my training at the knees of priests and nuns to become a martyr, and despite my stubbornness and belief that I could and would do whatever it took, there came a time when the often burdensome role of caregiving was too heavy to bear alone. It was time for me to come down off the cross.

When my marriage lost its function as an oasis and entered the status of "additional stressor," I was in deep trouble. My family of origin was unavailable to fill the gap and the few friends with whom I had been able to maintain relationships were jumping ship as they struggled with their own problems. I was leery of professional counseling—I had personal reasons beyond the general fear and mistrust of the public at large. But eventually it came down to bend or break. I bent.

During the period of my caregiving, I saw a few counselors for varying lengths of time. Some were better than others. More than once I went to someone who did not understand Alzheimer's and was unable to grasp what I was experiencing. Few of them understood grief.

Eventually I found a person who, while not familiar with Alzheimer's disease, was familiar with the feelings and reactions I was having to it. I came to call her the "heart lady." The heart lady was a woman younger than I who had personal and professional experience with trauma victims. Her specialty was helping people get in touch with the signals their bodies give them about themselves and what is going on in their lives. She quickly got a reading on my situation and worked skillfully to help me process and integrate the experiences I found so tumultuous.

The heart lady listened as the pain and loneliness of caregiving came pouring out. She recognized and validated my experiences as hellacious and gently directed me to others who could support me as a caregiver. She encouraged me to feel difficult feelings and share them in constructive ways. She encouraged the outlet of writing that had begun shortly after my husband's mid-life crisis began in the late nineteen-eighties. She provided hope and a safe haven in which to process and eventually move beyond the enormous pain with which I was dealing on a daily basis.

The heart lady taught me the difference between grief and depression. She worked long and hard to uncover the damage done by what had been for me a controlling church, and she encouraged me to work with a priest to heal the deep, painful wounds inflicted so many years before. She helped me uncover courage and strength I didn't know I possessed.

Finding a professional with whom I could work was one of the best decisions I made for myself in this painful journey. Family, friends and spouse as sole supports were simply not enough. I am grateful that I swallowed my pride, and overcame my prejudice and fear. Therapy was critical to maintaining my own health so I could make the right decisions for my mother.

As the heart lady helped me weave the anger and despair of Alzheimer's into love and commitment, I removed the superwoman cape that had been laid upon my shoulders at birth. She convinced me that I needed to let down, give in, and realize the importance of accepting and respecting my caregiving and grief as processes vital to my health. She assured me that I would survive. She helped me learn how to do the following which were critical to my survival:

- ❤ Identify Stress Relievers
- ❤ Change the Rules—Tell the Players (those who will be affected)
- ❤ Be Flexible
- ❤ Breathe
- ❤ Be Gentle with Yourself—Give Yourself a Break

The heart lady also helped convince me that I was entitled to be good to myself. The problem was though, on those rare occasions when I found the time, I was so exhausted I couldn't think of what I would like to do. In the earlier days of my caregiving, my husband remembered for me but once we were apart I had to remember for myself. The Spoil Me Box was something that worked for me. Maybe it could work for you too. So when you think of something it would be nice to do—write it down and put it in the box so you have ideas of what would "spoil you" when the opportunity arises. Why not get started right now by jotting down some things you'd love to do if you only had the time. One idea might be a hot bath with scented candles, a cold beer and a great book.

A hidden beauty of these is the fact that they can be more fully developed once the Alzheimer's journey is finished. Doing so can improve the quality of life of the caregiver long after they stop being a caregiver.

❤

In the middle of July 1993, I found myself on the doorstep of a rectory. It was the day before I was to tell my mother's physician of the decision to stop all curative treatment.

The priest I had gone to see was no longer in that parish so the tall, gawky high school boy who answered the door offered another priest.

When I said I didn't think so, the boy said "Father T is young and way cool."

What did I have to lose?

It was the heart lady who named the priest I finally connected with "the baby priest." When the "baby priest" walked in, I thought to myself, "He is not much older than my godson, what good can he possibly do?" But I was there, and he'd already sat down.

Within minutes I was in tears, relating the ordeal of my caregiving and my failing marriage.

At one point he smiled and said, "You know, I often haven't any idea at all what to say to people."

At that moment, a strange thing happened. I felt something deep inside "touch" a place of such goodness I was stunned. It happened in a flash and seemed to come through the priest. We talked for two or three hours. When I left, I was still upset but somehow calmer. In time, I realized that this connecting back to the part of my young life that had been so important was necessary for me to mature, to heal, and to reach my potential. It was also necessary to let my mother go.

I went to the priest many times. He came to the nursing home. He understood and met my mother's spiritual needs which I had been neglecting. He slowly dispelled my feigned disinterest in my own spiritual life and worked with me on the incredibly difficult end of life issues I faced with and for my mother.

The priest respected my rage and grief at an abusive church that came out slowly in my writings. He read these words and encouraged me to continue. He opened the door for me to re-establish a relationship with God. He often said that I had more faith than any ten people he had ever met. Although I couldn't understand this, I knew he believed it. He taught me the need to distinguish between feeling, thought and decision-making.

At one point in the spring of 1994, I mentioned a retreat. In answer to my concern that it was being held at a Catholic facility, although it was not religiously affiliated or focused, the baby priest urged me to go with an open mind and heart. He wisely advised me to take the day after the retreat off from work since people often find them exhausting.

As I left my home, I wondered if I had finally flipped. The house had been sold due to my impending divorce, I was moving in three weeks, and had months of packing yet to do. Yet this beautiful May evening found me driving sixty miles to, of all things, a retreat. "Maybe," I thought to myself, "my friend, who is at the house to clean out the refrigerator and mind the dog, will also finish packing!"

The retreat was called "A Gathering of Women"®. I was amazed at the power of the experience. The love and compassion throughout that weekend moved me several steps closer to the deep spiritual healing I so desperately needed. Although I cried almost all weekend, I was also deeply nurtured.

The retreat ended with a special service for Mother's Day. I experienced great difficulty doing the final exercise and I had a strange experience as I listened to a young woman sing "Amazing Grace" a capella. As I passed her in the closing ceremony, I asked if she would sing "Amazing Grace" at my mother's funeral. She agreed and asked me where and when. I said I didn't know. She gave me her phone number, which I tucked away.

The lesson of caring for myself has positioned me for a better, more fulfilling and healthy life. There is a part of me that is grateful I was forced to learn it. I survived Alzheimer caregiving, and, I am learning to live my life more fully and healthily day by day.

The crying and grief that I thought would never end are making way for joy and laughter, once again. I thank God for those who supported my self-care, and particularly those who were wise and courageous enough to encourage and help me to grieve. For now I am free to live and love without the incredibly heavy yoke that Alzheimer's placed over my life. ❤

Table 1: Needs Assessment Tool

Issue	Minimum	Adequate	Optimum	Current Status
Rest				
Nutritious Food				
Appropriate Exercise				
Nourishing Social Contact				
Spiritual Sustenance				
Laughter				
Tears				
Support				
Respite				

Physical Needs

Medical Care
Exercise
Food/Nutrition
Rest
Respite

Spiritual Needs

Oasis

Emotional Needs

Vacations
Stress Management
Relationships
Feelings
Letting Down
Grief
Humor
Anger
Joy
Relief

Rejuvenation/Replenishment

Music, Meditation and Massage
Yankee Ingenuity
Friendship
Patients helping Caregivers
Family
Colleagues
Professional Caregivers
Support Groups

Table 2: Sleep Log

SLEEP LOG Name: . _____ .				Date Log Started:			
Date	Time W[a]	R	N	Number of times up at night	Circum- stances	Interven- tions	Outcome	Staff Initials
Signature:								

a.   W (Waking) R(Retiring) N(Napping)

Table reproduced from: *Of Two Minds, A Guide to the Care of People with the Dual Diagnosis of Alzheimer's Disease and Mental Retardation,* Judith M. Antonangeli, RN, BSN, Fidelity Press, 1995., Chapter 7: Medical Issues—page 139.

Table 3: Coping Strategies

Feeling/Issue	Current Coping Strategy	Short/ Long Term	Effectiveness	Notes/Potential Coping Strategy
Anger				
Depression				
Exhaustion				
Fear				
Frustration				
Grief				
Guilt				
Hopelessness				
Isolation				
Loneliness				
Overwhelmed				
Relief				
Sadness				
Powerlessness				
Denial				

Table 4: Needs Assessment Tool

Issue	Minimum	Adequate	Optimum	Current Status
Rest				4–7 hours per night
Nutritious Food				weekly
Appropriate Exercise				none at all
Nourishing Social Contact				every two months
Spiritual Sustenance				rarely
Laughter				weekly at best
Tears				every other week
Support				monthly at support group
Respite				none

1. Jennifer Louden, *The Woman's Comfort Book—A Self-Nurturing Guide for Restoring Balance in Your Life*, Harper Collins Publishers, New York, NY, 1992, p.2.

2. Nancy L. Mace, M.A., Peter V. Rabins, M.D., M.P.H., *The 36-Hour Day (Revised Edition)*, The Johns Hopkins University Press, Baltimore, MD, 1991, pp. 225-227.

3. D. Goleman, *Emotional Intelligence,* Bantam Books, October 1995, p.ix.

Chapter 9:
Letting Go

Alzheimer's is a fluid, flexible process. It is also a process over which we have little control. So learning to "go with the flow " makes a certain amount of sense. And "going with the flow" often translates into "letting go." However, I must be honest about the fact that I did not want to let go much of the time. I often struggled to hold on. But when all was said and done, since I couldn't beat 'em I joined 'em and learned to let go.

The love of letting go

There were times when the best way I could show love was to let go. This love could be directed at me, my mother or at others. Regardless of who was the object of my love, the idea that letting go could be more loving than not letting go, was fairly new to me. Except with children who were spreading their wings, until that point in my life, letting go was not the typical way I showed love. But letting go became the most important way for me to show love to my mother and at times to myself. For we were bound and jailed by her Alzheimer's. And as it progressed, the truest most courageous act of love I could offer was freeing her.

It took me time to realize and accept that there were things I could control and things I couldn't. Once I did, I saved others and myself a lot of grief. The motivations and dynamics of large families are complex to say the least. The workings of institutions are also complex and the individuals with whom one comes into contact through Alzheimer's are varied, but all are human.

The grief and anger of Alzheimer's disease can be huge and horrific. In order to survive, I finally decided to concentrate on the things I could control, like my own behaviors, self-care, courtesy in dealing with others, and loving my mother. Once I learned this, I found I was better positioned to conserve my energy for the more important things like learning ways to be in relationship with my mother that preserved her dignity and actually strengthened love. I let go of anger at others who wouldn't or couldn't help.

In essence, letting go is about control. There were times when I felt I had no control. At times I felt I had complete control. Regardless of how I *felt and what I thought,* I either had control or I didn't. It wasn't until I accepted that I had control over some things and none over others that I began to understand the Serenity Prayer.

I had an attitude about this prayer because of the ways that some people had been spouting it. The frequency and vehemence with which they preached it was a total turn off to me. At some point, in order to survive, I made a commitment to trying to live the Serenity Prayer. It was then that I was both humbled and excited.

I also started a double list, on the left side of the page were things I could control, on the right things I couldn't. My serenity list helped me set priorities and use energy that was in all too short supply wisely. It wasn't easy but it was worth the effort for it helped me do what was right for my mother and started me on the road to self-care.

> *God grant me the serenity to accept the*
> *things I cannot change,*
>
> *the courage to change the things I can,*
>
> *and the wisdom to know the difference.*

Serenity List	
Things I Can Control	*Things I Can't Control*

One day the wife of an older gentleman who had fixed some chairs for me answered the phone when I called. When I explained that I wanted him to look at the top of a dresser I had damaged with a hot iron, Sarah said she didn't think Nick could help. After a bit of conversation, I convinced her to bring him over anyway. Sarah had to leave the room when Nick began to lovingly stroke the top of the dresser. He had been a skilled craftsman who did magical things with wood. But he no longer had the language to tell me what to do. However, he spoke so eloquently with his hands that it really didn't matter, at least to me.

When Nick fell asleep on the couch, Sarah and I went outside where she broke down as she told me the tale of his decline. We spoke of living wills and health care proxies and whether or not his guns should be removed from the house. By the time Nick awoke, Sarah had gathered herself together again. Nick gave me a big hug as they left my yard for the last time.

As I went inside, I remembered the first time Nick had come to my house. He stopped short in front of my fireplace recognizing it as one he had helped build when he was eighteen. I later found out from Sarah that it had been fifty-three years earlier. The fireplace was built of beautiful stones smoothed to perfection by the sands of time on a Cape Cod beach. I felt blessed each time I enjoyed this spectacular effort of such a sweet, talented man. Nick was eventually spared the full journey through Alzheimer's by an intervening cancer. I often remember with fondness the day I spent in his cellar as he fashioned a piece of oak into a heart-shaped frame to enclose a valentine poem I had written for my husband.

Another story of letting go was told at a support group by Kathryn who had finally unpacked her dad's tools, which had sat in the basement of her home for over two years. She found the experience comforting. To be able to hold the tools with which he had made such wonderful things allowed her to let go in some ways and stay connected in others. She spoke of adding pictures of tools and the things he had made with them to his memory book which they often looked at together.

The gifts of letting go

As my mother declined, she became more and more like a puzzle with missing pieces. And as the years passed and her Alzheimer's whittled away at her, I felt more and more like a puzzler attempting to puzzle without the picture. I wasn't willing to put the pieces back in the box and walk away, yet I didn't know what she or we would be in the end. A significant challenge of this ever changing puzzle was letting go. I found that in letting go, I discovered gifts I would never have expected.

There were many gifts of letting go. Tears made space for laughter, releasing anger made space for love and releasing sadness made space for joy. Letting go of the crushing responsibilities and old expectations when I was with her, allowed me to appreciate this softer, less defended mother. As we let go of our roles and learned to be together in this strange new place called a nursing home I found a wonderfully simple and loving woman who was more affectionate, more free with praise and better able to appreciate a kind word, and loving touch. It slowed me down for I knew we couldn't go any faster or be "productive" and accomplish tasks. We were forced simply to be.

Gifts I never expected

Everyone who deals with Alzheimer's disease must let go at many points and levels. What is difficult for one person may be less or more difficult for another. For me, what mattered as much as the actual things I let go was the process. I found that my acceptance of the process made letting go easier. Strangely enough, at times, I was even happy to let go, and sometimes, I was even happy, albeit in a sad sort of way, about what came next.

When my mother's understanding of her losses diminished, then finally disappeared, I was able to relax about being questioned by her about money. The transition from one wing to the next, like the emptying of her condominium, was something I had dreaded. Yet, when these events were completed I found myself in a state of acceptance and peace. We had negotiated another phase in the process lovingly and in my mother's best interest. She was better off and so were her children since moving to the wing where the staff was particularly good at caring for those who had advanced further into Alzheimer's.

For me, letting go was a process rather than single acts at discreet points in time. Along the road of letting go, I slipped back almost as often as I moved forward. But, once I accepted letting go as a bidirectional process I relaxed a bit and let it happen. There were many things I released; the traditions of a lifetime, ways of relating, and things I had counted on for years.

In many ways, I was letting go of the first and perhaps strongest foundation of my life—my well mother. I was not eager to let her go. Oftentimes I was not graceful in my letting go—particularly at the beginning. I often railed against the circumstances and changes that required it. But let go I did. I had to. And while letting go was more like an uncomfortable ride through a nasty, humid mosquito ridden swamp than a meander through a lovely summer garden, there were thrills to be had and lessons to be learned.

❤

I found a need to define my criteria for letting go. First and foremost, I learned to evaluate whether or not letting go was appropriate, timely, and healthy for me and for my mother. Over time it became clear to me that there were things that I chose not to let go. There were times when I chose to hold on.

Although some tried to convince me that my mother was no longer present, my own experience told me she was. Her emotions were intact to the end and when I was able to read and interpret them correctly we had real and meaningful communication. The more of these moments we experienced, the more I began to trust and nurture the ongoing connection between us and reconfirm my decision to remain committed to her care. Of course the enormous emotion between mother and child still keeps me holding on in some ways. A certain amount of holding on is healthy. Perhaps it was my inner wisdom all along that caused me to fight letting go of certain things.

A commitment to conscious caregiving

If a caregiver is even semi-conscious, the pain raised by Alzheimer's cannot be denied. Many people believe that to experience life fully, you must feel all emotions. For example, you must have pain in order to feel joy. But I did not know if I had the wherewithal to face the pain of Alzheimer's. I did not know if I was strong enough, or had faith enough, or was courageous enough to face loss after loss. Yet I knew that I had to find the resources to feel my painful emotions if I was going to make the best decisions for my mother, and, to come out in one piece myself.

So I committed myself to becoming a conscious Alzheimer's caregiver. Conscious caregiving had many components:

- ❤ Feeling all emotions
- ❤ Finding supports to deal with painful emotions

- ❤ Developing healthy ways of expressing those emotions
- ❤ Focusing on myself and my own felt experience
- ❤ Deciding to stay for the long haul
- ❤ Taking the process one step at a time
- ❤ Welcoming and honoring my tears
- ❤ Being gentle with myself

Periodically I wondered whether it was worth it to engage myself fully, and to what extent it was healthy. I found that I needed to recommit to the continuation of the painful process of conscious caregiving. Recommitment was most difficult in the darkest of times. The times when I was overwhelmed with the weight of grief and the burden of responsibility and duty were crushing.

I often wondered whether fully engaging was the only way to come out whole at the other end. I wondered how I could take one more step on this journey and where I would end up when it was over. More and more as time went on, my coping went from *day by day* to *hour by hour* to *minute by minute*. Finally, I had to release my judgments about myself and my coping abilities and strategies. I had to accept the fact that I could not always be strong.

I am a fighter. It is not easy for me to surrender. But this Alzheimer's thing was too big to handle well all the time, and it was too big to handle alone. In fact, there were times when it was too big to handle at all. As I let go of my pre-Alzheimer's self, I realized that it was OK to fall apart now and again, and that falling apart was not the same as having a nervous breakdown, or going round the bend for good. I also realized that confusion and grief came with the territory.

I had the benefit of the wise words of a school nurse I had met at my first professional job. Her words kept me sane as I struggled through the enormous grief over the death of my father. Sue said to me at his wake, "You are young and inexperienced with the loss of a parent, so I want you to know that your thoughts and feelings might seem crazy. But feeling crazy is normal at a time like this—it's called grief." Her words came back to give me an edge in dealing with the omnipresent, monstrous grief of Alzheimer's.

Letting go required courage. And it required faith and hope. But faith, hope and courage were in short supply more often than they were in abundance.

It seems to me that "just let go" has become a stock answer, a pat phrase that is used to avoid having to think, talk, feel or listen to others discuss certain situations and difficulties that arise in life. This phenomenon isolates Alzheimer's caregivers when isolation is the last thing they need. It often seems to be issued as a command or instruction, albeit sometimes in the guise of a wise bit of advice. Jon Kabat-Zinn has noticed this phenomenon too.

> The phrase "letting go" has to be high in the running for New Age cliché of the century. It is overused, abused daily. Yet it is such a powerful inward maneuver that it merits looking into, cliché or no. There is something vitally important to be learned from the practice of letting go.[1]

It disturbs me when I hear people in support groups apologize for their angst and anguish saying, "I know I just have to let go." Few of the situations and feelings to which this refers are simple. And situations and feelings *must be processed before they can be released.* The issues and emotions that accompany Alzheimer's disease are often foreign, and usually difficult and painful. Unless the difficult and painful parts of the disease are recognized, felt and processed, they cannot truly be let go. If they are not processed and let go, they can and will hang around, under the surface, wreaking havoc in the future. Unfortunately, there are no shortcuts.

So rather than telling caregivers to "let go," they may be better served by validating their difficult situation and feelings. They need to be *supported through processing* their feelings so they can truly start the sometimes iterative process of letting go which is often more akin to peeling an onion—one layer at a time. Sometimes this may mean letting go *temporarily* while one regroups and finds the strength and time to complete the process.

This does not mean that there weren't times when I had difficulty letting go when it was appropriate to let go. There were, but there were many more times when I was urged to let go when it was neither appropriate nor healthy, and I have seen countless others in the same situation. So it is important to assess the reason for the "advice" to let go. Is it offered as a gentle, loving aid to shift you to a better place? Or is it a bullying, judgmental comment by someone who is afraid of the depth of your emotion and the magnitude of the caregiving process in which you are engaged? Or is it really the person's defense mechanism or spoken by someone who pushes away that which they find uncomfortable?

In order to let go and finally reach acceptance, I had to dance with denial. For instance, I denied that my mother was no longer able to host holidays until my sister arrived at our mother's house on a Thanksgiving eve to find a can of cranberry sauce, a few potatoes and a box of squash. The fact that thirteen of us would arrive at my mother's house for dinner in less than eighteen hours made it eminently clear that my denial of her decline was no longer possible. My sister, the Matriarch-in-training spun into a flurry of activity to be sure Mom's "memory lapse" would not ruin Thanksgiving.

Out of this surrendering of denial came acceptance that things must change. No matter how much I ranted about it, or how creatively I railed against it, it was the way it was. My mother was different, and her children were different as a result, and none of us could do anything to change that. However, that didn't mean we were unable to do anything *about it*. In fact we learned in creative and sometimes funny ways that we could do something about these sad changes, and though we struggled to let go of the old, and faltered on our search for the new, we did it. It wasn't smooth, it wasn't pretty, it wasn't pain free, but it was possible. We were up to the challenges and accepted them along the journey of learning to let go.

Investing in divestiture

Equally important to letting go was accepting and investing in my changing mother. For to do what I had to do, I needed to become attached to the new mother who was replacing the old. This presented many challenges. If I hadn't become invested in my new mother, I wouldn't have been able to continue in the role of caregiver for such an extended period of time. The divestiture part of this process was letting go of my well mother. I couldn't invest in the new until I had divested myself of the old.

Several years into the journey, I wrote a poem about not remembering my well mother so I could stay involved with my Alzheimer's mother. I noted that it wasn't that I *couldn't* remember, sometimes I could. It was more that it was too confusing and too difficult to remember, for holding both mothers in the same emotional and cognitive space would have been overwhelming. It would have been too crowded. At some level, I also think it would have required a grieving so heavy that I would have been rendered unable to function effectively as a caregiver and unable to love my new mother.

I had to make room for the new mother. I was told by a professional mover during a discussion about how to pack my belongings that I had to purge. This meant it was time to clear out the closets of my old home and get rid of what I would no longer need. Throughout the Alzheimer's journey, I cleared the spaces of my heart and mind so I could make room for what I would need on the journey ahead. It was a process, with many fitful starts and stops. But if I hadn't been willing to negotiate the clearing out process, I would have smothered and buried myself trying to add the new.

❤

A counselor once explained to me that dissociation, like denial, can be a healthy coping strategy. I had always thought of dissociating as negative and counter-productive; but she explained it in a way that is similar to how I understand denial. Both dissociation and denial provide *initial* protection from situations so that the person can deal with the issues when they are in a better state of mind and heart to do so. This aids in controlling emotion and gathering the necessary internal resources to complete tasks and face realities, and this can be a prerequisite to ultimate acceptance of the changing landscape of one's life and all that leads up to it.

Although I got stuck at times, I never remained stuck. It is when people become or remain stuck in dissociation or denial that these coping mechanisms become unhealthy and problematic. I think it was dissociation that allowed me to distance myself enough to attend and hear what was being said in team meetings. This is not to say that I was not emotionally involved, it was more a matter of putting the emotion aside, for a time, so that I could be effective in gathering the information I needed and then in making tough decisions.

❤

It took me a while to figure out that I continued many activities beyond my mother's ability to enjoy or even care about them. These things I did for me, not her. Of course that was a startling revelation to me and one I wish I could have skipped. This was true of so many situations throughout the journey that I finally came to accept them as an integral part of Alzheimer's caregiving.

So, with many things I did not let go until *I* was ready. Continuing things that were for me, rather than for my mother, were indulgences I allowed myself until it became harmful or uncomfortable for her. Some were conscious at the time, others less so. Most were hard, and through the process of letting go, I protected myself when I could. When I couldn't protect myself from Alzheimer's striking blows, I learned to go back to heal myself.

After a while, it became almost impossible to buy gifts for my mother. She didn't notice or appreciate the concept, and she no longer needed anything—except of course our protection, advocacy and love.

For many years, though, I continued the charade of gift giving because I needed it. We continued this long beyond the point in time where she could appreciate any of it.

There was one situation that I am grateful I insisted upon. It was the year I told each of my siblings that they should get their requests to Santa soon since this Christmas would be the last year he'd be delivering to us. (Along with my other duties as my mother's surrogate, I had assumed the role of Santa.)

Being a lifelong Massachusetts Democrat and a staunch Kennedy fan, my mother had come with me when I bought a Kennedy rocker for my husband several years earlier. My request to Santa was for a matching chair. I found the Kennedy Rocker at a great price near our home on Cape Cod. Since my mother was almost a hundred miles away in the nursing home, and we had given up trying to get her to the Cape, I asked my husband to bring the chair to the nursing home. He thought this thoroughly ridiculous but grudgingly agreed after I told him that it would be impossible for her to understand the gift if she wasn't looking at it. He lugged the chair into her room in the nursing home where together they put a big red bow on it. Even my husband agreed that my mother's smile at her gift was well worth his extra effort.

♥

As with so many other things, my mother helped me learn to let go. At more than one point during her struggles to maintain her independence, she would say to me, "Well, honey, you can't fight City Hall." These words took on the scepter of graceful surrender rather than ignoble defeat. She went with dignity from one step to the next. Dignity was in her courageous battles, and sometimes less than easy surrenders. Self-respect was in her long-held right to voice her feelings and opinions, declining though they were. And dignity was in my mother's final surrender of the beauty of her body to the beauty of her spirit, which shone ever more brightly as her physical beauty faded. My letting go seemed to me less noble, and less dignified than hers.

♥

As my mother changed, her relationships changed. The loss of her ability to act as my mother was incredibly difficult and painful for me. While some of the changes were gradual, others were less so. Her determination to "beat this thing" had hidden deficits for a long time. Eventually, those deficits were revealed as her Alzheimer's marched relentlessly on. But despite this, in some ways, my mother never stopped being my mother.

The changes in her initiated my quest for ways to make her feel useful, needed, and loved. Although I acknowledged her anger at not being productive, I worked hard to show her that productivity was not the basis of our relationship. Even though I secretly grieved the loss of her counsel and wisdom and so many other parts of her, I eventually let them go. Much to my amazement, I found that there was much left as we learned new ways of being with each other.

The move from words and body hugs to heart-speak and eye hugs was incredibly poignant and loving. As the brilliance of my mother's spirit shone through eyes held captive in a ravaged body, I was awe struck, not only that love remained, but that it seemed so much more powerful, almost pure.

What Made My Mother My Mother?

What was the essence of my mother and what made her my mother? Obviously, the fact that she carried me in her womb for nine months and we shared genetics made her my mother. Certainly some of it was how she looked, felt, spoke and thought. The shared history and traditions of my lifetime and the fact that she raised me made her my mother along with how she laughed and cried and mothered her five children. Her reactions to experiences and how she chose to comment on them to me, her child, are a part of what made her my mother.

Although I had trouble finding language to describe it, the connection between us remained intact. In some ways it actually strengthened. I am still astounded that, although her physical beauty was devastated, although her teeth were gone, and her hair un-set for years, my mother remained beautiful to me. Her eyes spoke volumes. Her apparently meaningless body movements were expressive to me.

They told of a presence, something more than met the eye, but it was too elusive for me to touch or hold or describe. Surely part of it was love, but it went far deeper even than love. It was a connection I have not yet released and may never release (although I did not feel it immediately after her death). Perhaps I just don't want to, or am not yet ready. Perhaps I will never let it go. Recently, it seems changed. I feel I have integrated her—my mother's spirit seems now to be a part of me.

Since my journey I have come to believe that as my mother's defenses, which were constructed over a lifetime, weakened and eventually disappeared altogether, my defenses followed suit, at least when I was with her. Relinquishing our defenses left us free to invite and welcome our spirits, to be together through them, on their plane.

It was as though we had transcended the limits of our bodies when her ability to communicate in ordinary ways disappeared. The connection I felt with my mother was not of the physical realm. It was not something I would have sought had other avenues of connection not been removed. In some strange way, this was the ecstasy I found through the agony of Alzheimer's, although I did not view it as such until after the journey had ended. How strange to find this precious connection through the dreaded Alzheimer's!

It was as though we had scaled a mountain, all but the top of which had been under the cover of clouds. As we reached the top, the brilliance of the sun reflected through us, freeing our spirits. The climb had exhausted our need to protect our fragile selves. Reaching the summit through the decline of my mother's body, her spirit was freed. She made a gift of that spirit to me, soothing and comforting my grief by inviting *my* spirit to touch *hers*. By accepting her invitation, we created and experienced unconditional love.

My ability to respond to my mother's spirit seemed to calm and reassure her. It did the same for me. This 'spirit' connection, so deep it could not possibly have been held in the meager dimensions of a body, is what bound us.

Perhaps we have been together in other lifetimes. Perhaps our connection was too strong to be broken by mere bodily disease. Perhaps it was why we were put on earth. I don't know. All that matters is that for us there was something left when all else seemed to be gone. It was love.

That love is with me still. And though my mother's spirit has moved on, her love is always with me; a love that has lit some very dark pathways indeed, even since her death. It guides me still. If I can stay open to it, I'm sure it always will.

By seeking, welcoming and by accepting my mother's spirit, despite the deplorable and deteriorating condition of her body, the possibility existed for us to remain in relationship, to continue to love, to heal. And sometimes still, albeit faintly, I sense my mother's presence—her essence—her spirit. And when I can be open, gently present but separate, she seems to stay, *freely present*, neither grabbed nor held, for that, it seems, is antithetical to the very nature of spirit.

Perhaps my mother gained, or in the end finally showed, an inner quality of life which had been overshadowed by her physical beauty, only to be revealed when she lost her more visible or "outer" quality of life to Alzheimer's.

Alzheimer's patients need love right to their dying breath. They are entitled to dignity and compassion. Maybe, when all is said and done, quality of life is directly related to, or perhaps the same as, quality of love.

❤

A former backdoor neighbor told me a funny story almost a year before my mother's death. Tom was in his yard when he spied an older woman walking purposefully up his driveway. When he asked if he could help her, he was met with a none too friendly, "No thank you."

When he pressed further, the woman said, "I'm going to tend my daughter's roses."

My mother had been unable to drive to my house for several months preceding this encounter, but apparently, on this particular day, she was determined to find it, even if on foot. The only problem was that I no longer lived there. But—my mother loved roses.

At my mother's condominium complex, plantings were not allowed, but that did not stop her from asking us to give her two of her favorite rose bushes for Mother's Day. My godson John, who was also my mother's oldest grandchild, planted them.

When she left her home, I took my mother's roses to my yard. When I moved out of my own home shortly thereafter, one of the rose bushes moved with me. When I returned seven years later, the rosebush that had been too weak to move was nowhere to be found. But the following spring, I found and moved a rose bush that bloomed to beat the band. It was my mother's, the one we had left for dead several years before.

Because of my mother's great love and our shared connection with roses, I frequently stopped on the way to the nursing home for a rose. My mother still loved them, and even after she became nonverbal, she would light up when she saw the rose and sigh and breathe deeply when I held it to her nose for her to smell. The evening she tried to eat rather than smell the rose, I let go of roses.

❤

When I was getting married, my mother shopped for my wedding dress. Except for the one shopping trip to a bridal shop to which I had reluctantly agreed, she brought dresses home for me to try on. This compromise was reached because she did not approve of the dress I had bought just before we announced our engagement. My mother said the dress was too informal and would be a mass of wrinkles before we even got to the church. The arrangement worked well for us since I hated shopping and my mother loved it.

My mother finally found a wedding dress we were both happy with at Filene's Basement. Filene's Basement was the place where quality clothing from Filene's Department store went on sale, with a scheme for further reductions based on the time the item was in the basement. When my father's business associates came to Boston, my mother took their wives to "the basement." She was thrilled to brag to these often wealthy woman of the wedding gown that cost $19.99. And I was relieved that my parents did not spend a fortune on a dress that none of us could afford. On the morning of my wedding, I laughed when my mother lifted it to be sure I did not have cutoffs on underneath.

For the most part, I was pretty good about not getting angry with my mother. But I remember one particularly difficult day in Filene's during the early stages of her Alzheimer's. My mother was going over to the gloves when I told her she had several pairs. What I didn't mention, but was thinking, was that she was also going out less and less. And since I've never had much patience for shopping, I was predictably impatient to leave. My mother whirled toward me and yelled, "I'm a shopper. I have always been a shopper and I am not stopping now." My aunt shooed me away so she could help my mother select a pair of gloves she didn't need (and never wore). It was the last time I went into a store with my mother.

❤

The process of breaking up my mother's home was difficult, but this letting go was softened for me. The fact that my mother herself began to give her things to each of her children accustomed us to finding bits and pieces of our childhood home in each other's homes. It still warms my heart to walk into one of my brother's or sister's homes and see things from our childhood. By the time our mother died, there was really nothing of that home that had not been scattered to the five corners of her children's hearths and hearts. This was one painful post-death task we did not have to face.

❤

Home is where the heart is. For my parents, most of my siblings and for my husband and me, home was Cape Cod. The Cape was the place my parents took their first four kids and another couple for vacations, eight of us staying in a two room cottage. In time, my husband and I moved to the Cape.

Cape Cod is an island connected to the mainland by two bridges. Going over the bridge is a wonderful experience for those of us who can't seem to get "the sand out of our shoes." Shortly after my mother entered the nursing home, my husband and I decided to take her home—to the Cape. Since she talked of it often we thought she understood what and where Cape Cod was. But an hour into the two hour drive, she started to ask when we were going home. We were further confused when she talked of the nice day we had just spent on the Cape. Clearly, she did not understand what we thought she did. As her confabulations about the nice day on the Cape broke our hearts, we turned around and brought her back to the nursing home.

A year and a half later I wanted to bring my mother to see our new home. My husband was discouraging as he asked me how she would get upstairs to see the distant view of Cape Cod Bay, and who would change her diapers, and how we would manage her for two hours in the car. Upon hearing of this conversation, our new neighbors offered their help. Finally, although he thought it a big mistake, my husband agreed on one condition—that both of my sisters approved. That was the end of the trip to the Cape.

Cape Cod was just one more lost memory for my mother. Her Alzheimer's had robbed her of the place she loved most in the world. She could no longer go home and I finally accepted the fact that Cape Cod was our home now, but not hers. My mother's home had shrunk to a few hundred square feet, a hundred miles off Cape, in a nursing home.

❤

Although I had agreed to my mother's command not to cry until her death, I certainly was not able to honor it. However, I did respect what I later realized was her wish not to express my grief and

sadness in front of her and I did that faithfully except for one particular night.

I was upset and overwhelmed before I even got to the nursing
home when long-time nurse Gretta came in to see how we were
doing. Because I was so vulnerable to begin with, and because
Gretta was a trusted confidant, I "let it all hang out."

I was on the left side of my mother's bed talking to Gretta who
was on my mother's right. I was expressing anger and exhaustion at
the whole situation. I was struggling with ambivalence about my
mother's wishes and my own difficulty in letting her go.

In tears, I finally said to Gretta, "I feel like Katy!! (Gretta's four
year old). She's the mother, I'm the kid here! And I need to hear it
one more time. I need her to sit up and tell me again what I'm supposed to do. I can't do it alone!"

Gretta was listening with her usual calm, caring smile when she
was called out of the room. At that moment, as I moved to my
mother's "good side" I thought to myself, "Oh boy, I'm really going to
get it now," but when I got around and looked down, my mother
hugged me with her eyes. She was non-verbal and unable to move
but she was still in there and aware, at least at that moment, of me
and my needs!

Fully in character, my mother did, as she had always done, all she
could for me, her child. Somehow, it was enough. And to this day I
can feel my mother's compassion and love through that eye hug.

Holidays

Holidays are emotional times, which invariably raise memories of
times gone by, and they are particularly emotion-packed for Alzheimer's families. During the holidays, patients are faced with confusing situations that are often beyond their ability to handle, yet their
families are often reluctant to relinquish traditions that have been
with them for a lifetime. But eventually, traditions must change in
order to accommodate the Alzheimer patient. Many cling to old
ways of celebrating beyond the time when they are appropriate for
the patient. Eventually, even the accommodations families make to
include their loved ones in holidays simply stop working. While this
is sad and painful, it can also be healing and assist families in getting
on with their lives.

I was thrilled this Thanksgiving to hear my friend Alice's response to my query about her holiday.

"It was great." Alice gushed. "The best in years. There were twelve of us. We had a wonderful, relaxing time."

When I asked about her mother, Alice said she had visited her at the nursing home Thanksgiving morning and had a good visit, and on the way out, her mother's primary nurse June said, "Boy, have you come a long way!"

June was right. Alice had turned a corner; she was finally able to spend her holidays with family and friends without dragging her Mom from the place she felt safe—her small, secure world in the nursing home. Together we marveled at and rejoiced in Alice's latest letting go.

❤

Holidays were celebrated lavishly and loudly in the large Callahan family. Always presiding over these celebrations was the Irish Matriarch, my mother. The onset of Alzheimer's changed things irrevocably. These were difficult transitions for all of us. The letting go was eased by new plans but sometimes these backfired. It was extremely painful to let go of a tradition of happy memories. But let go we did as old traditions made way for new.

❤

My husband and I had our own special tradition with my mother. On December 23, the three of us went to dinner in the fancy restaurant of her choice. A few days before one of these wonderful celebrations, my mother had told me she had bought all of her presents. "All we have to do," my mother told me, "is wrap them."

She arrived looking like a million bucks, hair coifed, beautiful dress covered by her shiny mink jacket, and eyes radiant. I was shocked to find the car empty. But we spent a wonderful evening in a beautiful restaurant overlooking the lights of the city. The light snow made a magical evening even more memorable as we sat in the mahogany bar listening to my mother's stories of the days she met with her young friends there.

The next day my mother was as excited, fidgety and over-tired as a five-year old. As she bounced on our couch asking whether Santa Claus would come down our Chinese red chimney onto the blue tile hearth, my husband gently laid her down telling her she must close her eyes and nap. The phone woke her thirty minutes later. It was my sister saying her kids had been exposed to chickenpox and there was concern about the older people getting shingles. At that my mother became furious and insisted that she would spend Christmas with her grandchildren!

My husband went to the porch to get wood for the fire. When he came in, he told my mother that she might want to reconsider since phone contact seemed to have given him the shingles. When he lifted his shirt to reveal a stomach full of house shingles he had taken from the wood box we laughed so hard I thought we would die. The pall was broken as we giggled gleefully through the laborious process of showering, dressing and leaving for church.

In church, after the pageant brilliantly executed by the young parishioners, the priest came down from the altar and explained that the children would now find their families. As he told the shepherds to find their folks, a whirlwind of sheets and freshly scrubbed freckled faces flew around the church. Angels and kings were followed by the rest of the young actors. Shortly after the mass started my mother leaned over and told me it was time to go so she could "get into something dry." She was not to be dissuaded. We left, but the car was blocked by the chariots of other worshippers so we spent the next forty minutes repeatedly trying to explain to her why we weren't moving.

The following Christmas my sisters decided it was no longer appropriate to take our mother home. I was crushed and decided to have brunch at my house on Christmas day. My younger sister agreed to bring her family and pick up our mother on the way. My mother was unhappy and asking none too nicely, "It's Christmas isn't it? What's with the eggs? Where's the turkey, where's the roast, where's the ham?" She left with John, my godson and his brothers to go to their house where an appropriate Christmas feast was served. It was my mother's last holiday away from the nursing home.

For the rest of my mother's life, I continued to go to the nursing home at Christmas. Through most of these years, my mother didn't know it was Christmas. But almost until the end I insisted on going through the motions, bringing in a nativity scene and exchanging gifts. I always brought two outfits up to the nursing home the week before Christmas so my mother would look nice when the family came by. In 1990, I bought a royal blue jump suit for Christmas Day. When we arrived at the nursing home on Christmas morning, we were met by a woman in a wheelchair, telling us to call the police because she had been raped. After several deep breaths we climbed the stairs hoping for a better reception. Upon arrival, we saw the royal blue suit being wheeled by on another resident. I never did see it on my mother.

But even that visit was not all bad. Earlier in the week, we had bought a set of Santa Mugs as a gift for my sister and her husband. When I took a set for us, my husband returned them to the shelf saying we were way over budget. As we stood at my mother's bed on Christmas morning, my husband handed me my mother's gift to us. It was the two Santa mugs, which amazingly she seemed to recognize. Perhaps it was simply the joy on my face at such a wonderful gift that was familiar to her.

The first year my mother was in the nursing home, I found wonderful support in time spent with the activities director. Two evenings a week my mother and I went downstairs to "help" Heather get ready for the Holiday Fair. During those visits, I watched how Heather gently handled my mother's increasing confusion, and I learned new ways that love could be shared during a new and different preparation process for the holiday season. To this day, I cherish the bowl with the lobster molded into the cover that my mother took off the shelf one evening and presented to me as my "first gift" of the season. I also cherish the snowman broom she bought for me at our first nursing home holiday fair. I remember the pride with which she surveyed our donation to the fair's raffle labeled "Rita Callahan and family." We continued that tradition until she died.

❤

Since we lived so far away from the nursing home, I was able to let go of Mother's Day with less upset than I think I would have had if I was closer. A gift for Mother's Day was another matter altogether. The year we bought the new house I came up with a creative solution. Since there was a full three quarter acre lot to be sculpted and planted, I decided to buy a special bush for my mother each year which I planted in my new yard. I kept her apprised of this new twist to our Mother's Day celebration, and in the early years, she actually seemed to understand and be pleased. It was a way of honoring her as my mother and making her a part of my new home. When the house sold several years later, the family who bought it graciously told me I could come back for those plantings at any point in the future.

When she was first in the nursing home, my mother was concerned and verbal about her gifts to those she loved. By the time her first two grandchildren were graduating from high school she was non-verbal. But I brought graduation cards that I read to her and told her of the checks to be enclosed. Forgetting for a moment just how far she had descended into her disease, I asked the nurse if she thought my mother could sign the cards. The nurse said it was worth a try so we tried. I had to buy new cards because I thought her scribbles would upset the kids. But it was still worth trying, for seeing the results first hand helped me to let go of yet one more piece of my mother. These were the last gifts from my mother to those she loved so long, so well, so much—her family.

Wisdom from Within

The criteria by which professional caregivers, friends, family members and others measured my decisions were at times too loud, drowning my inner wisdom, my emotional intelligence and my "well mother's" ever more distant voice. In time, I learned to retreat from the maddening crowd and seek solace and wisdom within. This was a critical letting go for me.

Monday morning quarterbacks should be placed where they belong—outside the game, unheard, unseen, out of the play where their blithe, judgmental jargon cannot drain energy, raise doubt and cloud issues for caregivers. That is not to say that input is not valuable; in fact, I found input critical and imperative. That is not to say that motives and options and consequences should not be considered. They must be considered. But the motivation of the person who questions, aids and supports decision-making as a process must be to facilitate and work with the decision maker, not to act as judge and jury. Review of past decisions can be helpful, but the review must be constructive and objective, not a forum for others who were not involved or less involved to vent their frustration, guilt, grief, and anger. Unfortunately, the latter is all too often the reality.

There are those for whom the difficulties of the Alzheimer's caregiver are, apparently, crystal clear and infinitely simple. They seem, miraculously, to have all the answers. For them, the path is clear and straight. When such people offered advice they made things sound so simple. Those who truly face and deal with the issues of Alzheimer's know that Alzheimer's is not simple. Sometimes, however, because I was so exhausted, or because they were so persuasive or just plain loud, I forgot what I knew, disregarded my own inner wisdom, and fell prey to their toxic advice.

I remember one particular instance when a member of the extended family was giving one of my sisters a hard time about my mother's placement in a nursing home. To this person, who saw my mother infrequently, and only for a short time, our decision was ridiculous. I watched in horror as she shared her infinite wisdom which sent my sister into a tailspin of guilt and questioning that we all could have done without.

Such behaviors and input sometimes resulted in increasing my own doubt. At times I questioned my mother's decision for me to make decisions for her. I doubted my ability to do so well. I doubted the hard lessons I had learned over my tenure as a caregiver. Being battered by the rhetoric of someone who had no business in the affairs of my mother and her family did not, of course, make any of my doubts true. Sometimes, toxic advice resulting in my doubt came from within the family or from professional caregivers. This was even more damaging because I thought it so important to include family as much as possible in decision making and I needed to trust the professional caregivers to whom I looked for guidance.

However, there came a time when I had to shut out *all* unproductive input in order to survive. Occasionally this meant letting go of the decision I had made early on to seek input from all family members. The rest of the time, it meant letting go of those who were simply not helpful. Their oversimplification or pontificating about what and how things should be done was too draining. It was through these experiences of letting go that my strength was sorely tested.

What I needed most at times like these was to rediscover my own wisdom and find once again the faith that my mother's decisions and her children's decisions on her behalf were correct and in her best interests. My heart and spirit knew, at some deep level, that my motivation was love. But when I forgot that, it was courageous family members whose only agenda was my mother's best interests, or those special professional caregivers with whom we were blessed, who set me back on track.

Practice Makes Perfect

My eventual release of my mother in her *role* as my mother enabled me to slowly accept this new, smaller in stature, less controlling woman. Though I longed for my old mother, I found much to love about the new.

When I lost my temper or got so frustrated I thought I would scream, I remembered that nothing would be accomplished by pushing my mother into a catastrophic reaction or having to see the hurt on her face. It was at times like these that I got to practice surrender. Reaching to hug her or putting an arm around her offered a way to transform potential moments of hurt, or anger, to love. Although she couldn't share her wisdom through words, my mother shared it in non-verbal ways.

It would have been a shame to let go of my mother too early. I can imagine her saying what James Thomas said as reported in *The Loss of Self*:

> I am hungry for the life that is being taken away from me. I am a human being. I still exist. I have a family. I hunger for friendship, happiness, and the touch of a loved hand. What I ask for is that what is left of my life shall have some meaning. Give me something to die for! Help me to be strong and free until my self no longer exists.[2]

Letting go was a skill that required practice and support. I found that information and understanding the parameters and options of a situation greatly aided in the process I went through when letting go. I got better at it as time went on.

Although I was more ready for the ultimate letting go, when it came it was not easy. Like so many other things in this journey, my skill, ability and supports increased along with the increasingly difficult challenges I faced. If they hadn't, my exhaustion would have done me in. Over time, I had reached a point where I was clearly and loudly asking for divine help. I had said, 'Uncle' long ago, and despite my anger and hurt from the early religious abuses, I had to begin my recovery from them. I had to let them go, so I could survive this damnable disease and make decisions that were right and loving for my mother.

❤

My mother was a person who was always perfectly coifed. It was a sense of pride to her and seemed a part of her being. Her striking physical beauty was something her family took for granted, but as she declined her physical beauty faded. This happened for a number of reasons, some over which we had control, others we did not. While each of us reacted differently to these visible losses, we all found them enormously painful. For they forced us to face the less visible destruction raging relentlessly within.

I remember a discussion with my mother's nurses Gretta and Dot at my kitchen table two weeks after we buried my mother. I was upset at how the undertaker had been able to make my mother look like her old self after her death. It brought home to me the depths of her deterioration. I was crying about how awful her hair had looked for so many years.

Two or three years before, Dot and I had talked about the advis-ability of continuing to send my mother to the hairdresser in the basement of the nursing home. Doing so required moving her to a wheelchair, then sending her on the elevator to the beauty parlor so that her hair could be washed, set and dried.

I finally left the decision to Dot, saying it was best that she decide when to stop since it was she who witnessed on a regular basis my mother's reactions and ability to withstand these events. Comfort was the bottom line. Within a couple of weeks of this conversation, Dot informed me that, for the sake of comfort, visits to the hair-dresser had stopped.

At that point, we searched for other ways to keep my mother's hair clean and looking somewhat nice. I bought a 'bed shampooer' and hired aides to work on her hair on their off hours, but we were never able to get it right again and I had forgotten how it used to look. This realization hit me hard when later a stranger, the under-taker, made her look so much like my well mother.

As we sat at the table, Dot, in her wisdom, reminded me of our discussions and decision over two years earlier. She said that it would have been unfair to continue putting her through it. It would have been counter to my direction to choose comfort first. By removing the pain of hair-care as we'd known it, we had preserved my mother's comfort and dignity. What a long way I had come. What a painful journey it had been. How blessed I was to have learned to leave some of the decisions to others. How lucky we were to have had "angels" like Dot and Gretta along the way.

❤

One summer, a friend showed me the children's book *Love Me Forever* by Robert Munsch. It is a poignant example of the role reversal I was experiencing. Since I'd seen the book I had wanted to hold my mother, as one cradles a babe in arms. Due to her rigidity and my lack of strength, and because she was so frightened when moved, it was not to be. Somehow through the years, I had become much more protective of her body than I realized.

Because of logistics and because my father's funeral had been held out of my house, we had agreed as a family that my mother's would be out of my sister's house. That meant that my dear friend who is an undertaker would not be handling the arrangements. Although my sister and I had made the funeral arrangements and met the undertaker, it was years before.

My friends in the funeral business are not crazy about it, but the term 'Digga' was the first word I learned for undertaker. It refers to Digby "Digger" O'Dell, the undertaker character played by John Brown on the Life of Riley radio show which first aired in 1941 (I write it as Digga' to accommodate my Boston accent). I have never used or meant it as a form of disrespect. Rather it seemed to be the term that maintained a "safe distance" for me when talking about the disposition of my mother's body.

One night during the following fall, I arrived at the Support Group to find it was the wrong night but Marge, the facilitator, was there. We started to chat and all of a sudden I was talking about something that I had, apparently, been mulling around unconsciously.

In the course of the conversation I said, "I'm not going to let Digga' have her."

"Why not, Sal?" Marge asked.

"Digga' doesn't know her and she's so fragile now," I explained. "No one knows how to handle her except family and the nursing home."

"So what are you going to do with her if you don't let Digga' have her?"

"I'm not sure, but one of us must be strong enough to pick her up."

"Then what?"

"I'm not sure yet but I'll figure it out."

With more of Marge's gentle probing it became clear that I had a couple of issues to work out before my mother's death. We talked for a couple of hours, during which time Marge related the stories of her own parents' deaths.

When I went to leave, we hugged, and Marge said, "Hey Sal—let Digga' have her."

I smiled as I said, "OK."

I had had no idea that was an issue for me but I did one more thing to be sure I would be able to let my mother's body go. That weekend I called my undertaker friend Jed. After his wife and I chatted for a bit about my hesitation, she said I needed to talk to Jed. He and I talked for quite a while about my fears and by the time I hung up, I was OK.

Jed had suggested that I meet with 'Digga' but I no longer needed to talk to him. The night Digga' came for my mother's body, I remember standing at the nurses station thinking to myself, "Digga' knows how to do this, he'll be gentle with her—his father had Alzheimer's."

❤

On December 24, 1993, my nephew, Timothy Patrick, offered to drive me home on his learner's permit. For the next two days, Tim and I clocked well over a hundred miles. Although I drove several hundred miles each week, it had been a while since I had been the supervisory driver and I was freshly amazed at all that goes into what had become second nature to me. On Christmas morning, although I realized he might not be thrilled, I directed Tim to get off at the nursing home exit. Tim went on to tell me that he was angry about the discussion his mother and I had about not giving his grandmother medicine when she "got a cold."

When we got into the day room in which my mother was reclining in her cardiac chair, the woman behind Tim started yelling "I'm dying, I'm dying."

"Great," I thought, "the day the kid decides to come in someone puts on a real show."

On the continuation of our Christmas travels, Tim said he was glad he had gone in. I was surprised because my mother had not been responsive and had looked terrible. And of course, she could not take her piercing gaze, which seemed to me so painfully devoid of recognition, away from Tim's face.

In the language of a teenager he said to me "Although it sucked, Sal, I completely understand your decision not to treat Nan. And I'll be much more comfortable when she dies now that I've seen how she really is. You've made the right decision, that's no way to live."

Timothy Patrick had been nine when my mother left his house for the nursing home. He had been greatly troubled and affected by the tensions of that time. And he sorely missed the special relationship he had with his grandmother. In his own boyish way, Tim had supported my mother in her decline with the fun and love of a child.

And in some strange way, my experience with Tim that day helped me let go too.

♥

Sometime during the last several months of my mother's dying, I found myself practicing letting go. When I felt like going to the nursing home to tell her something, I would force myself to tell her from afar. I'd talk to her out loud as I drove knowing, I guess, that someday she would no longer be in the bed that had been her home for so many years. I practiced believing that she could hear me just as well as if I was beside her. I threw her kisses through the woods when I was near the nursing home and via the moon from my patio on the Cape. This was a transition period for me, this practicing for when she would be gone. It was in preparation for the final letting go. It was practice for the completion of the anticipatory grieving of my mother's long, slow march toward death, her release from Alzheimer's. This strange behavior somehow moved me more gently toward my mother's final transition, toward the end of her life on the earth that we had shared since my birth. ♥

1. Jon Kabat-Zinn, *Wherever You Go There You Are: Mindful Meditation in Everyday Life*, Hyperion, New York, 1994, p.53.

2. Donna Cohen, Ph.D., Carl Eisdorfer, Ph.D., M.D., *The Loss of Self: A Family Resource for the Care of Alzheimer's Disease and Related Disorders*, Plume, New York 1987, p.21.

Chapter 10:
End-stage Decisions

Our society deals with grief by *not* dealing with it. This, combined with judgments about self-determination can result in damaged relationships and treacherous struggles.

As the Alzheimer's patient enters the end-stages of the disease a number of difficult issues arise. Whether the patient is at home or in a long term care facility, family and professional caregivers face many challenges. It is a time when differences in understanding of the patient's wishes, differences within families and differences between family and professional caregivers rise to the surface. If not recognized, named and addressed, these differences can escalate into all-out war.

The length of the Alzheimer's process and the increasing difficulty in maintaining a relationship with the "person" who is no longer "there" is exhausting and wearing. Primary caregiver ambivalence about the patient and the primary caregiver's responsibility for that person is often overwhelming. The caregiver is cast into the position of making life and death decisions in a world of technology that can almost literally sustain "life" indefinitely. It forces the examination of quality of life for another with a cacophony of disparate voices in the media, among friends, associates, and professionals, and within families playing within the background. The strain is enormous, the grieving process protracted. The feeling of duty and responsibility can be crushing.

End-stage issues include, but are not limited to, medical conditions resulting from patient weakening through eating difficulties, skin tears, losses due to becoming non-ambulatory, infections, injuries, and a general decline in the body's systems that sustain life. A host of other conditions and diseases can also arise or worsen such as cancer and heart disease. Whether the Alzheimer's patient's medical problems are the result of Alzheimer's or of a secondary disease, the appropriateness of medical intervention must be faced. Some caregivers are comfortable leaving medical treatment decisions to medical personnel while others feel the need to make such decisions themselves.

Due to my mother's clarity regarding the withholding of medical interventions at the end of life, it would not have been appropriate to give medical personnel final decision-making power regarding her treatment. However, my decisions were guided by medical people including doctors, nurses and at the end, hospice. The advantages of having a long term relationship with my mother's professional caregivers and having already discussed so many of the issues I was facing as a surrogate decision-maker were many. The fact that my mother's children had come to believe that there was little or no quality left to her life made things somewhat easier in one way yet also more difficult, for we were finally having to deal with this enormous grief head-on. Our family history of loss and grief played into our reactions and decision-making process. This, I have come to learn, is a very familiar happening in such situations.

There were a number of painful truths that I had to face in order to come to a place inside myself where I could honor my mother's wishes to be kept comfortable but not to be kept alive, to be allowed (if not helped) to die:

- ❤ My mother could not be cured of her Alzheimer's disease.
- ❤ With excellent care and technological and chemical medical intervention, my mother's body could be kept "alive" almost indefinitely.
- ❤ It would be a struggle to let her go.
- ❤ I might meet with resistance from family and/or professional caregivers no matter what decisions I made.

Facing and accepting these truths was one of the greatest challenges of my journey. It required faith, strength and courage seemingly beyond my capacity. Perhaps most frightening of all, the one to whom I had always looked for faith, strength and courage was fading

fast. She would not be able to remind me of her wishes or assure me
that the decisions I made were right.

I found the need to "search my soul" often during these last several years. This was no small feat given my exhaustion and difficulty
in letting my mother go. I often required help from outside the family to get a different perspective on the issues and how they fit with
my mother's wishes. Although I finally made decisions with which I
am now comfortable, reaching these decisions was not without cost
to me. In fact, when the first hospice team left in February of 1993,
they advised me to stop asking for family input. It was their opinion
that the family meeting had not been constructive, did not improve
my mother's care or the decisions regarding her care, and were too
upsetting to me. While there were times that the cacophony of
voices was overpowering, I still saw the advantage of everyone having
had the opportunity to put in their "two cents." For it was only when
I heard the disagreements, some of which were barraging me in my
own head, that I could finally face the complex difficulties inherent
in Alzheimer's and choose the course of action and treatment that
was best for my mother.

Eating and Feeding Difficulties

The first incident we faced about eating/feeding issues was late in
the winter of 1987, little more than a year after my mother had
entered the nursing home. At that time she had trouble eating and
was put in a small feeding group. I was on vacation at the time.
When I returned my sister and I met with the Director of Nurses.
When asked if we would use a tube to feed her if faced with that, we
answered simultaneously. I said, "No." My sister said, "Yes." This
was the first time we were aware of our difference of opinion about
our mother's treatment. My negative response was due to having
heard how difficult, if not impossible, it was to remove feeding tubes.

We thought we agreed on medical and quality of life issues, yet
when push came to shove, it became clear that our definitions were
different and the timing of certain treatments and withholding of
treatments were not in sync. It was hospice and the priest who
helped me work through most of these discrepancies. I never, at any
point in time, questioned the motivation of my siblings, but I did
think at times that they lacked a full understanding of what certain
decisions would mean in the long term.

The next feeding incident arose in the fall of 1992 after my
mother was hospitalized following a choking incident. She had pre-

viously had problems with swallowing and choking. Thickening agents were considered but not introduced at that time. My sister was quite upset about that hospitalization and started going to the nursing home daily to feed my mother. The nursing home told me that my mother was eating complete meals while my sister told me our mother was spitting the food out. My sister believed our mother did not want to eat but was forced by nursing home staff.

In an effort to clarify the situation I contacted hospice. After bringing in a hospice aide to feed my mother several times a week, the hospice team told us that our mother was not being forced to eat and that she had stabilized to the point where we should discontinue hospice until she required their services again. During this difficult time I found out that some in the family believed that my mother had been force fed from the time she could no longer feed herself. This was a very difficult issue that came up a number of times over the years and eventually led me to write an article on end-stage feeding dilemmas that was accepted for publication in an Alzheimer's professional journal.

In January of 1994, I was asked to feed my mother. Since I was rarely at the nursing home during meals I had difficulty at first. After being shown how by an aide, I found myself pushing the food through my mother's tightly closed lips, cajoling and pleading with her to swallow. It took one hour to get a pile of pureed food, half the size of a child's fist, into her. When relating this experience to hospice, those dreaded words "forced feeding" were uttered.

When the second hospice team used the words "force fed," I was understandably upset. Their raising of the issues was not pejorative in any way and actually clarified my mother's wishes and rights. After two weeks of discussions with hospice they requested a full team meeting at the nursing home to discuss the overall care plan. At that meeting, they raised the feeding issue and suggested that my mother's feeding be altered in the following manner: Each tray would have yogurt or ice cream on it (because she had seemed slightly more interested in the crushed brownie in milk than the rest of the food). If she did not seem interested in the meal, she was to be offered the ice cream or yogurt. If she was not interested in that, feeding was to stop for that meal.

When I spoke to the doctor about the proposed strategy, he supported the plan but noted that it might be difficult to get aides to follow it who were trained to be aggressive in the feeding procedure. However, my mother's nurses were willing to monitor the situation and encourage the aides, particularly after the doctor spoke to each of them. Since it was impractical for the family to be at the nursing home three times a day to feed my mother, we had to rely on the nursing home staff to follow the new feeding protocol. The fact that we had an interdisciplinary team in place was particularly helpful in resolving this emotional issue. Although I was never entirely comfortable with the feeding/eating situation, I realized that we were fairly typical when I read the following:

> When eating difficulties arise, reactions of families tend to be guided by the care setting. If the person with dementia is still cared for at home at this late stage, families are clearly in charge of decisions regarding a feeding strategy. On the other hand, if the demented person is being cared for in an institutional setting, physicians, administrators, and others may feel compelled to pursue aggressive measures for fear of liability. Consequently, the authority of the family may be jeopardized, and a power struggle may ensue between the family and various professions. ...Families need to be apprised of the burdens and benefits of aggressive measures at a formal conference involving an interdisciplinary team. ...Without advance directives from the demented person, helping families to retain their rightful role as surrogate decision makers should be of utmost concern to human service professionals....[1]

Sometimes it seemed as though the decisions I made were based on "non-objective" data. One night I felt compelled to go to the nursing home, thinking en route that there was a reason. I was convinced of that when I walked into my mother's room while she was being fed. I could see her tonsils from the door, three beds away! It was abundantly clear to me that she knew she was being fed and she wanted more food. To me, the fact that my mother exhibited, almost in caricature, that she was, in fact, able to open her mouth, swallow and indicate her desire for more food, reaffirmed my decision to follow the hospice plan.

Comfort Measures

"Quality of life," "comfort measures," "heroic or extraordinary measures," and "burden vs. benefit" are terms that Alzheimer's caregivers will encounter if they are lucky. However, the luck stops with encountering the terms, for although there are definitions for these terms, they can be confusing and, at times, contradictory.

Legal definitions are made through courts in cases where people challenge the norm, current law, or a particular group's outlook. Ethical decisions are greatly affected by value systems. Religious, moral, and ethical decisions are similar but not always the same. They too can be confusing and contradictory. Wordsmiths, those people who use language to make a living—lawyers, counselors, writers, ethicists, etc.—can be helpful or hurtful in trying to sort all this out.

The bottom line is: the one who finally makes the decision must be comfortable that she understands the issues, has considered all definitions, and makes decisions that honor the patient's wishes and beliefs. Whether they are legal, ethical, moral, in alignment with or against the perceived cultural norm, is not what the decision-maker ultimately must live with. This is not to encourage illegal, unethical, immoral decisions, but at times, it is in fact the laws, the values, and the actions of society that are examined, challenged and eventually changed through the decisions of people who do not or cannot accept them in certain circumstances.

"Kindness," "compassion" and "common sense" were words the first nursing home doctor used with me in response to my clumsy efforts to convey my mother's lifelong stated wishes. At some level, I was grateful for his concise description of a phenomenon that heretofore had been theoretical, something Mom always talked about and seemed so clear on. Although I used *kindness, compassion,* and *common sense* in everyday speech, I had never used them in that manner to describe those issues. "Phew! Thank God!" I said to myself. "At least someone here knows how to get through this."

Yet over time, the meaning of kindness, compassion and common sense became less clear. What became more clear was that professional and family caregivers did not always agree on these terms when forced to define them in the context of Alzheimer's.

I have yet to meet a person who did not agree that comfort should be a goal in treating Alzheimer's and that kind and compassionate care, liberally laced with common sense, was a laudable treatment goal. It is the individual interpretations of these goals that present challenges that become increasingly difficult to manage. End-stage issues are when heads nodding vigorously in agreement start to slow and even stop. Then tongues start to wag, fingers to point, and voices to whisper in 'tsk-tsking' noises.

Hospice

Hospice is a philosophy of patient care that is driven by the use of palliative measures. Palliative treatment is anything that provides comfort. In the hospice philosophy of care, you take no measures, use no tools or strategies to extend life. The goal is not to *cure* but to *keep comfortable*. The hospice philosophy is to ease the patient's journey, respect her choice to refuse or to stop treatment, and to support the patient and her loved ones by offering people to listen to and help them sort through their fears, concerns, feelings and hopes.

Integral to the hospice philosophy is an acceptance that the patient will die. The hospice model in the US is the only one in the world that is an oncology model, based on the presumption and in fact the doctor's statement that the patient has six or fewer months to live. Hospice also offers support to survivors as they come to terms with the death and negotiate through the grieving process. This support is typically available for one year after the death of the patient.

Soon after my mother entered the nursing home I called hospice which I knew to be a group who worked with families and their dying patients. Although my mother was still walking and talking, I understood that Alzheimer's was terminal. I am sure my call was prompted at least in part by the fact that my mother had always been a vocal proponent of hospice. Her sister had died of cancer and my mother often expressed her wish that hospice had been available when their father was dying of cancer.

Hospice seemed to be the single professional group to whom I could turn for guidance and support, but they were not available to us because my mother was not likely to die within six months. This left me floundering and feeling very much adrift and potentially at the vagaries of other professionals who may or may not embrace the hospice philosophy.

Hospice came to the United States almost thirty years ago. I am amazed at the misunderstandings that people have expressed to me about hospice. Particularly those who think that hospice means a choice to end, or have someone else end, the patient's life. The first hospice team had been very clear that they did not support euthanasia. Also surprising to me is the misconception that once a person chooses hospice, they cannot have treatment.

We participated in hospice treatment because we knew it to be consistent with our mother's wishes for herself. Others in the extended family had used hospice. Hospice provided a way for me to make decisions that were consistent with my mother's clearly stated wishes. But hospice is not a philosophy to which everyone adheres. Obviously, for those people, hospice would be inappropriate. But before making a decision about supplementing professional care with hospice or any other adjunct group or therapy, it is important for the surrogate decision-maker to have an accurate and thorough understanding of the adjunct groups and therapies.

One of the advantages of hospice was their commitment to educating nursing home staff on a number of issues that arise in the end-stages of Alzheimer's. These ranged from feeding to pain management to comfort. Because hospice was a "guest" in the nursing home environment, they worked within the parameters of the facility. Some long-term care facilities, perhaps many, are hesitant about their involvement. Some at the nursing home saw hospice involvement as an intrusion on their territory while others saw it as an indication that their care was "not good enough." I was confronted with both attitudes initially but in time, and with reassurance from both hospice and me, the facility staff came to see hospice as the adjunct, supportive therapy it was intended to be.

Many facility staff welcomed hospice insights on how to manage dying patients and how to support me in making difficult decisions. In fact, since 1992, when we began with hospice, this nursing home has changed considerably. The organizational structure of the place has changed and long-time nurse Gretta and my mother's primary nurse Dot have been promoted. Hospice care is now routine and the education process for families and staff has been woven into the fabric of this facility.

What I didn't learn until much later in the journey was that hospice works in predetermined benefit periods. At the time of my mother's illness the first two benefit periods were 90 days each. The third was thirty days. The last benefit period was unlimited. (The rules have changed since 1992 so you should check with your local hospice.) When the first hospice involvement began in November of 1992, my mother had stabilized within the first benefit period so we agreed to save the rest.

A different hospice team was introduced several months later. Prior to beginning the third benefit period, which was only thirty days, I called the doctor. He said he did not think my mother would live through the thirty-day period. She did and we went into the unlimited benefit period after much consideration by hospice. My mother actually lived a full ten months on the unlimited period. Medicare paid her hospice benefits. The issue of continuing with hospice was less about money and more about the potential for her living a long, long time beyond the six months. However, at that point in time, I had come to rely heavily on hospice and would have felt abandoned and likely unable to advocate as effectively for my mother on my own. The nursing home was in the very early stages of hospice in those days and many did not accept my mother as terminally ill or hospice involvement as appropriate in the nursing home setting.

In the Alzheimer's Association 1996 Annual Report, the issue of hospice for Alzheimer patients is explored.

> Hospice which provides dying individuals with comfort and care, is too often unused by, or not available for, those in the last stages of Alzheimer's disease. In part, this is because the sophisticated care needed to treat those who have lost so many mental capabilities is not always available. It is also because hospice is intended for those in the last six months of life, a prognosis difficult to determine in individuals with Alzheimer's. As a result, some hospice programs have not admitted such patients or have discharged them. During the year, the association commissioned the Hastings Center, a leading medical ethics institute, to identify barriers to providing hospice care to people with Alzheimer's disease. The outcome of this initiative, which is continuing into the coming year, is to create partnerships among physicians, payors, providers and consumers to make hospice services accessible and affordable for Alzheimer families.[2]

Working with hospice and others in the final months of my mother's life, I came to see our journey through Alzheimer's somewhat differently. Hospice provided legitimacy to my profound sadness, which had for many years been hidden in the ignominy of others' discomfort with it. Hospice removed the shroud of invisibility in which my mother and I had been cloaked more and more as the months and years dragged on. It provided a way for me to think about, discuss and make decisions that were in concert with my mother's clearly stated wishes. Hospice provided a structure from which to begin to assimilate and share the extraordinary experience of being the primary caregiver for a demented loved one. I came to view hospice, like so many others along the way, as angels sent to shore up my eroding foundation. These people seemed, somehow miraculously, to understand that the losses, though not yet final, were real and painful indeed.

The Right to Die

It seemed that because my mother had Alzheimer's and lived in a modern institution, she had *lost her right to die*. This was not right. But it was hard for me to fight for her right to die when I did not want her to die. So how was I, a grieving daughter, supposed to effectively convince, and if necessary fight, a medical establishment, the foundation of whose values were care and treatment run by people who were trained and had taken an oath to cure and do no harm? It seemed as though they equated *do no harm* with *cure*. This was problematic. How was I to convince them that my mother had the right to refuse treatment? What gave me the right? And what would be effective in convincing them that she would no longer want to be alive?

Yet, on the other hand, what gave them the right to *force* treatment or care that could and would have harmed my mother by prolonging her suffering? There seemed to be a clear confusion about curative being right no matter what—while I saw it as an abuse of power that was harmful to my mother. It was almost as though they did not think about the outcome and consequences of treatment.

My mother could not be cured. By definition, her disease would kill her. Were the actions of some professional caregivers bordering on ethical violations? Whose life was it anyway? Wasn't this within the purview of her surrogate voice, her family? As time went on and my struggle continued I became more comfortable with the burden of responsibility, and our role reversal. Perhaps most important of all, I learned to trust my mother's decision to give her voice to me, followed by my own ability to make decisions in her best interest and according to her wishes.

In retrospect it is clear to me that I was making decisions in a climate of confusion. The mores on end-stage care were in a state of flux. The population at large, family caregivers and medical spokespersons were often at odds. I think in some ways the general confusion of society added to my burden as I tried to sort through mixed messages. In this way I carried this burden for more than myself. I was acutely sensitized to the issues and felt fingers pointing from professional caregivers while I was being nagged on another front to

let her go. I couldn't win either way. I was either a murderer or a tor-
turer. It was difficult to find a calm spot in which to think and reach
thoughtful decisions that were right for my mother.

The time finally came when I had to face the need to make a decision about withholding curative treatment. Like all decisions, it was
a process. I included my brothers and sisters in evaluating the alternatives, but when all was said and done, I was the one who relayed
our decision to the doctor that no more medical interventions would
be used.

The decision to withhold curative medical treatment was met
with a variety of reactions from my mother's professional caregivers
ranging from full support to open hostility. This decision was the
one around which my mother's five children rallied as a unit.
Although it was incredibly difficult for each of us, we knew the time
had come to let "nature take its course." Although we came to this
realization at differing times and in different ways, we were committed to defending it. We did this individually and as a unit. We tacitly
agreed to circle the wagons to protect our mother's rights, particularly and specifically her right to die.

Withholding Treatment

There is a crucial distinction between taking life and allowing the
natural death of someone already dying. With good care and modern
medical technology, it is possible to keep a patient comfortable and
pain-free for many years. But at what point do you stop maintaining
the body of a person who is no longer self-determined, can no longer
care for herself, and has no hope of recovery? How long do you prolong the agony for the patient, caregiver and family? The traditional
stance of both medical ethics and law has been that life itself, without regard to its quality, must be sustained.

The decision to withhold treatment to allow the natural process
of death should be a thoughtful one rather than one of benign neglect
or inaction due to denial or emotional paralysis. The need for guidance exists but beware of the "Monday Morning Quarterbacks,"
those "know-it-alls" who have nothing to offer but glib opinions.

What would my mother consider "the living dead"? When would
she have determined that her life had slipped into the category of
having no quality? When would she choose death over life? Would
it have been when the hospice nurse described her as an infant? (I
can tell you that this comment caused a bit of a quake in my own

heart and soul.) Would it have been when she became incontinent or had to be fed or when she became bed-bound? I didn't and wouldn't know the answers to these questions. The only one who could provide them wasn't able to tell me so I had to rely on myself, my family, and my mother's professional caregivers.

A conversation with the emergency medical technician (EMT) who was returning my mother to the nursing home after the trip to the hospital emergency room opened my eyes to a number of issues. He stressed the fact that calling him indicated a call for help. Regardless of whether or not patients had DNR (do not resuscitate) orders, he would "jump on their chest" to save them. If there is a DNR order, it is not always shared with emergency medical technicians. If it were shared with him, his response would be, "Why did you call? If I transport, I treat." This EMT was very clear that given what I had told him, my mother should not be transported out of the nursing home *for any reason*. This was the only way, in his opinion, that we could guarantee that she would not be treated. Given the problems we had just had within the nursing home, it became clear to me that there was really no way to ensure treatment or withholding consistent with my mother's wishes if she left the facility. Since our journey, some states have instituted "compassion acts" that apply to emergency medically trained professionals. It is important to discuss such vehicles to clarify patient wishes early in the process and to be sure professionals with whom you deal are aware of and respect them.

There were times when my response to a situation was a manifestation of my own ambivalence. Although I had made the decision not to treat my mother with anything other than comfort measures, when she became physically sick I found myself asking the staff to do something to help her. Because of the long term trusting relationship I had with my mother's professional caregivers, they took the time to evaluate the mixed message I was giving and to explain that what I was asking for was contrary to the decisions I had already made. Their compassion and patience at these particularly emotional times supported me in being true to my mother's wishes.

Professional caregivers also were careful to point out that certain actions such as testing to find the cause of a fever or hematuria (blood in the urine) would likely result in treatment by an on-call physician, which would not be consistent with the decisions made for comfort measures only. It was at times like these that relationship building with staff really paid off in terms of protecting and ensuring my mother's rights and wishes.

❤

The terms *DNR* and *Heroic or Extraordinary Measures* are often bandied about by patients, patient families and professional caregivers. What these terms mean to each of these people as individuals and as groups is where the trouble starts. When actual, concrete, real life situations arise, agreement can quickly disintegrate. Putting a DNR order in place does not automatically ensure that other "heroics" will not be performed. Some people consider antibiotics a comfort measure, while others consider them more curative in nature.

Even in the best of circumstances, the protracted time period coupled with the enormity of decisions, losses and the emotional turmoil render end-stage decision making extremely difficult. The issue of a child facing a decision to stop treatment for a parent, although the parent may have been perfectly clear and consistent about wanting and expecting that decision to be made, is complicated. The decision over life and death for another is more complex than for one's self.

Interpreting my mother's wishes was very difficult. Although she had been consistent for many years about how she felt and what she wanted for herself, her declarations were regarding cancer, not Alzheimer's. There were few medical people who told me that Alzheimer's was the same as cancer in regard to her wishes. It wasn't until the second doctor from the nursing home became involved that I was told that directly. This may have been because my mother was already in the final stages of the disease. I now realize that a progressive, terminal disease is a progressive terminal disease. I wish someone had told me sooner.

There was no doubt about my mother's primary emphasis on quality of life, her wish not to have her life prolonged, and her choice to be allowed to die and not be a burden, but when actually faced with withholding or changing treatment, I found myself ambivalent. I struggled to let her go. But my mother had been crystal clear about her wishes. In respect of these wishes, I made decisions not to treat, not to test, and not to use extraordinary measures. I worked hard to protect her rights regarding life and death within the institutional setting. I made the decision and, at times had to fight to allow my mother's dying to continue unimpeded.

The medical community has only recently (and grudgingly at that) begun to include patients and family caregivers as equals. Great courage, leadership and grace are needed to open the hallowed, sacred doors of medical decision-making to the ones who know the patient best—the family. The patient's voice, through the one who speaks for him or her, must be preserved at all costs.

One of the most difficult areas of medical decision-making is how far to go in treating illnesses and conditions that arise in the Alzheimer's patient. Many, although not all, come to a point where they consider withholding treatment. What to withhold and when, and under what circumstances, are complicated, difficult decisions. Once the decisions are made within families, hopefully with guidance from medical and spiritual advisors, doctors, professional caregivers and surrogate decision-makers, the decisions must then be communicated to all caregivers.

This can be particularly tricky if the patient is institutionalized. The problem in our case was not lack of facility with language or a desire of any of her caregivers to intentionally harm my mother, the patient. The problem was not usually one of control and power. The problem was values, belief systems and pain. The pain was emotional for all caregivers and, though most acute for family members, no less real and potentially clouding for professional caregivers. The problem was that all involved were human beings, and their human pain, their active suffering over what they were witnessing and felt helpless to control, was getting in the way.

Sometimes the terms were never discussed or even thought about until they were raised in crisis. At those times the differences in understanding, definition and values entered the scene like a runaway locomotive. That was when emotions were already boiling over. Those moments were when the grace of God was needed most—to calm things down, and bring the issues forward in ways that encouraged and supported cogent, calm, meaningful discussion, with the wishes and best interest of the patient as guiding lights.

This is easier said than done. These terms are best discussed and defined before a crisis occurs, preferably in an interdisciplinary team approach where family and professional caregivers view themselves as allies, and co-advocates of the patient.

Over the last few years, I wrestled frequently with the decisions to continue or withhold treatment for my mother. Although I knew when someone reminded me that the decisions were really her own, spoken to all of her children over most of our lives, I often did not remember anything except the fact that I was the one repeating them. I was the one responsible. I felt like an executioner.

A story told to me by a hospice social work intern helped turn my feelings around. When her youngest son, 10-year-old Timmy, had learned about his relapse with leukemia and the option for a bone marrow transplant, his eyes filled with tears, and he said, "I don't want to die, Mommy. What's it *like* to die?"

His mom held him in her arms on the bed—then told him that while she didn't know for *sure*, there were people who weren't afraid to die anymore because of things they found out at times when they had "died" and been revived.

She proceeded to read from Dr. Raymond Moody's book, *Life After Life*, short anecdotes by people who had been considered "dead" for several minutes, and what they had felt or experienced. At that point in time the woman was fascinated but also skeptical about near death experiences. She viewed the book and concepts as therapeutic tools.

Timmy's reaction was, "Oh, that's not so scary," as he went off to play.

Months later, on his fifth day in intensive care (after having been twice resuscitated) the brain biopsy was definitive. The battle was over—Timmy was dying. Tim's mother gathered her other sons and told them that this time their little brother wouldn't make it home— he could never recover. She further explained that she and their dad wanted to remove the respirator so as to set Timmy *free*. It was now clear that his *death*, rather than his *life*, was being prolonged.

Timmy died peacefully in his mom's arms later that day, minutes after the removal of the respirator.

Approximately one week later, Timmy's brother relayed a special message to his mother: "Mom, Timmy wants me to thank you for all your care when he was sick—and he asked me to *thank you* for letting him off the machine!"

After telling me her story, the social work intern said, "Perhaps you should think of yourself as your mother's liberator rather than her executioner."

This professional's courage in sharing her own story shifted my perception from a view of my responsibility and role as agonizing executioner to that of loving liberator.

The decision to withhold all but palliative interventions was one that I found myself questioning on more than one occasion. The moments when I seriously questioned my decision to stop antibiotics resulted in a litany of questions about what kind of a daughter would withhold curative treatment. Why was I stopping them now when she had been treated with antibiotics all along?   Was it due to my own exhaustion and need for release from the role of caregiving more than in honor of my mother's wishes?

Now that I am years beyond this excruciatingly painful decision, I recognize that an exhausted daughter was beating herself up over finally finding the courage and support from family and professionals to carry through with her mother's wishes. While my questioning could probably not have been avoided, I have long since come to respect and accept my decision to stop all but palliative treatment as being consistent with my mother's wishes, hard as they were for me to accept, communicate and ensure.

❤

On the Wednesday before Labor Day of 1993, the nursing home called about my mother's rising fever.   Things were serious but Gretta told me not to come to the nursing home that night because my mother was asleep and I was clearly upset and exhausted.

When I got there the next morning, I was too upset to go into my mother's room. As I sat at the nurse's phone, my mother's primary nurse by my side, I explained the situation to my sister-in-law.

Although she had expressed her opinion earlier that she would not stop curative treatments if the decision were hers, she calmed me down by explaining that the decision was made when my mother was not in crisis. We did this for a reason. She reminded me that it was a calm and thoughtful decision about which my mother's children had all agreed. She pointed out that now that the decision was made, we must work with the nursing home to determine what would be appropriate in light of it.

The nurse pointed out that to request tests would give a mixed message and that the on-call doctor would then likely insist on treatment. After a few more minutes on the phone, I was calm enough to go in to see my mother.

On Labor Day, the nursing home social worker suggested that we consider involving hospice again. I met with her the next morning and, with family agreement and the doctor's approval, a different hospice team became part of my mother's professional caregiving team.

When the second hospice team came on board, I was thoroughly exhausted by the decision to withhold treatment. When the hospice nurse explained that we would take each situation as it arose, making decisions about treating or withholding individually, I thought I would snap. The strain of making the decision to withhold all but palliative treatment had nearly broken me. To think that I would have to repeat that process with each and every new situation was too much for me to contemplate. The decision had already been made to maintain comfort without curative interventions.

❤

Communicating with my mother became infinitely more difficult as she progressed into the disease. Her inability to respond verbally left me in the position of trying to interpret her nonverbal reactions. Some believed that these were random and unrelated to what was happening around her. For a number of reasons I did not believe this. At times she seemed to have no reaction at all, but I found some strange comfort in the presence of her body—her eyes, her smile, her hands that could still sometimes hold mine.

The thing that I found most difficult was using the "*D*" word with her. *Death.* Part of my problem with this was my own fear of facing a life without my mother, but I was also vigilant about not upsetting her. She was trapped after all and it seemed cruel to add upset and fear.

The first time I remember actually talking about death in front of her was when hospice and my husband and I went to tell my mother about the situation with her eating. I was standing at the head of my mother's bed. When I announced that I had said my piece and tried to leave, the hospice nurse, who was at the foot of the bed, said, "You're not finished yet Sally, tell your mother all of it."

I, of course, wanted to bolt but couldn't because my husband was so close behind me I couldn't turn, let alone run.

So I took a deep breath and said, "You can go to Daddy and Aunt Kay whenever you're ready."

Even at that point, I wasn't able to utter the *D* word so instead used a euphemism.

It wasn't until we decided to stop all but palliative care that my mother was officially considered a dying patient. That was when we started to learn about the terminal care which would be in place until her death. During those months I came to finally and fully accept the inevitability of my mother's imminent passing from this world along with her body.

With remarkable support from the nursing home, hospice, the "baby priest" and others, I became strong enough to face and take the final steps in our Alzheimer's journey.

There were times when I said, "Leave her alone—please no more—let her be." Strange as those words had seemed to me for so many years, they had finally become comfortable and right. They had become the most loving words I could say to my mother's professional caregivers. I was finally ready to let my mother go. She was becoming ready to leave.

Antibiotics

Despite discussions among family members, the doctor and hospice, as of May of 1993, no clear resolution had been reached regarding the issue of treating infections with antibiotics. In the meantime, my mother developed a sensitivity which some called an allergy to antibiotic creams such as Bacitracin. This meant that when her skin was torn and an infection set in, the antibiotic creams that were standard treatment were no longer effective. Each infection, whether a full-blown congestion in her lungs or a simple skin tear on her arm or leg, further compromised her physical health.

My decision not to treat anything followed a very serious congestion my mother had. This episode was treated with an antibiotic that was started several days after the onset of the congestion. My attempts to reassure and comfort my mother raised my own ambivalence to the surface over her plight. With her clear statements about quality of life, there was no doubt about her wishes not to have her life prolonged. However, when actually faced with withholding oral antibiotic treatment I found myself struggling to let her go.

The first time I saw my mother so physically ill, in May 1993, I panicked and ran. I think it was the fear in my mother's eyes. Whether it was a reflection of her fear or mine, I'm not sure, but it was there and I ran. My visceral reaction was a shock to me at a point in time when I thought I could no longer be shocked by this brutal disease. The dull aching sense of dread and responsibility that was usually present in the background was now front and center all the time. Nothing seemed able to distract me, not even a walk on the beach or a great book. These heretofore lifesaving activities were beyond my ability to escape into—I was trapped. There was no getting around it. I had hit the wall.

❤

I began the anguishing decision to withhold treatment and had a series of discussions with the doctor who encouraged me to call often. This helped develop a relationship of openness and trust. He offered to always be on call for my mother, so that covering doctors would not act out of protecting themselves from liabilities with families and patients they did not know.

❤

Finally, two months later, after a minor skin infection was automatically treated with an antibiotic, I raised the issue of withholding treatment with each of my siblings individually. In this way, we came to as much of an agreement as was possible for us.

In mid July of 1993, the doctor and I agreed that no treatments other than Tylenol for fever and other such non-curative comfort measures would be initiated from that point forward. Six months after discharge from the first hospice team's care, my mother's five children had reached a consensus to withhold all but palliative treatment. This decision not to treat was tested during an episode of fevers and hemutoria six weeks later. At the suggestion of the nursing home, hospice was reinstated. My mother gradually declined.

Antibiotics are great because they can *cure* illness. Their primary function is curative. Comfort resulting from the use of antibiotics is secondary. While this may seem like nit picking, it became the deciding factor in a final discussion between my younger sister and me. I asked her to talk to her friend in the pharmaceutical industry. His answer was clear. Antibiotics are curative in nature, intent and design. If comfort was the goal, drugs and strategies other than antibiotics should be used.

We were face to face with the words we had heard time and again from our mother: "Comfort only. Keep me comfortable, but let me go."

Autopsy

I finally found the courage to do one more distasteful, incredibly difficult task—arrange for an autopsy so we could obtain a definitive diagnosis.

After much discussion over a period of years we had decided to donate our mother's brain for research purposes. At the suggestion of my mother's physician, I arranged for the autopsy at the hospital in which she had been diagnosed, the place she had stormed out of years before. They had her records and were well respected, so it made the most sense.

The decision to have a brain biopsy was a difficult one, but I suspect less difficult for us than most. Our mother had agreed to an autopsy following our father's death, which was requested by the heart specialist who had done what was considered "radical" treatment at the time. He had brought my father to medical symposiums and used his case to alter the approach to his specific medical problem. My mother's agreement to the doctor's request for an autopsy was immediate and unequivocal. I was sitting with her when she called the doctor to tell him of our father's death. I heard her side of the conversation. Her message to her children was that we should agree to have an autopsy if doing so could help someone. I did not know until many years later how difficult our father's autopsy was for two of my siblings.

Shortly after my mother had been moved to the second floor of the nursing home, where she was deteriorating rapidly, the head nurse urged me to arrange the autopsy. I remember thinking for several months, which spilled into years, that it was something I had to face but just hadn't been able to.

As I experienced later when arranging my mother's funeral, the people on the other end "knew how to do this." My phone call was received by a professional, who was grateful for our consideration of an autopsy, and clear and calm in describing the options:

- ❤ We could simply have a small piece of brain tissue evaluated for the purpose of diagnosis.
- ❤ We could donate part or all of the brain for research.
- ❤ We could have a full body autopsy performed.

Materials describing the process were sent. Written permission was required from me, as my mother's legal surrogate, to prearrange the autopsy. Nursing home cooperation was required. Verbal permission would also be required at the time of death.

Finally, I negotiated with the hospital to pay the additional charge of transporting my mother's body from the nursing home to the hospital then back to the funeral home. There was no charge for the autopsy, no matter which of the available choices we ended up using.

Finally, the autopsy would not delay a wake or funeral and it would not affect how my mother looked if we chose to have an open casket.

I shared this information with my brothers and sisters. My sister suggested that each of the five of us should give written permission; she was afraid that after our mother's death, one or another of us might say we'd never agreed. This way we would have proof that we had all agreed. Because we all signed the papers, any of the five of us could be called at the time of death. I asked that each of us keep the papers in a handy place. I followed through with my mother's nursing home doctor. He explained that it was impossible to guarantee cooperation adequate to ensure the autopsy happened since so many factors could affect it. The importance of the swift transfer of my mother's body to the hospital, accompanied by a signed death certificate, was known to be necessary but could not be guaranteed.

These arrangements were made years before they were needed. During those years, it became increasingly more important to me to know for certain whether or not my mother actually had Alzheimer's disease. The intervening years were so stressful and bizarre, I needed a definitive diagnosis. Brain biopsy is the only way to obtain a definitive diagnosis.

A final word about autopsy is warranted. Our family had a precedent, set by our mother, to guide us when it came to autopsy. But it is important that no person within the family feels coerced into doing something that is not in keeping with the patient's or the family's value system. To this day I feel badly about my insensitivity in discussing the subject of autopsy with a friend whose mother had Alzheimer's. Her mother had been in a fetal position for several years and her father had died within the past couple of years from cancer. Of course there was no way for me to know that her father had made some very strong statements to his daughter about his aversion to autopsy. His daughter transferred these feelings and wishes to her mother. Clearly, for that family, autopsy would not have been in keeping with family values.

Spiritual Preparation

As I said in a previous chapter, my attention to my mother's spiritual needs was essentially non-existent. This was a function of my own anger and confusion in that area. It was not fair to my mother. Meeting with the hospice chaplain was the first time I really started to think about this portion of my mother's care. It was shortly before the involvement of the second hospice team that I started to meet with the "baby priest". Because of our work together, he became involved on a regular basis. Had I not had access to him, the hospice chaplain would have become more involved.

Pastoral care can be very helpful to families and patients. The opportunity to share my anger at a God with whom I was not on good terms, directly with one of his representatives was very important in my journey. The baby priest (to whom I am now sure I was led) respected my anger. He welcomed and validated *all* of my feelings as he helped me untangle the knots of confusion and rage that I had buried deeper and deeper. Not only did this hard work prepare me for and hold me in good stead for the ending of this journey and the beginning of the next—it also allowed me to help my mother in new ways. The involvement of pastoral care counselors early on could have been helpful to my mother and to me. Alzheimer's certainly threw me into a major spiritual crises that lasted many years. Given my mother's history as a devout Catholic, spiritual support at an early stage certainly couldn't have harmed her in any way. ❤

1.   D. Kuhn, "The Normative Crises of Families Confronting Dementia", Families in Society: *The Journal of Contemporary Human Services*, Family Service America, October 1990, p. 457.

2.   A world without Alzheimer's disease, *Alzheimer's Association 1996 Annual Report*, Chicago, IL, 1997, p. 7.

Chapter 11:
Saying Good-bye

As the end-stage "baby in the bed" became more frail and I more exhausted, I thought about the children's story, *Alexander's Terrible, Horrible, No Good, Very Bad Day*, a book my mother loved me to read to her in my early days of teaching. Now every day was like Alexander's—terrible, horrible, no good and very bad.

Perhaps at such difficult times it was natural to move backward in time to the things of childhood. Or perhaps it was just that children's stories had been part of our lives from the beginning or maybe children's stories are "simple" and safe enough to help us understand what is so overwhelming to us as adults. Whatever the reason, I found my mind and heart in strange places during the last fourteen months of my mother's life. The involvement of hospice, the baby priest, the heart lady, and some people at the nursing home during those months, were critical to my ability to function at my best as a surrogate decision-maker.

I wondered often about what was happening in my mother's damaged mind. The thought that she might be frightened but unable to be reassured was hauntingly terrifying to me. Perhaps I was projecting my own fear onto her. Whatever it was, I wished I lived in *Peter Pan* and could do what Mrs. Darling did each night after her children—Wendy, Peter and John were asleep:

> It is the nightly custom of every good mother after her
> children are asleep to rummage in their minds and put

things straight for next morning, repacking into their proper places the many articles that have wandered during the day. If you could keep awake (but of course you can't) you would see your own mother doing this, and you would find it very interesting to watch her. It is quite like tidying up drawers. You would see her on her knees, I expect, lingering humorously over some of your contents, wondering where on earth you had picked this thing up, making discoveries sweet and not so sweet, pressing this to her cheek as if it were as nice as a kitten, and hurriedly stowing that out of sight. When you wake in the morning, the naughtiness and evil passions with which you went to bed have been folded up small and placed at the bottom of your mind; and on the top, beautifully aired, are spread out your prettier thoughts, ready for you to put on.[1]

There was no way of course for me to know what was in my mother's mind anymore than anyone knows what is in another's mind. Since I had never been a mother myself, I had never quite found that "Mother's School" where women learn how to do what Mrs. Darling did. Yet I felt so protective of my mother and so frightened of what we were facing that I tried to imagine what might be there in her mind.

With all my heart I hoped that whatever was happening in my mother's mind was pleasant and safe for her. I thought more than once during these last months that she sometimes hovered above her body, above me—betwixt and between, neither here nor there, out and about but not really anywhere. I had no hard evidence of this. It was more a feeling than anything else, and an elusive feeling at that. She could not tell me and I would not have asked, but it seemed at times that she was almost "testing the waters." J.M. Barrie describes this phenomenon in *Peter Pan and Wendy*.

Children have the strangest adventures without being troubled by them. For instance, they may remember to mention, a week after the event happened, that when they were in the wood they met their dead father and had a game with him.[2]

But I digress. Of course it's clear to me why. I am avoiding now what I would have given anything to avoid then, that for which we had been rehearsing and preparing for what seemed like eons, the final event, my mother's death.

The Final Event

Over the last year of my mother's life, I came to use the term "Final Event" when referring to her death. I am sure at some point I must have read it, or heard it spoken of by professionals. I guess it provided some protection from the reality of finally losing her. Whatever it was, it had almost happened so many times and was anticipated with longing for relief and horror of what it meant, that it didn't seem to matter what I called it. My denial was no longer strong enough to protect me from its inevitability. I was as ready as I could be. I was exhausted and crying for relief. Now the question became, was she?

I had taken to bringing music when I visited. It seemed to relieve some of the need for that one-way conversing of which I had grown so weary. As Barbra Streisand says in her introductory remarks of the album "Higher Ground"— "Music is the connective tissue among souls." Together we listened to a tape that seemed to speak to the situation I couldn't bear to raise with my mother directly. It is called "Living with Loss" by Robert Gass. It has several songs that are beautifully rendered by a host of forty voices. While not liturgical, they were similar to that type of music. These songs always calmed my mother. I don't know whether or not she understood the words or was just reacting to the music or my reaction to it. Whatever it was, it was helpful to both of us and prepared us in a strange way for our last hours together.

❤

In August of 1994, for the first time in several years I took more than just a "crisis break." Although the shadow of caregiving was still there, I was able to ignore it for awhile, even beyond the "crisis relief." The time was right, my mother was stable and another was willing and able to take over for a time. I had struggled for months to actually take the break; but once I did, I felt like I had been released.

Even in a short time, I recognized the value of distance in providing a perspective I could not otherwise have had. When I returned after that last respite, my mother was congested. Over the next four and a half weeks, the congestion would worsen, improve, and then worsen again. My whole being felt, more than ever, as though I was on a roller coaster.

During that break I was overwrought with concern about my brother who was undergoing the first of two rounds of chemotherapy. When I returned "to duty" and my mother gave me some guttural greeting or other, I said, "Knock it off. You don't have throat cancer, he does." I then told her he seemed to be fighting strong and we were all with him on this. I had insisted to my sister that she tell my mother the night I was told. She scoffed at first but my words were enough to convince her to follow through. Without thinking I said, "She knows anyway, he's her child."

People often ask about the appropriateness of telling the Alzheimer's patient bad news such as about an illness or death of someone they love. Since my bias has always been truth, I usually recommend it, but there comes a time when it is clear that telling is no longer reasonable.

❤

Thursday morning found me back at the nursing home for a team meeting which had been moved up from the following Monday. At the team meeting I raised a number of concerns. The first was that I had noticed an order in my mother's chart for oxygen and morphine. I was told, this was simply "to be ready." The second was that I had had a disturbing thought a few nights earlier about the full-body autopsy. Again I was unable to identify the source of my discomfort. The hospice social worker agreed to call the hospital where we had arranged for the autopsy to clarify the protocol.

We also discussed the issue of pain and pain management at length. When hospice personnel had come on the scene, they concurred with what doctors and nursing home staff had told me about pain. It came down to the fact that we would know my mother was in pain as one knows with an infant. She would grimace and screw up her face into weird contortions and she would become restless. "How," I asked, "could someone who can barely move become restless?" I was assured that they would know and I would know. In May of 1993 and on other occasions I found they were correct. They knew and I knew that my mother was in pain. There was no mistaking it, subtle as it was.

Another thing the team discussed that day was whether or not to suction my mother. (Suctioning removes secretions (phlegm) from the throat.) A friend who had been suctioned in an emergency room while he was awake and aware had told me how uncomfortable suctioning was. We had pretty much decided not to suction my mother for this reason and also because once it was started, it would most likely continue. Suctioning takes oxygen along with the secretions it is designed to remove. It also stimulates the gag reflex and makes the throat sore. Finally, the level of discomfort is affected by the skill of the person doing it. I knew that not suctioning would mean that my mother might eventually drown. I also knew it was likely to be some sort of infection that would take her in the end. It was clear that short of a quick fatal heart attack, the cause of her death would require comfort measures.

We also talked about a Scopolamine Patch, which had been discussed by the first hospice nurse as a way to lessen congestion by drying secretions. My mother actually had two patches earlier that week, but by Thursday morning they were removed because her primary nurse did not feel they were effective. Because I was not willing to put my mother through the discomfort of suctioning and had been assured that pain medications could establish and maintain comfort, I was willing to brave hearing her struggle when not suctioned. We had settled the fact quite a while earlier that oxygen would be provided.

At some point a few years before, I had been crystal clear that I wanted to be with my mother at the end. On that Thursday morning, I was asked again and said "yes" although I was more frightened than I had been in the past. I also felt ambivalence that had not been there before. The strength of the team gave me the courage to say "yes." As difficult as those last couple of days were, it was critical to me to be present. Being there allowed me to finish the cycle and has facilitated my grieving and, ultimately, my healing.

The priest had recently told me about the religious ritual (sacrament) to release the fear of the dying. I wondered if there was a comparable religious ritual for those of us left to release the fear of losing the person who is dying.

That Thursday morning, for the umpteenth time, the team discussed pain management. Two nurses with whom I was particularly close and both hospices told me similar stories. All had been involved with a dying patient who was on a narcotic hourly. More than one nurse had skipped doses or had administered them late because they felt the patient was not in pain. In each of these cases, within a short time, the patient was in agonizing pain. It was explained that pain management narcotics worked by reaching and then *maintaining* a level of the drug. To skip or hold dosages for later, interrupted and limited the ability of the drug to provide comfort and ease pain.

Once again I raised the issue of what could happen if a nurse who either didn't understand or didn't agree with using the narcotics correctly was assigned to my mother. I was particularly worried about this happening when she started to die or when the team with whom I had become so comfortable was not on duty. I was assured that the word had been passed and that hospice, at least, was available to us twenty-four hours a day should concerns arise. I felt totally confident that everyone understood my mother's wishes and that they would be followed no matter who was on duty.

At the end of the meeting, the hospice nurse asked the nursing home nurse whether she thought my mother would "pull out" of this congestion.

The response was "Who can tell with Rita?"

They agreed that the next forty-eight hours would determine what happened; she would either fight it off or worsen.

Since the next day was my mother's eightieth birthday and I knew that at least some of the others would come, I asked if I should warn them.

The team said, "Why don't you talk to them tonight about the autopsy. And it would probably be wise to tell them not to bring a frappe."

❤

Around 1:00 PM Friday, one of the younger nurses called to say that my mother had taken a turn for the worse. I asked to speak to the nursing supervisor who told me that I should plan to come up since this looked like "it" but she noted there was no big hurry.

Then I called hospice who told me to wait to hear from their nurse. While waiting I called a couple of friends and tried to figure out what I should do. It was clear that I would be gone overnight at least, and maybe longer, so I decided to "pack." My neighbor later told me that I moved most of my clothes from my closet to the car. I also insisted on bringing the five pounds of London broil that was marinating in the refrigerator.

I prayed and cried all the way to the nursing home. The hospice nurse had said there was no need to speed as there was time. However, she had also told me that my sister needed me more than my mother did right then. Until several months later, I thought I had driven ninety miles in forty-five minutes.

When I arrived at the nursing home, I took a deep breath and raced up the stairs. Before entering the room I remember stopping at the door to gather myself together.

My mother's breathing was terribly labored and she looked awful; clammy, almost wet. The change in thirty hours was beyond belief! She was struggling. The oxygen machine was large and in the way of me getting close to my mother.

When I think now about "gathering myself together," I think of pulling each part of my body in close around my heart to tie it together tightly, with strong rope. This seems to me now to have been the weaving of a protective net, protective to my breaking heart and also to gather together the pieces of me that were flying hither and yon. The shock at my mother's appearance barely penetrated my mind; yet I thought that what did penetrate would kill me. I considered running until I saw my sister standing at the foot of the bed. I vaguely remember saying to myself, "It's just the next step, you can do this!"

I approached my mother's head and kissing her said, "So you put on a command performance to get us all together on your eightieth birthday."

When I moved toward my sister, she asked, "How do you want to do this?"

"I want one of us with her all the way through," I replied. "If I have to, I'll do it myself."

"No," my sister said, "There'll be at least three of us."

At some point I remember my brother and his wife, and then my other sister and her husband around the bed.

❤

Earlier, before I arrived, the hospice nurse said there should not be conversation around my mother but, of course, there was. We were acting in character as we spoke of funeral arrangements and other things.

One of my sisters who was standing by the bed said to the nurse tearfully, "Why aren't you doing something. This is wrong! Just put her to sleep!"

The nurse said, "We're doing all we can."

My sister cried, "Then get the bat!"

Later, when my sister and I went to get a bite to eat, we talked about the discomfort our mother was in and what to do about it. We agreed to a schedule. When we got back, I introduced her to one of the "old time nurses" who said that there would be coffee all night

whenever we needed it, and whatever else we needed would be ours
for the asking.

❤

The first physician had raised the issue of feeding and/or hydrating through intravenous means. It was his opinion, which we all
accepted, that Alzheimer's patients feel differently or less than others. He said that when they are at the point of dying, they feel neither hunger nor thirst and, in fact, some believe they feel a certain
euphoria when they stop eating and drinking.

I was not concerned about artificial nutrition and hydration. The
morning before at the team meeting, the use of lemon glycerin swabs
to prevent drying of the tongue and lips and the use of pink "water
sticks" to provide fluid was discussed. Since my mother's death I
have also learned of saliva substitutes and that mouth care can be a
big job if the death is lengthy. The hospice team had brought a very
concise statement on what we should do which was posted at the
nursing station. When we were standing around the bed on Friday
night, I got a copy for my siblings, all of whom seemed comfortable,
as we recalled together the meeting with the doctor years before during which this had been discussed. Since that time I have read a
number of articles on the issue. Clearly professionals disagree on
whether the dying experience pain or hunger or thirst from the withholding of food and water.

Despite the fact that some in the medical professions believe that
withholding food and water from dying patients causes pain, others
believe the opposite—that offering food and water to a body whose
systems are shutting down can actually cause pain. Pain is not due
to the hunger or thirst, but to the disease.

While we recognized the disagreement among professionals, we
were all comfortable with the position we had reached long before.
The fact that hospice had reiterated the first physician's opinion
solidified us in this regard. There would be no tubes of food or water.

❤

The issue of pain management was another matter altogether. As
I had feared, it was Friday night and the "team" was off for the weekend. Thankfully, the nurse in charge had worked with our hospice
nurse for many years and had a 'take charge attitude,' but his shift
ended at 11:00 PM.

Earlier in the day, my mother had been started on the beginning dose of 4 mg of morphine each hour sublingually (under the tongue) to be titrated up in four mg increments to a maximum dosage of 20 mg per hour.

The nursing supervisor had also assured us that the hospice-ordered morphine dosage of up to 20 mg per hour sublingually would be adequate to get my mother to a comfortable level. But relief from pain was not to be for many hours and clearly the nurse who came on was uncomfortable with the dosage. She actually said to me, "Sally, we're going to kill her with this much."

Morphine is a depressant that works on the central nervous system. Administered sublingually, my mother would not have to swallow; it would be absorbed directly into her system. By the time I left, it was up to 12 or 16 mg. I stayed longer than planned and during that time, my mother became increasingly restless.

At midnight, when the nurse came in to give my mother her hourly dose of morphine, my mother opened her eyes for a moment. They were strange eyes, not the clear blue loving eyes of my mother, but vacant, almost dead, perhaps the drugged eyes of a person in a semi-coma. The nurse and I spoke about her restlessness as I followed the nurse to the station where she called the doctor on-call.

The doctor on call did not agree to the hospice-recommended increased dosage of morphine up to 20 mg, which was still within the limit ordered by hospice and approved by my mother's doctor. When the nurse hung up the phone she was in tears. I found it inhumane and excruciatingly painful to watch my mother thrash in the bed, gasping for breath as her temperature went up and down like the whistle-stop in a cartoon. Furious, I went to the phone and called my mother's doctor. Although I knew he was not on call, I insisted he be contacted. Within two minutes he called and told the nurse to follow the hospice recommendations. I remember thinking that I would give the medicine to my mother myself if the nurses refused. Although I didn't realize it at the time, the narcotics were locked up so I couldn't have had access to them.

It was clear to me that there was some confusion, misinformation, and/or discomfort about the appropriate titration of morphine for a dying patient. We were not dealing with managing pain in a recovering patient but with managing pain in a *dying patient*. Titrating down to a lower dose for recovering patients makes sense. Titrating up to reach and maintain comfort in a dying patient also makes sense.

The supervising nurse on the evening shift had shown us how to lower my mother's temperature, which continued to spike and plummet, at one point from 105 to 96 within twenty minutes. I became quite adept at applying a cold compress to the base of my mother's neck and a towel that had been soaked in cold water then folded lengthwise, under her armpits and across her chest. These things worked to lower her fever. They provided me with something helpful to do. I could see that they provided comfort.

Although I had done little actual hands-on care over the years, I did much in those last thirty-six hours which was quite important for me. To this day I take comfort in the fact that I changed my mother's wet gown a half-hour before she died. To this day I wish her head had been cradled by her own flowered pillow case and that someone had pulled down the sides of the bed and invited me to hold my mother.

❤

Saturday morning found me back at the nursing home. When my brother expressed concern about the use of addictive psychotropic drugs, I went downstairs to discuss this and the fact that two nurses had expressed their discomfort with the medication with the nursing supervisor. I told her that a nurse had told me we were *killing my mother* the night before and that it was repeated to me by another nurse the next morning. I asked about the use of psychotropic drugs. She explained that my mother was dying and that nothing was important now except comfort. The psychotropic drug Ativan was to ease agitation and whatever anxiety or fear she might be experiencing. In terms of the nurses' hesitation to administer the morphine, she said "If the nurses aren't comfortable administering the medication as ordered, the supervisors will do it."

Those minutes with the nursing supervisor, whom I had known for many years, were a sanity break for me. She provided what I'd been asking for years, a reality check and calm, cogent explanations so I wouldn't panic and change the decision to let my mother go. She clearly understood how to do this dying thing. I had full faith in her. She had always been open and honest. She was a professional at her best. Her words worked wonders on my agitation—until the change of shift.

I spent the next several hours alone with my mother. I had brought my bills and checkbook since it was the end of the month. Sitting on the next bed, which had been left empty, I paid my bills and balanced my checkbook. I was struck by the scene; my mother's labored breathing only a few feet away as I balanced my checkbook and paid my bills in the way she had taught me almost thirty years earlier; the funny way I marked each check, flipping it over so they'd be in order.

As I look back on those hours, I realize how numb I was. Although I tended to my mother when she became agitated, I also needed to break to a mundane task. I paid the bills and tried to balance an unbalanceable checkbook. The physical discomfort in standing vigil for hours on end was too much for my exhausted body. At one point, the nursing supervisor suggested I take a nap in the empty bed. I couldn't.

I had never seen a person die before. I was terrified. I was furious and felt helpless that the last thing I could do for my earth bound mother was to make and keep her pain-free. These nurses who told me we were killing my mother were not "bad" people. They were loving professionals who faced a dilemma. One of my siblings believes that at least one of the nurses also faced a deeply held moral issue where her religious beliefs were in conflict with what Rita Callahan and her children had clearly stated as the patient's wishes. This person, my sibling feared, was covert about her dilemma and simply moved more slowly, thus increasing my discomfort.

This same sibling, on the other hand, says those days were the best she had ever spent in the nursing home. She believed that our mother was already gone, hovering about somewhere. While my sister was in some ways shocked that the hustle and bustle of normal life continued as we watched our mother die, she believed our mother was not in pain because she was not really there.

It wasn't until much later that I realized that I didn't know how to do the dying thing. It had always been my mother's thing, not mine. Perhaps she had been as frightened and out of her element as I was, but I find that impossible to believe thinking back on the many deaths we had gone through already and her consistently reasoned, calm approach. When her sister was dying, my mother seemed almost comfortable. I think that came from her experience with their father's death, which they viewed as long and painful. By the time her sister was dying, hospice was involved and my mother was relieved that her sister was spared at least some of what their father had endured. Even when my father died, my mother seemed completely in control, unafraid, confident. But I, at my mother's side all these years later, was another story altogether. I was Humpty Dumpty sitting on a wall, unable to move.

Years later I read the story about Elisabeth Kübler-Ross working with the mother of a dying child. Dr. Kübler-Ross explained that the child's drawing of the purple balloon floating up all by itself, totally disconnected from the rest of the child's picture, spoke of her awareness of what was happening and her readiness to die. What a lovely image that was, clearly the child was not as frightened as her mother.

❤

When my sister came in later she said, "You're exhausted, go home and get some sleep." We talked about the morphine, how it had been administered later and later as the day went on. I told her what the supervisor had said.

My sister said "When her breathing slows too much, when her respirations get to 8 per minute, they'll stop the morphine."

"No," I said, "The supervisor and I specifically talked about that and they won't." From there we exchanged words which became more heated until I stormed out. I landed in the supervisor's office. She called hospice. Help was on the way.

The nurse from hospice, whom I had never met, was incredibly calm and helpful. She assured me, through my hysterics, that the dosages were fine and she would see to it that they were administered on time.

When she asked to speak to the supervisor, I realized, by listening to her end of the conversation, that she thought my mother had stopped breathing more than once when she had been with us a couple of hours earlier. I was aware of the Cheyne-stoking, a pattern of breathing that is somewhat irregular, shallow breaths followed by deeper ones then long pauses between breaths, and I had asked her why the blood wasn't pooling in my mother's extremities. She had checked and said, "You are right, that's not happening."

The door opened and we were told there had been a change and we should go back up. I must have taken those stairs twelve at a time because all of a sudden I was running into the room. I stopped just short of the curtain and pushed the supervisor in front of me. She looked, then left.

My sister was at the foot of the bed and said "She's gone but she didn't fight." So typical of the younger sister, I replied, "No, we did."

I walked up to my mother, kissed her, and removed the canular from her nose. My sister acknowledged how much I had done over the years.

"Turn it off," I said, referring to the oxygen.

When she didn't move, I said it again, "Turn it off."

Finally, she switched off the machine.

Then my sister said, "Sally, close her eyes."

As though I did this on a regular basis, I reached over and closed my mother's eyes, just like I'd seen a hundred times on "Bonanza." I was taken aback but not frightened when they opened again. The next time I tried, they remained closed.

A few more words were exchanged before I collapsed in sobs on my sister's shoulder. As I lifted my head, I saw the most incredible sky I had ever seen. Soft, fluffy clouds of sky-blue-pink were moving toward us.

I said, "My God, there she goes!"

We stood in awe for a moment or two. Then a nurse came in with the crackers and ginger ale, which my sister had demanded when she realized I had been asking for food for hours. My sister left to call the others.

I sat alone with my mother for almost forty-five minutes, speaking to her as I watched the sunset. I sat there saying good-bye, telling her once again that I had done the best I could, and that I loved her. I also told her that we would be all right. I was incredibly comfortable and peaceful sitting with my mother's dead body, sipping ginger ale and eating saltines as I watched her set into a spectacular sunset.

When she returned, my sister and I were curious about a number of things. We weren't scared—just curious. We talked like two young children might talk about a phenomenon with which they were not familiar. Perhaps, it was because it was *our mother's body and our mother's death* that it was safe and all right for us to be curious.

But my reaction and our curiosity were a surprise to me, a pleasant surprise. Dead was different. Dead was quiet. Dead was peaceful and dead was curious but dead was not scary. As the others arrived we told each of them, "She's better, much better." Each of my mother's children had time alone with her. This time was important for all of us.

❤

I remember feeling calm after I left my mother, but also impatient, waiting for the pathologist to call back about the autopsy. The night before our mother died, my sister told me an agreement had been reached among family members about the autopsy. We would donate our mother's brain and get a diagnosis, but not allow the full body autopsy. She was clear that consensus had been reached in that regard. When I spoke to the hospital shortly after my mother's death, I conveyed this. I was told it would have to be put in writing. I wrote the changes, and the four of us who were present signed the document, and it accompanied our mother's body to the hospital.

I had been told that the protocol for the autopsy was for the undertaker to bring my mother to the hospital, and then bring her back to the funeral home. The pathologist said that was not what would happen. He explained that the team did not assemble until 8:15 the following morning so Digga' would take my mother to the security guard at the hospital who would "flash freeze" her. Although this conversation with the doctor may sound crass, he was amazingly sensitive and kind. He made what could have been a horrific conversation one that I experienced almost comfortably. Another professional at his best. As this conversation was ending, my brother accompanied our mother out of the building and helped Digga' get her settled for the first of her rides in the hearse.

❤

One of the things I remember about the night of my mother's death was my sisters coming into the house in hysterics. They had left the nursing home earlier than the rest of us to go shopping (at Filene's Basement of course, where else) for "funeral attire." The dress had been agreed upon years earlier but at the nursing home Digga' had asked about under garments. When the shoppers returned, they pulled out the sexiest, royal blue panties I had ever seen, not exactly Puppy's old style, but what's the difference—she had just put on a spectacular sunset so maybe she was ready for anything. Along with that was a 32A bra that wouldn't have held half of one of my mother's breasts—so like her daughters in the sixties, she went braless. As we roared hysterically, we moved into the den where the serious talk of what was to come began.

The funeral

Funerals are different for different people. I remember thinking when my father died, how important his wake and funeral were for me—and how horrific. We had spoken years before about our mother's funeral. We had arranged it. Now, it was time to live it, not in the nightmares of caregiving exhaustion, but in the flesh and blood of a family who could finally begin to close a long, painful chapter. We were now a family of adult children—some of whom had more than half a century of history together—who had no one in the front line but themselves. We were a family who had awaited and dreaded and hoped for this funeral for more time than most people likely think about most things.

As we spoke about the funeral I explained that everything was paid for but I would split whatever extra anyone else wanted to do. "It's Mamma's funeral, it's for us. Anything any one wants is all right by me. All I want is a blanket of roses for her casket." My sister said she would have the blanket of roses designed by a wonderfully talented floral designer.

On Sunday, I went home to wait and rest. I remember stopping three times on the ninety mile ride home. I was crying so hard, I couldn't catch my breath, and I couldn't see, but I finally made it. I was sitting at my kitchen table with my new and former neighbors when I found out that one of them had taken a picture of Puppy's Sunset.

♥

On the morning of the wake, I did a marathon at the mall. Not being a morning person, I was surprised to see that it was not open until 10 a.m. I marched around that mall as I had marched around the nursing home during the death watch. At 10 a.m., I was the first one in, where else—Filenes.

There I found two angels, sent I am sure by my mother. I was in the dressing room when I asked a woman about ten years my junior what she thought of a particular dress. In the next few minutes, she realized it was for my mother's wake and funeral which was to start in four short hours. A few minutes later, her mother took over, discarding one dress, sending the sales lady for another until in no time at all, I was dressed and ready to go.

Earlier, as I marched around the mall, I spotted an Irish store. I bought a claddaugh ring and asked if I could return it if it didn't fit on my dead mother's finger. The lady looked twice before saying, "Certainly dear."

On the way out, I passed a store with black, diamond and white earrings. They reminded me of the wonderful earrings my mother wore when I was a child. Since they matched my new dress perfectly, I bought them. I also bought several George Winston tapes to be played at the wake, and a blue heart necklace for my mother.

On my exit, through Filenes, I passed a box of five rings on sale. Since the Mastercard was still hot I thought, "Why not! Didn't Mamma think of Daddy's wake as a party, changing her clothes and hair between shows?" I ran to the car with a full funeral ensemble, marveling at how much damage I had done to the Mastercard in a couple of short hours.

When I got to the funeral home, I remember walking down the long hall toward the room where my mother was. As I looked into the casket, I remember thinking how nice it was to see my old mother, Puppy. Her hair was perfect and the blue dress she'd worn ten years before, on her seventieth birthday was healingly familiar. I pulled out the box of rings (there were seven by then) and handed them to Digga'.

When he asked, "Which one?" I said, "All of them."

He looked at me as though I had seven heads and said, "Only one."

"No," I said, "She needs more than that."

Now my mother had never been one to wear lots of rings so I'm not sure what I was thinking but he put the blue heart around her neck and asked which hand and finger for the family ring. As I watched Digga' struggle to get the ring on her finger I realized that she would be wearing only one. So I put the claddaugh on my own hand and when my sisters, sisters-in-law and niece came in, told each of them to pick a ring. When they asked what these were I replied, "Funeral favors, what else."

We had delayed the funeral for several days in the hopes that our brother could gather enough reserves to help us lay our mother to rest. He did, although he had to leave the afternoon wake. The wakes were a mob scene. When we went back that night, three of us agreed to try to keep the typical family line by the casket. We were not successful. I was amazed at the people who came to pay their respects. Two of my father's colleagues had flown up from Connecticut, neighbors from decades before swarmed to our sides along with nursing home staff, and friends from work who had made the long trek.

Old, dear friends, whom we hadn't seen in decades, came too. During the waiting day I'd had on the Cape, I called one of my mother's old friends and went to see others. I was shocked at their question, worded identically, "Sally, how could you have let this go on? You know how your mother felt." It was remarkable how natural their words sounded, how true they rang, how much of a reminder of my well mother they were. I cried as I told them, "I couldn't stop it. There was nothing I could do. I couldn't take her life."

I had learned that I was unable to take my mother's life. I was afraid that when we went to bury her, she would open the box, and come to me, her finger pointing and say "Didn't I tell you? How could you have allowed this?" I had no idea what I would say.

I was incredibly comfortable with my mother's body. I remember as a child how comfortable my mother had always been with our dead, fixing their beads, fluffing their hair, kissing them each time we left. Somehow, it seemed that she had left that trait to her two youngest daughters and eldest son. Our other brother and sister were unlike us in that regard, in fact our familiarity with our mother's dead body seemed to freak them out.

The night she died, I wanted to help prepare my mother's body. Although I didn't know exactly what that meant, I knew it was something I wanted to do. It seemed respectful to me, but because my wishes to do so upset my brother, I didn't. I later found out that more and more people are caring for their dead; picking them up, preparing their bodies, and waking and burying them themselves.

In true family tradition, we had to have some fun—even during the wake. It was my brother, who was without a voice during all of this, who brought Barbara, the forty-four year-old doll the size of a four-year-old to sit her across the room from our mother. Silly as it may sound it was in no way disrespectful; it was appropriate. Barbara belonged at Puppy's funeral as much as the rest of us. My sisters had found many old family photographs, framed them and set them around the funeral home. Our mother's funeral was personalized. But we had forgotten one last thing—rosary beads. Since none of us could find our own, Digga' made a mad dash to another funeral home to correct that oversight.

The funeral home felt comforting and I had no trouble as I leaned over to kiss my mother for the last time just before my husband and I walked to the limousine. We ended up walking youngest to oldest behind the casket. My sister and I covered the casket with the shroud. My mother was carried by the youngest men in the family, three of whom were still in their teens. The baby priest officiated at the comfortingly familiar funeral mass.

The sight of my mother's own carrying her was of enormous comfort to me. It seemed right somehow, that this wonderfully loving woman who had taught us how to love was now being carried to her final rest by those she had loved so well. My sisters and one brother read and the singer I met at the retreat seventeen months before sang "Amazing Grace" at the grave.

The funeral was touching and beautiful in its own sad way. As my niece Sarah said later, "Puppy's wake and funeral were probably the best days in all the final stages of her illness." My mother's funeral was a fitting ending designed in love, and executed in the unique style of those who knew her the longest, those who loved her the most, her children and theirs. We were sad, but in the tradition of our family, as we had been taught, we laughed too—as we moved closer to the head of the line.

❤

As I sat at my kitchen table weeks after my mother's death with two of her nurses, I asked them what they thought the autopsy would show. Both were somewhat surprised and said, "Without a doubt, Alzheimer's." I expressed my strong doubts saying I thought my mother had been too aware to have Alzheimer's. They said that was what made Alzheimer's different from the other dementias. With the other dementias, people tended to be truly out in "never never land" with no knowledge of their plight. Alzheimer victims, however, knew what was happening. (The last evidence I saw of my mother's awareness was the single tear in the corner of her eye as my brother and I stood by her side as she lay restlessly on her deathbed.)

The nurse's comments about my mother's awareness were not a comforting thought. In fact, I found it quite disturbing. To think that my mother was aware through all those years was beyond my ken. Yet in another way I found it comforting for it meant that she truly understood the depth and nature of my loving care.

The result of the autopsy was moderately severe Alzheimer's. A secondary diagnosis of mild arteriosclerosis was noted. When I spoke to the chief of the unit in which my mother had been diagnosed, he said that all people of her age had some arteriosclerosis. It was simply the result of too much ice cream, which my mother loved. The doctor was surprised when I asked for the full report, but he forwarded it. Upon reviewing that, I learned that the two mild sub lunar infarcts were not in fact strokes at all. Although the word *stroke* started appearing in my mother's chart four or five years prior to her death, she had never in fact had a stroke.

A few words on narcotics

Morphine is a narcotic. Since my mother's death, several medical people have told me that nurses in nursing homes are unfamiliar with narcotics and that some schools of nursing teach that hospice's recommended dosage of morphine is too high. In this litigious society, what nurse would not be fearful of doing something that could land him or her in court on a murder charge?

Yet it was excruciatingly difficult to watch my mother thrash in a bed because someone had been taught that the dosage needed to keep her comfortable was too high. Nurses need to be taught how to use pain medications effectively and, once taught, they must be supported in the proper use of them for pain management.

It was not until recently that the American Nursing Association's position paper on the titration of pain medication for dying patients was sent to me. It states:

> The American Nursing Association believes that the promotion of comfort and aggressive efforts to relieve pain and other symptoms in dying patients are obligations of the nurse. Nurses should not hesitate to use full and effective doses of pain medication for the proper management of pain in the dying patient. The increasing titration of medication to achieve adequate symptom control, even at the expense of life, thus hastening death secondarily, is ethically justified.[3]

The nurses had obviously not seen this when told me they were killing my mother. Even if they had seen the position paper on pain management, I wonder what it's impact might have been. I have several other questions in relation to the position paper. Does it depend on the values of those who run the nursing homes? How would a corporate attorney view it? How do nurses keep up to date on such things? What if they don't agree? What if facility policy is in conflict? What should a family do if faced with a nurse who does not or can not act accordingly?

While my mother was clearly dying and in pain, we were faced with at least two nurses that were not comfortable with the administration of the hospice-prescribed pain medication. Hearing their doubts and discomfort regarding the medication was not something I needed at that point. Although they were well-meaning, I was exasperated that they were unable to keep my mother comfortable through the last hours of her life.

Since my mother's death, I have gone through the episode in my mind on more than one occasion, and I actually ended up back at the nursing home a few months later to discuss it with a nursing supervisor. She assured me, once again, that reliving such an event is normal and that I might actually relive it a few more times yet before I fully integrated it. When I said I was afraid that we had actually killed my mother, she assured me that the medication levels had been appropriate and that those nurses were speaking from fear born of ignorance. The fact that my mother was dying made the higher doses of morphine appropriate despite the discomfort of some nurses and doctors. My mother could not and would not live. Fulfilling my promise to keep her comfortable in her last hours was the last gift I could make to her. ❤

1. J.M. Barrie, illustrated by Edmund Blampied, *Peter Pan and Wendy*, Charles Scribner's Sons, New York, NY, 1940, pp.5-6

2. J.M. Barrie, illustrated by Edmund Blampied, *Peter Pan and Wendy*, Charles Scribner's Sons, New York, NY, 1940, p.8

3. Originated by: Task Force on the Nurse's Role in End of Life Decisions, Promotion of Comfort and Relief of Pain in Dying Patients, *American Nurses Association Position Statement*. Effective date: September 5, 1991, Washington, D.C.

Chapter 12:
Moving On

My mother had died. My role as a caregiver was over. I had experienced grief before, many times. The most significant loss had been the sudden death of my father in 1975. At that time I was still a bride, married only sixteen months, and my father, my husband, and my mother were three of the most important people in my life.

Having grieved before, I knew the toll it would take on me. I knew I must grieve again, but this time it would be different. My mother's death was not like the death of my father; she had been sick for years, he died suddenly. I was almost twice the age I had been when he died. I was now separated from my mate of more than twenty years. I was in a more tenuous position with my siblings. This time my grief would be more isolated—without the strength of a parent, the love and comfort of my husband.

Except for the black dog with the white chest and brown eyes with whom I shared my life, I was alone for the first time in my forty-four years.

But I had friends and neighbors who were older and wiser than my friends and neighbors had been in 1975. In those days, no one else seemed to have a clue about grief—I was the expert on it. This time, I found myself surrounded, most gently, by a number of people from whom I expected little, perhaps because of my earlier experience with grief.

I was terrified that grieving for my mother would be as painful and long as grieving for my father. I was wrong but I was also right. It was less painful. It was more painful. It seems shorter. It may be longer.

I was weakened by exhaustion but strengthened by maturity and experience. I knew I had survived before. I knew I would again. I knew I could do the unfathomable. I had already done it. I knew there would be angels to help me along the way. I was frightened but I had courage. I was weakened but I was strong. I had doubts but I had faith. I was alone but I was not alone.

One thing was distinctly different though: I was now an orphan. I remember the difficulties my husband faced with the death of his father, which left him an orphan. He joked about it but it wasn't really a joke at all. It had the potential to redefine his life. Both of his parents were gone now. Although my mother had been gone in many ways, she was not physically, or spiritually, gone until her death. This meant that my years of practicing to be an orphan were now over—I was full fledged, I had joined the club, I had no living parent.

I was given the following at a hospice grief group which I attended five months after my mother died. The group, which met eight times was helpful although the experience of the others as caregivers and survivors was so different from my long-term experience that I felt somewhat alone. But the group and the following Jewish prayer helped me find the courage to grieve. It reaffirmed what I already knew, that the only way out was through the feelings.

> Through the gateway of feeling your weakness lies your strength.
>
> Through the gateway of feeling your pain lies your pleasure and joy.
>
> Through the gateway of feeling your fear lies your security and safety.
>
> Through the gateway of feeling your loneliness lies your capacity to have fulfillment, love and companionship.
>
> Through the gateway of feeling your hopelessness lies true and justified hope.
>
> Through the gateway of accepting what you lacked in your past lies your fulfillment now.

The grief group forced me to slow down enough to respect and face my grief. Scheduling time and having that time structured was very important to this very busy mourner. And even though the thought of actually scheduling time to grieve bothered me, I knew it was necessary. I had a fear of falling into the grief pit and never getting out. I even considered not taking any vacation for if I "slowed down" to grieve what break would that provide? But of course grief is a process, and experience had taught me that I could never be truly happy if I didn't attend to that process, offering it my full attention, at least at times.

Grief

Most of the literature on grief points out the difficulty of grieving in a society that has no use for grief, an energetic society that wants fun and to be upbeat all the time. A society which had rendered me all but invisible as I struggled through the years of my mother's Alzheimer's disease. The anticipatory grieving I had managed for years had become legitimate, but only for the afforded week or two that is offered to get grieving under control and out of sight. Then I was on my own, sent off with a hope and a prayer that I would have the decency to get on with life, but above all, grieve in private.

Many of the people around Alzheimer's caregivers expect them to be relieved when the patient finally dies. They seem to expect that the difficult journey to the final event, death, has provided enough time and energy to grieve. Now that the caregiver is free, she should be happy the yoke of dementia has been removed from her shoulders. But that was not my experience. For more than a decade I had been a primary caregiver; my mother's Alzheimer's had changed my life. Her death tore a wide hole in the fabric of my life. It changed my schedule and my activities. I had little trouble understanding and accepting she was dead. And I was happy for her release, but my own release was more complicated. Just as it was hard to find acknowledgment and support for my feelings while she was alive, now that she was gone it was more difficult except during the time immediately following her death and funeral.

The pain was sudden and sharp. And while I knew I would survive it and that I must feel it, I was often stunned by the intensity of it. Practicing communication from afar certainly helped but there were many moments when I desperately wanted to hold my mother's hand, gaze into her eyes, see that she was still here.

When some urged me to forget the Alzheimer's journey, I was angry. It was too soon. Society's expectations were unrealistic. I needed time to grieve. To truly move on and be healthy, I needed to integrate my mother and my journey with her into myself.

♥

When I returned to work the following week, anxiety set in. I found myself uttering a non-stop litany of "Mamma's OK, she's safe, nothing can hurt her now." The sunset told me my mother was free, met by those who had gone before and they were partying up a storm after all her years of being trapped in a body deteriorating from a debilitating dementia. She had looked like a million dollars all decked out in blue with her blanket of roses. She had been carried by her own and gently lain in her grave. She was with God now, but what I remembered was Puppy in the casket. What had happened to the baby in the bed? Where had Rita gone? How could we have wiped clear that image of her so quickly, so fully, so completely?

It was to the baby priest that I went with these questions. His answers were typically calm and loving. "It's our society," he explained. "We dress and position the dead as though they are sleeping, wanting no sign of the pain and illness that took them from us. So we hide the signs of that pain as swiftly, as surely as we are able. We are masters at it. We've worked hard to perfect the changing of our dead into fully dressed, sleeping people—displaying our loved ones in beautiful boxes.

"Our funeral rites keep us clean," he said. "We don't see our loved ones buried. We don't handle the shovels or the dirt. We walk away from the gleaming, rose covered box in our clean clothes. We don't do dead, Sal. This is hard for you. You lived the illness with your mother. You were by her side throughout this journey, you sat by her bed after she died. But they took her away and cleaned and dressed her like our society expects. It's not surprising that you're off kilter wondering where the baby in the bed went. Your grief will sort things out. But not before it confuses things even more. Just hold on for the ride. Remember it's normal. Pray. Let yourself feel. You're not alone. Neither is your mother."

♥

I knew I had to take care of myself, make myself my top priority for the first time in my life. While that frightened me in some ways, I was still within the protective bubble of shock. I was numb. My body was protecting me as it recovered from the years of exhausting caregiving and the loss of my two primary relationships—my mother and my husband. My shock and numbness allowed me to rest for the most important challenge of all—becoming me, fully and independently.

❤

I had enough experience with grief to know that the burial was not the end of it. I knew that there would be times during the coming years when my grief would sneak up from behind me when I least expected it. It would descend upon me in an instant with no warning. I would feel upset and emotional for no apparent reason until I noticed that the date coincided with some significant date in my mother's life.

As the second anniversary of my mother's passing approached, I was stunned by the return of my tears. These weeks, which turned into months, brought back my grief and tears with a vengeance. I was both surprised and pleased to realize how long it had been since I cried so hard, so often.

I received a strange sort of gift near the second anniversary of Puppy's death. As I sat at my computer working on this book, I noticed a strange change in the lighting outside—from a nasty rainy day to a peculiarly strong sunlit afternoon. When I saw the change, something told me to grab the dog and head for the beach. Upon my arrival, an enormous bank of storm clouds was being transformed into the fluffy brilliant pink of my mother's sunset as she had left her body. Of course this made perfect sense to me since it was her birthday which is also the eve of the anniversary of her death. Two years later and she was still sending sky signs!

Once again I accepted anniversary antics as part of grieving. I would learn, this time, to anticipate and to be gentler with myself during these bouts. I recognized and accepted them as normal, something I could not avoid if I was to be healthy. Running from them only pushed them down, not away. The piper, like the Alzheimer thief, would be paid—one way or another.

A few weeks before the third anniversary I awoke one morning to a Puppy pink sky—but it was sunrise, not sunset. Why was Puppy's sunset transforming into sunrise? Perhaps the dream signified another letting go. Perhaps there was hope that my memories would reverse and I would get back to remembering my well mother.

The power of family support

I was surprised when my brother arrived to put up my storm windows. My arthritic brother who was weakened by two rounds of chemotherapy, and compromised by the heavy radiation in which he was embroiled, got himself over to put up my storms. I had trouble understanding this, for I could not have cared less about my storms, or the impending winter replete with oil bills and a shortage of funds. But I cared very much that my brother had come. In his weakened condition, he strengthened me. In the following months, it was he more than the others with whom I spoke of our mother. He, who had been the most detached during the actual journey, was there to help me complete it. He who was so sick, was now caring for me. Thank you, God. Thank you.

In fact, I was concerned about little in those early days after my mother's death. I was moving along in the molasses of grief that I knew to be normal. I was less surprised by my wandering thoughts, disintegrating memory, and deteriorating organization. These too, I knew to be normal. I was unconcerned by my crazy thoughts and feelings as they tumbled about in the sludge of my inner landscape. I was grateful for my dog, who knew before I knew that a storm of grief was about to descend upon us. I was apparently unchanged on the outside, though I was a fledgling orphan on the inside.

My brothers and sisters kept in touch in one way or another. Although in some ways our relationships were strained, they put that aside and despite their own grief and exhaustion they kept in touch. How I needed that connection! How important it was for each of us! These were our first tentative steps at saving our family. As time has passed, we have taken more steps and grown stronger. Strangely enough, their reviews of this manuscript have opened the door to discussions and offered insights. It has been a healing experience, at least for me.

Many things changed that year. I hosted my first Christmas Eve dinner alone and invited the whole family. It was wonderful and healing. The bulbs I had planted weeks before my mother's death came up that winter in the New England climate that never saw bulbs until Spring. The Christmas cacti bloomed at Thanksgiving, Christmas and then again on Mother's Day. The sky was a new found friend, my old home a new haven.

Forgiveness

I had many things to forgive. I had many people to forgive. More than a decade of Alzheimer's added to four decades of life in a large family and a quarter of a century of marriage with a single partner leaves lots of opportunities for forgiveness, but I didn't know how. For the first several months after my mother's death my forgiveness work was directed at myself. Despite all I had done, I still thought there were things I could have done better, or differently. It was in my upbringing to go on and on ad nauseum about the single tiny thing I had done poorly in a field of remarkable achievement. It was part of being a woman. It was time to change. It was time for me to begin the serious work of forgiveness.

> Forgiveness! That was a term that was not within my capacity at that time. [Tom told me that forgiveness doesn't absolve people of the intent behind their deeds. It means that you have stopped needing to prove you're right. It means letting them be, as they are, to live their lives and learn their own lessons while you get on with your own].[1]

I also had to forgive my mother and others. My mother was a particularly hard one. For years I had wondered what to do with my anger at her. How could I share it, especially once she had become a baby in a bed? While I knew it would only fester and grow if I ignored it, coming out in inappropriate ways if I didn't deal with it, how could I? There were professional caregivers and others I also needed to forgive. And of course there were those situations and scenes with my siblings that needed forgiveness. It was forgiveness all around, but I was as confused about forgiveness as I had always been. I equated it with acceptance. It wasn't until I was referred to Robin Casarjian's book, *Forgiveness: A Bold Choice for a Peaceful Heart*, that I started to realize that I might yet learn how to forgive.

Although I honored my mother's insistence on confidentiality when she made me her legal surrogate, I was angry at the tension and grief it caused for me and for my brothers and sisters. Eventually I realized my mother had done the best she could. I thought of how much worse things might have been if she had not named a surrogate at all. And I realized that although she was my mother, she was a fallible human being.

There was nothing to be gained by carrying my anger around with me—my load was heavy enough so I set this anger down by the side of the road knowing I could pick it up whenever I chose. I walked by it often enough and noticed it with a familiar regard until one day I saw that it just wasn't there anymore. I have done fine without it, actually I realize I am better off without it. And it is easier to love my mother now that it is gone.

Valuing Elders

Because my mother was a senior citizen, she was at risk of being devalued by society. When she got Alzheimer's, she joined the ranks of the devalued earlier than she otherwise might have. Some minimize the death of people like my mother. They do this because these people are old, and they have been sick for a very long time, and because they think that grieving family members are relieved. At some point in time, relief sets in. But an acute sense of loss is also present. It is not a linear process. It is grief.

While it is true that Alzheimer's robs people of skills and abilities they once possessed, it also opens doors and provides opportunities for growth and development in other ways. People who lose their memories and cognitive abilities are forced to live in the moment. They experience life moment to moment. Alzheimer's caregivers who are willing to enter their patient's world have an invaluable opportunity to live in the moment, to slow down, to accept this person *as they are*. They have an opportunity to rewrite a relationship that may benefit from some rewriting. Many say their Alzheimer's patient is easier to be with than when they were well.

Alternative Therapies

More than eight years of involvement in a long term care facility changed me. As traditional therapeutic interventions became less effective, I became more open and willing to try new approaches. Toward the end of this journey, I considered the use of holistic practitioners from non-western backgrounds to address some of my mother's and my own needs. I moved with great caution in this area—first because I was unsure of my own reaction to these non-traditional mediums and second, because I did not want to offend or displace those who cared for my mother on a daily basis.

One avenue of healing that I discovered through the Gathering of Women® retreat was a type of energy work called the LUMarian Method. It was developed by Elizabeth Lawrence, a pastoral counselor who works in a community south of Boston. Elizabeth uses

Energy Medicine, a technique to release painful memories from the cell level. This is a releasing of attachment to memory. The LUMarian Method uses Centering prayer, the "laying on of hands," and living out of an intention. I can't describe what happens but know that I have been greatly moved by it on more than one occasion.

I also experimented with the use of "light" and sending positive energy to alleviate what appeared to be sources of emotional discomfort to my mother. I recently met a woman who has been working with Alzheimer's patients for almost two decades. She told me she is, among other things, a Reiki practitioner who has repeatedly seen an amazing clarity in Alzheimer's patients immediately following a Reiki session. My skepticism seems to wax and wane on these alternative therapies but it is hard to deny experiences that were so powerful in my own healing. It is clear to me that being open to them is a requirement for their effectiveness.

Unconditional Love

The rewards of Alzheimer's caregiving are many: a job well done, a relationship that would not have been possible otherwise, new ways of living and loving. Unconditional love was a gift my mother made to her family. I was able to give it back to her through caregiving.

Over time I learned the value of releasing my expectations and desires and just flowing into the unconditional love that was there with my mother when I would recognize and allow it. It was not really something one or the other of us gave to each other, it was more an experience we needed to be open to. There were countless times when my mother seemed to come out of her Alzheimer's and be the mother again. It was not upon command, more as a result of the letting go we both learned over time.

It is hard to describe the sense of wonder and joy I could reach when I let the love come. In a sense, I had to get out of my own way, stop struggling for that which could be no more and accept what was. Then the love would appear on its own. And what a love that was. It seemed much stronger than other love to me. It was certainly precious. There are many times still when I am able to feel the love of that journey. I am always grateful when I do.

As my niece Sarah so eloquently says of her Nanny-Puppy,

> "She was a proud woman, proud of the children she had
> raised, proud of her children's children, proud of her

appearance. She was always so beautiful, inside and out. I grew up a lot over those many long, difficult years. I grew to understand and appreciate just how precious life is and the responsibility of each and every one of us to live it fully and happily. I grew to learn that although at times I yearned to be a seven year old playing on the oriental rugs of my grandmother's Cape house, those days were gone. Nan was ready to go and all we could do was give her that momentary pleasure, to keep her comfortable, out of pain, to die with dignity. We all needed to be selfless and thoughtful of the wishes of our [original] caretaker, the one whose unconditional love had enveloped each of us for so many years."

Blessings

When someone told me to count my blessings while I was in the middle of my caregiving years, I wanted to slap them. I shouted my rage "Blessings! How dare you speak to me of blessings!" Two ways I might have been better able to count my blessings were if I could see how far I had come and see how much better off I was than others.

At the time, I had neither the insight nor perspective to realize these things. But time has moved me to another place. I now count my blessings regularly. I wonder, if I had had more courage and support, could I have counted my blessings as a caregiver? Perhaps. Perhaps not.

But I am grateful for my ability to count them now, for they are many. Below are lists of blessings I had as a caregiver and those I have as a result of having been a caregiver.

Then
- ❤ Opportunity to grow
- ❤ Opportunity to give back
- ❤ Opportunity to love
- ❤ Easier, less defended relationship
- ❤ Simpler, less demanding time with mom
- ❤ Wonderful humor
- ❤ Writing
- ❤ Facing spiritual conflicts
- ❤ Learned to breathe
- ❤ Learned to let go

Now

- ❤ The sky
- ❤ Easy laughter
- ❤ Rest and relaxation
- ❤ Pride
- ❤ Writing
- ❤ Opportunity to make a difference in the lives of Alzheimer families
- ❤ Resolution
- ❤ Relationship with me as #1
- ❤ Letting go

Out of the Mouths of Babes

As I come to the conclusion of this manuscript, I think, once again, about all of the aspects of this disease I did not encounter or do not feel competent to write about. Since I know the impact that Alzheimer's can have on a generation of grandchildren, I invited my nieces and nephews to share their thoughts and feelings with me.

The following is from Sarah's poignantly shared thoughts on family:

> "My grandmother suffered the physical effects of Alzheimer's. None of us would feel the pain for her. Nonetheless, the disease that Nan suffered too many years, all of my family suffered too. We suffered with each visit to her nursing home, only to find an increasingly more weakened woman than that which we had left on our previous visit. We all suffered through the difficult financial and medical decisions that were made. We all suffered the many, often tense, phone conversations that her children had regarding her care."

One of my sisters often had my mother to her home for dinner, sharing her older, much loved children with their grandmother. My sister recently told me that those dinners were a way to give back to and continue to receive from our mother. My brother and my sisters shared one of the most important things in our mother's life, children. They gave a gift to our mother the rest of us could not, the gift of her grandchildren.

These children learned by the actions and expectations of their parents about illness and how to treat elders. I was moved by the lesson of love Sarah learned from her grandmother's Alzheimer's, as is shown in her story:

> "The years made it more and more difficult to go see Nan. We, the younger members of the family, had become unrecognizable to her first. I guess because she had known us for the shortest amount of time. She recognized the older members of her family longer, both immediate and extended until finally she knew no one. She was equally affected by the arrival of a nurse to comb her hair as she was that of her son and his family.
>
> I hated that: I remembered her and loved her equally as much on my last visits as I had as a young child when she'd comforted me with a skinned knee. I wanted a sign that I was special to her. I needed something visible or tangible or even a voice to show me that she knew me. But, that was out of anyone's reach. Our family visits became more and more depressing. We would leave the building in silence and make our journey home with an ominous cloud of sadness above us. We all searched for that sign. That one I had been dying to find.
>
> My sister pointed out what that sign was. She said, 'Nan knows we're there. Her eyes light up when we walk up to her and touch her hand and say hello.' I didn't understand her, at first thinking that's only momentary pleasure. How can that be the sign I was seeking?
>
> 'Don't you see?' Julie said. 'All we can do for Nanny is make her comfortable and bring her that momentary pleasure. She knows we're there. She knows she's loved. She always knows that, and always will.'
>
> From that moment until her death, I knew that that was what we all had to do for Nan."

The Healing Time

Things are different now. It is a time of letting go—again and again and again. It is a time of seeking and solidifying peace and learning forgiveness. I seem gentler now somehow. Even those of us who were most at one another's throats seem to have backed off somewhat. We seem to be moving forward with hands outstretched, hearts more open, minds a bit more free. Our ability to offer and accept love seems greater too. But the old stuff, the non-Alzheimer's stuff that got played out through our mother's illness, must still be within.

Despite our difficulties before, during and since our mother's Alzheimer's, my brothers and sisters and I are family. We learned of commitment and the importance of excellence from our parents. Along with the tough stuff of families we have the love which we learned at our mother's knee. We have risen above the pain and loss of Alzheimer's to continue this tradition of love.

We have all grown some since our mother's death. We are somehow managing to get beyond the horrors of the Alzheimer's years. It seems to me that we want to stay connected. While that is not easy, it seems more possible now. My mother used to say how great it was that her kids all "liked one another." Well, I'm not sure that was always true through the years of her demise.

Maybe now, with our mother in a better place, with more access to the grace we need, we can fully heal. But if not, at least I hope we will stay on this path of less resistance, seeking less control, learning better how to respect and accept one another in love. I know that as time goes by, it is the love of my mother's eye hugs, and her toothless smile, more than the tears of rage and grief that I remember. It is the loving care and support of so many rather than the difficult family dynamics that I remember now. It is the dedicated care rather than the self righteous, dysfunctional acts of a few professionals I remember.

Occasionally, or perhaps more regularly than it felt at the time— an "angel" of one sort or another would appear to help me scale yet one more hurdle, jump through one more hoop, make yet one more good decision for my mother. I hope those angels will continue to appear in my life, help me in my healing, and move me closer to a life of meaning and of love.

❤

Alzheimer's changed my life. It took my mother from me. It changed who I am, what I care about, what I do and how I spend my time. Although I have laid my mother's Alzheimer's to rest, there are others who are still waging this war. Others who still feel the daily pain of loss. Others who still live the horror of watching their loved one being stolen away. I cannot sit still knowing of this pain. I cannot turn my back. I cannot ignore the Alzheimer's War.

In my own small ways, I wage the war still through advocacy, support and education activities. I serve on my local Alzheimer's Association Board and chair their Patient and Family Services Committee. I continue to educate myself and I train others. I follow, more closely than ever before, the research on and costs of Alzheimer's. I write, I speak, sharing my experiences privately and publicly. I facilitate a support group. With the support of my college president and colleagues, our college is collaborating on a number of projects with the Alzheimer's Association. I am not alone in these activities. Many who have survived Alzheimer's do similar things. Some of my brothers and sisters are still waging the war too in other ways. We all know enough to offer an ear, a smile, a hug. We know enough to be there for those who are on the front lines.

Above all, my mother's voice must not be lost. It must be heard by those in power, those who allocate funds for research, and those who make and change the laws that govern funds for Alzheimer's patients. I will continue to use my knowledge, my passion, and my talents to share our story to educate others about Alzheimer's. I can do nothing less. Perhaps, if enough voices are raised against the formidable Alzheimer's foe, we will win. Perhaps we can change the statistics, turn the tide, free the afflicted. Perhaps with enough prayers and work, we can create an Alzheimer's-free world.

In the meantime, we must treat every Alzheimer's patient with respect and dignity. We must protect their rights to decisions that are in keeping with their wishes and values. And we must ensure that they have access to loving comfort throughout their journey through Alzheimer's.

Alzheimer's has altered me in many ways. I have been humbled by it. I hate it. I am afraid of it. I am grateful for every day I was unaware of my mother's Alzheimer's. I am not finished with Alzheimer's. Perhaps it is not finished with me.

❤

Simple comforts soothe me now. A walk on the beach, a pat from the dog whose name my mother thought so ridiculous, a long overdue connection with an old friend, a hug from a child, a chat with my family, a laugh with a neighbor, an outing with a friend. These are the things I enjoy as I hadn't been able to in years. I once again allow the right side of my brain to balance the left. I am becoming more and more proficient as a woodworker. I build what I can't afford to buy. I am moving on.

Please remember that the bottom line for my mother, for her children and grandchildren and for all human beings, is love. And love was the method through this madness called Alzheimer's. Love takes many guises. Love changes. But it was love that got us through this terribly challenging journey. Recognizing the love of letting go has left me, at least, some semblance of peace. I will never let go of love. For if I can love, if I am loved, I am blessed and I will be well. And when all is said and done, I have sunsets that mean so much more to me now, and my heart is at peace. And at times, I even believe that my mother has left me her courage and strength, her faith; the gifts I asked of her so often at the end of our journey. ❤

1.   Beverly Bigtree Murphy, *he used to be Somebody: A Journey into Alzheimer's Disease Through the Eyes of a Caregiver*, Gibbs Associates, Boulder, CO, 1995, p. 263.

Afterword

A couple of years ago I met a woman from a family who carries an early onset gene. Her mother began her descent into Alzheimer's many years ago. Her aunt also fell victim. More than thirty years later, Alzheimer's has reappeared—some of her siblings are now showing signs of the disease. As my friendship with this woman grows, I am struck again by the devastation of the disease that changed my life. But in this family, as it is affecting several young people directly and simultaneously, the rage and fear I know too well is multiplying exponentially.

How, I wonder, can I support this woman on the brink of her fortieth birthday, as she is surrounded by so many of her siblings marching relentlessly into Alzheimer's? What hope can I offer? What gift might I make in the face of such tragedy? What difference could I possibly make in the life of this mother, wife and sister?" Amazingly, as our friendship has developed, my offer to support her has been met in kind. I am continually astonished at her unrelenting courage as she struggles to live her life day by day.

When I admitted to my friend that there was a period of my life during which I withdrew from and avoided meeting people over the age of fifty in an attempt to protect myself from the pain of losing them, she pointed out that she might get Alzheimer's. I had already considered that fact, but too late, for she had already captured my heart.

The night before that conversation, I found myself searching desperately for a solution to a problem we shared. She was having difficulty remembering her sister before she got sick, as I had experienced with my mother. Exhausted, on my way to bed, her

317

words beckoned. Knowing I wouldn't sleep, I reached for a pen and
wrote:

A box is all you need.
A box with shelves and drawers that float and melt.
A box to beckon, shine, and hide.
A willing box that opens upon command, at the slight-
est wave of your hand.
A quiet box to hold firmly, guard staunchly all she
meant to you.
A strong box to withstand the whipping, chill winds of
loss.
A clear box through which you can see the memory once
so close and real.
A foggy box to protect and hold you in the eye of the
storm.
A box with strength enough to meet and catch the rage
that builds with each new loss.
A gentle, velvety box to cradle the love in safety until
you can hold it again.
A magic box to hide you from the thief that steals your
heart with each new beat as you frantically race to
remember what is no more.
A brave box to shelter your grief in the wildest of times.

A box is all you need.
A simple, gentle, strong, clear, foggy box to shield you
from the fearsome grip of the mind thief as he steals
away another bit of your breaking heart.
A box to store her body and eyes as she follows him
away.
A box to rescue the pieces of her you so treasure.
A box to catch the warm soft breezes she shuns.
A box to untangle the web of confusion and fear that
bludgeon the gentle oneness that flowed so freely
once.
A box in which to store the pieces of her whole as she
fades and storms away, raging from—then turning
toward the thief, the goddamned thief, who came
before.

A box is all you need.
A simple, gentle, clear, strong, foggy box to shelter and
save the love he can't destroy.

> A box to hold her memory clear and near as she slowly
>   slips away.
> A magic box to deliver courage and patience, hope and
>   faith, peace and joy as you bravely march by your
>   familiar stranger's side down the same sad road
>   you've crawled before.
>
> A box should do it.
> A box to hold safe what you're losing.
> A heart-shaped, satin lined, flexible, fluid, filtering box
>   to hold her memory fast as you falter and lurch by
>   the side of the thief's new bride.

As we sat together, she and I, comfortable in our fledgling friendship with a history short yet rich and deep, I read to her of the box. Sharing slowly, in the zigzag way we do, we spoke of ways to build the box. Ten minutes a day, each and every day, to capture the memories. Her daughters could help, and others too. Or she could do it alone, going back to times and places when she and her sister were one with each other's hearts, before the thief had returned to her family. She could build the box slowly, a memory at a time. Tears would keep the hard fine wood supple, as laughter raised it to the heavens, blessing it with love while she slowly preserved the woman who was once the breeze beneath her wings. She could store the cool, calm breezes they had shared before the memory thief violated them again. She could store them in the box to retrieve when she needed them herself, or save them for someone else. Yes, a box could be built to cherish what she could not now hold.

Perhaps I could build a box, too. Perhaps I could slowly retrieve my memories of my well mother—the ones that are still so far outside my mind or hidden deep within. Heart memories are here and fine but the mind memories—those are not accessible yet— maybe the box could work for me. If I could find the courage, if others might help, memory by memory, maybe I could find my well mother again, and lay the sick one to rest.

Please support those who face the challenges of Alzheimer's. And please support research and education on Alzheimer's disease so that one day, those in my friend's family whose gene might force them to face the Alzheimer's thief head on will simply smile at the thief and say: "No more thief—you're finished. We surrender no more of our lives and love to you. We are free at last!" ❤

might help, memory by memory, maybe I could find my well mother again, and lay the sick one to rest.

Please support those who face the challenges of Alzheimer's. And please support research and education on Alzheimer's disease so that one day, those in my friend's family whose gene might force them to face the Alzheimer's thief head on will simply smile at the thief and say: *"No more thief—you're finished. We surrender no more of our lives and love to you. We are free at last!"* ❤

Appendix 1:
How To Help

Offer to stay with the Alzheimer's patient so your friend or relative can get a break. Suggest they go to a movie, or visit with a friend, go out for a meal, or take a walk.

Help your caregiving friends by offering friendship; listen to their concerns, frustration, and grief. If they need information on home or community based care, offer to call for them. If they need information on long term care, offer to go with them. If they are not taking good enough care of themselves, encourage them to do so, make them a nutritious meal, offer respite, do their shopping, tell them a funny story, hold them while they cry.

Gather a group from your church or club who are willing to provide an hour or two of respite to local Alzheimer caregivers. Your local Alzheimer's Association should be able to provide training.

Write or visit your senators and congressmen to be sure they are aware of the difficulties Alzheimer's families and patients face and let them know how they can help.

Alzheimer's Association chapters all over the United States raise money for research and fund local services to patients and caregivers through the *Memory Walk*. Find the one nearest you through your local chapter. Some chapters have incorporated a *run* into that day's events. Call your local Alzheimer's Association for information. If you can't walk or run, sponsor someone who can. If your patient can walk, or ride in a wheelchair, bring her along.

A Massachusetts family with *FAD* (Familial Alzheimer's Disease) sponsors a long *bike ride* (www.memoryide.org) each year. The Alzheimer's Association of Eastern Massachusetts forwards one hundred percent of the funds raised from that event directly to Alzheimer's Research.

Call your local Alzheimer's Association to find out about fund raising events. On Cape Cod, we have an Annual *Dessert Cruise*. The local eating establishments donate wonderful desserts and for $25.00, on one of the Island ferries, we cruise around in Nantucket Sound and watch the sunset. (Three years in a row, Puppy has provided a sunset.)

Call your local Alzheimer's Association and ask for a list of support groups in your area. If necessary, accompany your caregiving friend or relative or stay with their loved one while they attend.

Send a donation to your local Alzheimer's Association, consider naming them in a bequest and invite people to send a donation in lieu of flowers when your friend or loved one dies.

Offer your time by volunteering at the local Alzheimer's Association office. You needn't have any particular skills if you are willing to offer your hands to do what needs to be done. Stuffing envelopes for mailing, maintaining member database lists, computer skills and answering the phone are typical volunteer opportunities.

If you and your pals are golfers or bridge players, why not host a fund raising event to support your local Alzheimer's Association. You could specify that the money should go towards respite for an exhausted caregiver, go toward the cost of mailing an advocacy alert, or buying Alzheimer books for the office or local library. Another way to raise money is through a neighborhood yard sale.

Buy an Alzheimer's book for your local library, or better yet, ask one of your State's community colleges to build a special collection to be loaned to all local libraries in the State's interlibrary loan network. These might also be loaned to individuals. For information on the library component of the *Lifting the Veil* collaborative between Massasoit Community College and the Alzheimer's Association, call (508)588-9100, x1141.

Host a barbecue for your friend's support group. Invite patients and caregivers. This will offer opportunities for social engagements which are probably few and far between. Knowing others will understand and accept the Alzheimer's patient's behavior will make it "safer" for families to attend.

Donate your special talent or company's resources. Many in the community help the Alzheimer's Association do their important work. Newspapers donate advertising space and announce support groups, restaurants provide food or snacks for educational conferences, churches and hotels rent their facilities at reduced rates. Some even allow employees to spend a day a month providing respite breaks. Other ways to help include: providing postage for mailings, maintaining computer databases, working in the Alzheimer's office, providing transportation to doctor's appointments or day-care, making meals for caregiving families, or answering the hotline (training would be needed). The sky is the limit with this type of generous contribution. Why not ask your local association how you can help. ❤

Appendix 2:
Music, Meditations
And Tape Seminar
Resources

Music

Name	Label	Year	# on Spine	Media
Conversations with God - a Windham Hill collection	Windham Hill	1997	01934-11304-2	CD
Living with Loss	Spring Hill	1993		Tape
Meditation Volume 1				CD
Timeless Motion - Daniel Kobialka	Li.Sem Enter-prises Inc.	1991	DK 102 Stereo CD	CD
Higher Ground - Barbra Strei-sand	Columbia	1997	CK 66181	CD
by heart - Jim Brickman	Windham-Hill	1997	01934-11164-2	CD
Inspirational Songs - Liam Rimes	CURB Records	1997	D2-77885	CD
Return to the Heart - David Lanz	Narada	1991	ND-64005	CD

Music

Music for Relaxation - Sounds that Sooth - Jim Oliver	Relaxation Company	1992	CD582	CD
Tranquility - Hennie Bekker	North Sound	1994	NSCD 29552	CD
Pacific Blue - Stefan Schramm and Jonas Kvarnstrom with authentic sounds of whales	North Sound	1991	NSCD-20642	CD
Music for Meditation Volume 3	Creative Music Marketing	1995	CMM 507-2	CD
Hymns Naturally	North Sound	1996	NSCD 24582	CD
On Wings of Song - Robert Gass	Spring Hill Music	1992	SHM-6002	CD
Heartsounds - David Lanz	Narada	1983	ND-61003	CD
Pachelbel Ocean	North Sound	1994	NSCD 25942	CD
Healing Harmonies - Music Composed to Balance and Soothe - Jim Oliver	Relaxation Company	1992	CD3205	CD
beloved - A David Lanz Collection	Narada	1995	ND-64009	CD
Ocean Surf - The Relaxation Collection	Madacy		C-5605-1	CD
Rainstorm- The Relaxation Collection	Madacy		C-5605-2	CD
Mountain Retreat - The Relaxation Collection	Madacy		C-5605-3	CD
Country Stream - The Relaxation Collection	Madacy		C-5605-4	CD
Angel's Kiss	Unisom Music	1995	CNCICD3	CD
Music of the Angels - Gerald Jay Markoe	ASTRO-MUSIC	1994	Astro - 011	CD
Music for Meditation Volume 2	Creative Music Marketing	1995	CMM 506-2	CD
Classical Relaxation Meditation - Vol. 1	M Music		31-051	CD
Classical Relaxation Meditation - Vol. 2	M Music		31-052	CD
Dan Gibson's Solitudes	Harmony	1989	CDG100	CD
Natural Sleep inducement	Solitudes	1998	CDG150	CD
Pachelbel, Forever by the Sea	Solitudes	1995	CDG121	CD

Meditations

Name	Label	Year	# on Spine	Media
Heart of Perfect Wisdom On Wings of Song and Robert Gass	Spring Hill Music	1990	SHM-1012	Tape
Living with Loss	Spring Hill	1993		Tape
Opening the Heart - Guided Imagery and Music - Robert Gass with On Wings of Song	Spring Hill Music	1991	SHM-4001	Tape
Your Body's Inner Wisdom - Linda Marks	Institute of Emotional Kinesthetic Psycho-therapy	1990		Tape
On Wings of Light, Meditations for Awakenings to the Source - Joan Borysenko	Mind/Body Health Sciences, Inc.	1992		Set of Tapes
Love is the Lesson - guided meditations to support healing in mind, body and spirit (Joan Borysenko)	Mind/Body Health Sciences, Inc.	1990		Set of Tapes

Tape Seminars

Name	Label	Year	# on Spine	Media
The Power of the Mind to Heal, Renewing Body, Mind and Spirit - Joan Borysenko	Nightingale Conant		10410A	Set of Tapes
Women, Power & Self Esteem - Take Charge of Your Own Well-Being	Career Track Publications	1990-91		Set of Tapes
Controlling Anger, How to Turn Anger into Positive Action - Dr. Carol Tavris	Career Track Publications	1989	10009	Set of Tapes
Self-Empowerment, Achieving Your Potential Through Self-Awareness - Jeff Salzman	Career Track Publications	1991		Set of Tapes

How to Contact Resource Companies

Company	How to Contact
Astro Music	P.O. Box 118 NY, NY 10033
Career Track Publications	(303) 440-7440
Creative Music Marketing, Ltd.	P.O. Box 994, Chadds Ford, PA 19317
CURB Records	Nashville Tennessee
Harmony - Exploring Nature with Music	Castlewood P.O. Box 38149, 550 Englinton Avenue West, Toronto, Ontario, M5N 3A8
Institute of Emotional Kinesthetic Psychotherapy	(617) 965-7246
Li.Sem Enterprises	(800) 726-3924
Madacy	P.O. Box 1445, St. Laurent, Quebec, Canada H4L 4Z1
Mind/Body Health Sciences, Inc.	393 Dixon Rd., Boulder, CO 80302 (303) 440-8460
Narada Productions, Inc.	(414) 272-6700
Nightingale Conant	(800) 323-5552
North Sound - Harmonizing Nature with Music	(800) 336-5666
Spring Hill Music	P.O. Box 800 Boulder, CO 80306
Solitude Ltd.	1131A Leslie St., Suite 500, Toronto, Canada M3C 3L8
The Relaxation Company	20 Lumber Road, Roslyn, New York 11576
Unisom Music	P.O. Box 141000, Nashville TN 37214-1000
Windham Hill Records	(800) 495-1976

Appendix 3:
Useful Contacts

The *National Alzheimer's Association* was started by family members. It has a wealth of information and can tell you what to believe and what not to believe. There are over 200 local chapters nationally. Check their website or call them at (800) 272-3900.

Eldercare Locator links anyone in the United States with information about services. Their toll free telephone number, (800) 677-1116 is answered 9 AM to 5 PM EST.

The *Health Care Financing Administration* (HCFA) is a federal agency that oversees two types of insurance, Medicare and Medicaid. Their address is US Department of Health and Human Services, Health Care Financing Administration, 7500 Security Boulevard, Baltimore, Maryland 21244-1850. Along with numerous other agencies, they offer a number of publications which are good for the lay person.

"Human Genome News", Betty K. Mansfield, Managing Editor, Oak Ridge National Laboratory, 1060 Commerce Park, MS 6480, Oak Ridge, TN 37830. Phone: (865) 576-5454 Fax: (865) 574-9888.

An Annotated Reading List is published annually by the Alzheimer's Association of Eastern Massachusetts at 36 Cameron Avenue, Cambridge, MA 02140. Phone (800) 548-2111.

Appendix 4:
Useful Videos

The *AD: National Feeding Techniques Video*, was made by the Bedford Massachusetts GRECC (Geriatric Research Education and Clinical Center). It is distributed by Terra Nova Films, 9848 South Winchester Avenue, Chicago, Illinois, 60643. (800) 779-8491   Fax (773) 881-3368.

The Great Brain Robbery, is a moving, five-minute video by Joanne Koenig-Coste. This collage of beautiful photographs of people with AD is accompanied by Ms. Koenig-Coste's poetry and voice speaking the thoughts of those depicted. It is distributed through the Alzheimer's Association of Eastern Massachusetts at 36 Cameron Avenue, Cambridge, MA 02140. Phone (800) 548-2111.

Someone I Love Has Alzheimer's Disease is an award-winning Video and Curriculum Guide for children available through the Alzheimer's Association of Eastern Massachusetts at 36 Cameron Avenue, Cambridge, MA 02140. Phone (800) 548-2111.

Appendix 5:
Useful Websites

(Correct as of 5/15/99)

National Alzheimer's Association
 Includes: Fact Sheets, Benjamin B. Green-Field Library Specialized Reading Lists and much, much more

http://www.alz.org

Saskatoon Alzheimer's Association

http://www.sfn.saskatoon.sk.ca/health/alzheimer/index.html

Caregiving Support Resources

http://www.caregiving.com/support/html/resource.htm

Family Caregiver Alliance, San Francisco

http://www.caregiver.org

Caregiver—Northwestern University Medical School

http://www.brain.nwu.edu/core/caregive.htm

Personal home pages on AD and Caregiving

http://home.hiwaay.net/~bparris/homepages.html

AARP Answers Page

http://www.aarp.org/answers.html

Cambridge Scientific Abstracts
   Hot Topic #1 Alzheimer's Disease

http://www.csa.com/alz.html

The Alzheimer's Disease Web Page
   (Bedford GRECC at Boston University Medical School) A site
   dedicated to the distribution of information to investigators,
   families, caregivers & others interested in AD

http://www.visn1.og/Alzheimer/

The dilemma of feeding end-stage Alzheimer patients

http://www.visn1.org/alzheimer/callahan.htm

Alzheimer's Disease Research Center

http://www.bcm.tmc.edu/neurol/struct/adrc adrc1.html

Northwestern University Medical School
   Links to research and other Information

http://www.brain.nwu.edu/research/linksto.htm

Human Genome Project, US Dept. of Energy

http://www.er.doe.gov/production/ober/hug_top.html

Research, Office of Biological and Environmental Research

http://www.ornl.gov/hgmis/research.html

Clinical Diagnosis of AD (for physicians and other health care professionals to self-evaluate their clinical diagnostic knowledge of AD)

http:www.alzheimerdrsrvy.com

Online Alzheimer Publications

http://www.alzheimers.org/pubsonln.html

The Alzheimer's Bookshelf, Elder Books

http://www.elderbooks.com

An Alzheimer Newsletter (U of Kentucky)

http://www.coa.uky.edu/ADReview

Alzheimer's Disease Center University of California—Los Angeles

http:www.adc.ucla.edu

Mandel Alzheimer Caregiving Institute at Case Western Reserve University

http://cwru.edu/affil/alzcare/home.html

Cognitive Neurology and Alzheimer's Disease Center, Northwestern University Medical School

http://www.brain.nwu.edu/

Alzheimer's.Com

http://www.alzheimers.com

Administration on Aging

http://www.aoa.dhhs.gov

http://www.aoa.dhhs.gov/factsheets/alz.html

National Institute on Aging—Alzheimer's

http://www.alzheimers.org/nianews.html

Food and Drug Administration

FDA Talk Papers are prepared by the Press Office to guide FDA personnel in responding with consistency and accuracy to questions from the public on subjects of current interest. Talk Papers are subject to change as more information becomes available. Talk Papers are not intended for general distribution outside FDA, but all information in them is public, and full texts are available upon request.

http://www.fda.gov

Government Information Locator Service

http://www.access.gpo.gov/su_docs/gils/gils.html

NIH—National Institute of Health

http://www.nih.gov/

Hospice

http://www.nho.org

Last Acts

http://www.lastacts.org

Choice In Dying—nation's leading experts on end-of-life-issues

http://www.echonyc.com/~choice

Choice In Dying (Advance Directives)
    http://www.echonyc.com/~choice/ad.htm ❤

Bibliography

Alzheimer's

Antonangeli, Judith M., RN, BSN, *Of Two Minds, A Guide to the Care of People with the Dual Diagnosis of Alzheimer's Disease and Mental Retardation*, Fidelity Press, 1995.

Cohen, Donna, Eisdorfer, Carl, *The Loss of Self A Family Resource for the Care of Alzheimer's Disease and Related Disorders*, Plume, 1987. ISBN: 0-452-25946-0

Feil, Naomi, *V/F Validation: How to Help Disoriented Old-Old*, Edward Feil Productions, 1992. ISBN 1-878169-00-9

Gray Davidson, Frena, *The Alzheimer's Sourcebook for Caregivers*, Lowell House, 1993. ISBN: 1-56565-080-8

Hurley, A. Bottino, R, Volicer, L. "Nursing Role in Advance Proxy Planning for Alzheimer Patients", *CARING* Magazine, August 1994, p.73.

Mace, Nancy and Rabins, Peter, *The 36-Hour Day*, Revised Edition, Johns Hopkins 1991. ISBN: 0-8018-4034

McGowin, Diana Friel, *Living in the Labyrinth*, Delta Trade (Dell Publishing), 1993. ISBN: 0-385-31318-7

Murphy, Beverly Bigtree, *He Used To Be Somebody: A Journey into Alzheimer's Disease Through the Eyes of a Caregiver*, Gibbs Associates, 1995. ISBN: 0-943909-14-7

Rogers, Joseph, *Candle and Darkness: Current Research in Alzheimer's Disease*, Bonus Books Inc. ISBN: 1566250951

Rose, Larry, *Show Me the Way to Go Home*, Elder Books, 1996. ISBN: 0-943873-08-8

Sheridan, Carmel, *Failure-Free Activities*, Elder Books, Forrest Knolls, CA, 1987. ISBN: 0-943873-05-3

Strecker, Teresa R., *Alzheimer's: Making Sense of Suffering*, Lafayette, Louisiana, Vital Issues Press, 1997. ISBN: 1-56384-133-9

Volicer, L., Rheume, Y., Brown, J. Fabiszewski, Brady, E., Chapter 10 "Ethical Issues in the Treatment of Advanced Alzheimer Dementia: Hospice Approach", in *Clinical Management of Alzheimer's Disease*, Aspen Press, 1987.

Volicer, Ladislav, and Hurley, Ann, *Hospice Care for Patients with Advanced Progressive Dementia*, Springer, 1998. ISBN 0-8261-1162-9

Caregiving

Berman, Claire, *Caring for Yourself While Caring for Your Aging Parents*, New York, 1996. Owl Books, Henry Holt and Company, Inc., 1996. ISBN 0-8050-4109-5

Grollman, Earl A., et al., *Your Aging Parents, Reflections for Caregivers*, Boston, MA, Beacon Press. ISBN 0-8070-2799-5

Grollman, Earl A., *Caring and Coping When Your Loved One is Seriously Ill*, Boston, MA, Beacon Press, 1997. ISBN 0-8070-2713-8

Louden, Jennifer, *The Woman's Comfort Book— A Self-Nurturing Guide for Restoring Balance in Your Life*. Harper Collins, 1992. ISBN 0-06-250531-9

Schiff, Harriet Sarnoff, *How Did I Become My Parent's Parent?*, Hammondsworth, Middlesex, England, Penguin Books, 1997. ISBN 0 14 02.3714 3

Sanford, Linda Tschirhart, et. al, *Women & Self-Esteem: Understanding and Improving the Way We Think and Feel About Ourselves*, New York, 1984. ISBN 0 1400-8225 5

Children

Munsch, Robert, *Love You Forever*, Willowdale, Ontario, Canada, 1986. ISBN 0-920668-36-4

Potracke, Rochelle, FSPA, *Nanny's Special Gift*, Paulist Press, 1993. ISBN 0-8091-6615-1

Wahl, Jan, *"I Remember!" Cried Grandma Pinky*, Troll Medalion, 1994. ISBN 0-8167-3457-7

Leighton, Audrey O., *A Window of Time*, NADJA Publishing, 1995. ISBN 0-9636335-1-1

Ethics

Humphrey, Derek, *Dying with Dignity: Understanding Euthanasia*, Carol Publishing Group, 1992. ISBN 1-55972-105-7.

Peck, M. Scott, *Denial of the Soul: Spiritual and Medical Perspectives on Euthanasia and Mortality*, Harmony Books, 1997. ISBN: 0-517-70865-5

Post, Stephen G., *The Moral Challenge of Alzheimer Disease*, Johns Hopkins, 1995. ISBN 0-8018-5174-2

Wicclair, Mark R., *Ethics and the Elderly*, Oxford University Press, 1993. ISBN 0-19-505315-X

"The Care of Dying Patients: A Position Statement from the American Geriatrics Society", *AGS Ethics Committee*, Prepared by Greg A. Sachs, MD; reviewed and approved by the AGS Ethics Committee and the AGS Board of Directors, May 1994., AGS 43:577-578, 1995.

"Promotion of Comfort and Relief of Pain in Dying Patients", *American Nurses Association Position Statement*, Effective Date: September 5, 1991, Washington, D.C. Originated by: Task Force on the Nurse's Role in End of Life Decisions.

Genetics

To Know Ourselves, The U.S. Department of Energy and The Human Genome Project, July 1997

Human Genome Project Reports, Part 1: Overview and Progress, The U.S. Department of Energy and The Human Genome Project, November 1997.

Pollen, Daniel A., *Hannah's Heirs, The Quest for the Genetic Origins of Alzheimer's Disease*, Oxford Paperbacks, 1993. ISBN: 0-19-510652-0

Bristow, Lois, *Will I Be Next? The terror of living with Familial Alzheimer's Disease*, Hope Warren Press, 1996. ISBN 0-9648885-0-5

Grief

Aiken, Lewis R., *Dying, Death and Bereavement*, Allyn and Bacon, 1991. ISBN: 0-205-12650-2

Callahan, Maggie & Kelley, Particia, *Final Gifts*, Posiedon Press, 1992. ISBN: 0-671-70006-5

Colgrove, Melba, et al., *How to Survive the Loss of a Love*, Los Angeles, California, 1976. ISBN 0-553-07760-0

Kubler-Ross, Elisabeth, *To Live Until We Say Good-Bye*, Simon and Schuster, 1978. ISBN 0-671-76547-7

Kubler-Ross, Elisabeth, *Death: The Final Stage of Growth*, Prentice Hall, Inc., 1975. ISBN 0-13-196998-6

Moffat, Mary Jane (editor), *In the Midst of Winter: Selections from the Literature of Mourning*, Vintage Books, 1992. ISBN 0-679-73827-4

Randoe, Therese A., *How to Go On Living When Someone You Love Dies*, Bantam Books, 1991. ISBN: 0-553-35269-5

Taterbaum, Judy, *The Courage to Grieve*, Perennial Library, 1980. ISBN: 0-06-091185-9

Vozenilek, Helen, *Loss of the Ground-Note: Women writing about the loss of their mothers*, La Mesa, California, Clothespin Fever Press, 1992. ISBN 1-878533-07-X

Walsh, Monica & McGoldrick, Froma, *Living Beyond Loss, Death in the Family*, W.W.Norton, 1991. ISBN: 0-393-70203-0

Wild, Laynee, *I Remember You—A Grief Journal*, Harper Collins, 1995. ISBN: 0-06-251090-6

Healing

Borysenko, Joan, *Minding the Body, Mending the Mind*, Reading, MA, Addison-Wesley, 1987. ISBN 0-553-34556-7

Borysenko, Joan, *Guilt is the Teacher, Love is the Lesson*, NY, Warner Books, 1990. ISBN 0-446-39224-3

Casarjian, Robin, *Forgiveness - A Bold Choice for a Peaceful Heart*, New York, Bantam, 1992. ISBN 0-553-35236-9

Chopra, Deepak, *Creating Health—How to Wake up the Body's Intelligence*, Boston, Massachusetts, Houghton Mifflin Company, 1991. ISBN0-395-42953-6

Fox, John, *Poetic Medicine The Healing Art of Poem-Making*, New York, Tarcher Putnum, 1997. ISBN-0-87477-882-4.

Heard, Georgia, *Writing Toward Home,* Heinemann Publishing, 1995. ISBN: 0435081241

Kabat-Zinn, Jon, *Wherever You Go There You Are*, Hyperion, 1994. ISBN: 0-7868-8070-8

Lerner, Harriet Goldhor, *The Dance of Anger*, NY, Harper & Row, 1985. ISBN 0-06-091565-X

Spirituality

Borysenko, Joan, *Fire in the Soul*, New York, Warner Books, 1993. ISBN 0-446-51466-7

Borysenko, Joan et. al, *On Wings of Light, Meditations for Awakenings of the Source*, New York, Warner Books, 1992.
ISBN 0-446-39225-3

Carlson, Richard et. al, *Handbook for the Soul*, Boston, MA, 1995. ISBN 0-316-12812-0

Kabat-Zinn, Jon, *Wherever you Go There You Are, Mindfulness Meditation in Everyday Life,* New York, Hyperion, 1994.
ISBN 0-7868-8070-8

Moore, Thomas, *Care of the Soul A Guide for Cultivating Depth and Sacredness in Everyday Life*, Harper Perennial, 1994.
ISBN 0-06-092224-9

Myss, Caroline, *Anatomy of the Spirit*, New York, Three Rivers Press, a division of Crown Publishers, Inc., 1996.
ISBN 0-609-80014-0

Norwood, Robin, *Why Me—Why This—Why Now—A Guide to Answering Life's Toughest Questions*, New York, Carol Southern Books, 1994. ISBN 00-517-59850-7

Peck, M. Scott, *The Road Less Travelled: A New Psychology of Love, Traditional Values and Spiritual Growth*, Simon & Schuster, 1978. ISBN 0-671-25067-1

Rinpoche, Sogyal, *The Tibetan Book of Living and Dying*, San Francisco, CA, Harper, 1994. ISBN 0-06-250834-2 ❤

Index

F

G

H

I

J

journal writing 199

joy 210, 226, 236

K

Kevorkian, Jack 37, 45, 78

knee-jerk reactions 42

Koenig-Coste, Joanne 11, 12

Kubler-Ross, Elisabeth 204, 292

L

laughter 36, 51

Lawrence, Elizabeth 308

legal competence 85

letting go 233, 236, 237, 239, 240, 241, 242, 246, 249, 252, 253, 254, 258, 305, 309, 312

levels of care 157

life insurance 108

listen to the emotion 61

living will 14, 86, 87

loneliness 38, 150, 216, 223

long term care 18, 135, 138, 139, 140, 141, 145, 152, 162, 196, 219, 259, 266, 308, 321

long term care insurance 111

Louden, Jennifer 191

love xix, 2, 5, 7, 10, 14, 18, 20, 21, 22, 23, 24, 26, 28, 33, 34, 37, 48, 51, 53, 54, 56, 59, 68, 71, 72, 75, 78, 79, 120, 121, 122, 126, 135, 142, 144, 145, 146, 149, 160, 187, 190, 191, 192, 196, 201, 203, 204, 205, 207, 209, 210, 216, 217, 219, 220, 221, 223, 226, 233, 234, 236, 237, 240, 242, 243, 245, 246, 247, 248, 251, 253, 257, 267, 281, 284, 292, 293, 298, 301, 302, 304, 309, 310, 311, 312, 313, 314, 315

LUMarian Method 308, 309

lying 96

obtaining a diagnosis 47

orphan 302, 306

P

pain 215

pain management 284, 285, 288, 299

palliative 274, 275, 277

palliative care 158, 159

palliative measures 44

paralysis 10

Patient & Family Services Committee 122

patient history 50

Peck, Scott 24

personal-need allowance 107

perspective 27, 34

PET 50

Physical Examination 50

pneumonia 180

power of attorney 85, 86, 88, 89, 90, 91, 95, 100, 101, 102, 155

PRN basis 186

probate 110

professional caregiver 17, 38, 42, 44, 68, 86, 139, 141, 146, 147, 148, 150, 158, 159, 160, 174, 180, 182, 183, 184, 187, 207, 218, 220, 252, 260, 268, 269, 270, 271, 272, 276, 307

Psychiatric and Psychological Assessment 50

psychotherapy 199

psychotropic drugs 140, 290

Q

quality of care 141

quality of life 13, 37, 41, 47, 53, 54, 55, 59, 61, 65, 67, 68, 74, 119, 135, 141, 168, 224, 245, 261, 263, 271, 276

Other Books from
The Alzheimer's Bookshelf

Failure-Free Activities for the Alzheimer's Patient

by Carmel Sheridan

This award-winning book describes hundreds of simple, non-threatening activities which are suitable for persons with Alzheimer's disease. The author describes how to focus on the abilities that remain rather than the patient's deficits and shows how to create activities which capitalize on existing strengths. $10.95

Coping With Caring:
Daily Reflections for Alzheimer's Caregivers

by Lyn Roche

Coping with Caring is designed to ease the day-to-day stress of caring for the person with Alzheimer's. In an easy-to-read format, each page provides an inspiring daily reflection, followed by a related caregiving tip. Designed for daily use, this unique treasury serves as a support group, a place where caregivers can recharge and gain new insights. $11.95

Alzheimer's: The Answers You Need

by Helen D. Davies and Michael P. Jensen

This is the only guidebook written for people in the early stages of Alzheimer's disease and their caregivers. This first-of-its-kind book contains not only the expected 'What is Alzheimer's' information, but helps patients come to grips with their many daily frustrations. It contains tips for improving the quality of their lives. Virtually every question is addressed that co-author Helen Davies has heard in her fifteen years counseling Alzheimer's patients and their caregivers. $10.95

Surviving Alzheimer's: A Guide for Families

by Florian Raymond

Easily digestible, this book is a treasure house of practical tips, ideas and survival strategies for the busy caregiver. It describes how to renew and restore yourself during the ups and downs of caregiving, and shows you how to take care of yourself as well as your family member. $10.95

Show Me The Way To Go Home

by Larry Rose

Larry Rose was a vital gifted engineer in his forties when Alzheimer's struck. In this first-person account, Rose shares his heartbreaking experiences with the disease he has been battling since 1992. Show Me The Way to go Home is a highly individual personal experience with universal appeal. $10.95

For information about other books, visit the Alzheimer's Bookshelf at www.ElderBooks.com

Order Form

Send Order to:

Elder Books PO Box 490 Forest Knolls CA 94933
Ph 1-800-909-COPE (2673) FAX: 415-488-4720

Qty		Price/copy	Totals
_____	*My Mother's Voice*	$14.95	$_____
_____	*Failure-Free Activities for the Alzheimer's Patient*	$10.95	$_____
_____	*Coping with Caring Daily Reflections for Caregivers*	$11.95	$_____
_____	*Alzheimer's: The Answers You Need*	$10.95	$_____
_____	*Surviving Alzheimer's: A Guide for Families*	$10.95	$_____
_____	*Show Me the Way To Go Home*	$10.95	$_____

Total for books $_____

Total sales tax $_____

Total shipping $_____

Amount enclosed $_____

Shipping: $2.50 for first book, $1.25 for each additional book; California residents, please add 8.25% sales tax.

Name _____

Address _____

City _____ State _____ Zip _____

Visit The Alzheimer's Bookshelf at http://www.Elderbooks.com